THREE
DAYS IN
JANUARY

ALSO BY BRET BAIER

Special Heart

THREE DAYS IN JANUARY

DWIGHT EISENHOWER'S FINAL MISSION

BRET BAIER

WITH CATHERINE WHITNEY

WM

WILLIAM MORROW
An Imprint of HarperCollinsPublishers

HarperCollins books may be purchased for educational, business, or sales promotional use. For information, please email the Special Markets Department at SPsales@harpercollins.com.

FIRST EDITION

Library of Congress Cataloging-in-Publication Data has been applied for.

ISBN 978-0-06-256903-5
ISBN 978-0-06-267799-0 (Books-A-Million signed edition)

17 18 19 20 21   DIX/RRD   10 9 8 7 6 5 4 3 2 1

To our sons, Paul and Daniel, and their generation. Please allow history to inform your decisions in the future.

CONTENTS

FINDING IKE

I put the white gloves on as the librarian came over with the gray cardboard box. She untied the cover flap and slowly lifted out the first folder inside. Her movements were deliberate as she placed the folder on the giant wood table in front of me. On cue, I followed suit by slowly removing the papers from the plastic sheeting inside the folder, trying to mimic her movements. It was then, as I held the final draft of President Dwight D. Eisenhower's farewell speech, that I started truly trying to imagine and describe the closing moments of the thirty-fourth president's term three days before the inauguration of the thirty-fifth.

The typewritten page was clear but it was filled with pencil markings from President Eisenhower: accents, underlines for emphasis, and additional words or phrases that would make it into the teleprompter version. The top of the page read, "My fellow Americans: THREE DAYS [capitalized] from now, after half a century [underlined] in the service of our country, I shall lay down the responsibilities of office as, in traditional and solemn ceremony, the authority of the Presidency is vested in my successor. THIS EVENING [capitalized] I come to you with a message of leave-taking and farewell, and to share a few final thoughts with you, my countrymen [double underline]."

Reading through the speech with Eisenhower's notations, I

could imagine him scribbling the final adjustments at the Theodore Roosevelt desk on January 17, 1961, before preparing to deliver the speech from the Oval Office that night. This moment, holding his speech in my gloved hands, had been three years in the making.

Every journalistic investigation begins with a flash of curiosity. That happened for me in the spring of 2013 when I rediscovered Dwight D. Eisenhower in a personal way. I had just come off an exciting but brutal year and a half covering the 2012 presidential election. From my daily show every weeknight, moderating debates through the primaries, covering primary and caucus nights, co-anchoring convention coverage and the general election debates—it all culminated in a long election night that finished with President Barack Obama's reelection by big numbers.

The presidential election every four years can seem to happen in a fishbowl, with an excessive focus on the daily sound bites. Significant historical references give way to the drama of the trail. But I've always been drawn to the ways our current political debates are informed by the past.

Some people look at our nation's history as a series of explosive events and larger-than-life personalities. We easily get sidetracked from the most important stories by the flash, while the true jewels lie undiscovered. So even as I was reporting on the political horse race in 2012, I was thinking about how I could tell a fuller story. And a serendipitous experience a few months after the inauguration opened a door for me.

AN AVID GOLFER, I received the Holy Grail of golf invitations in spring 2013 through a friend who is a member of the Augusta National Golf Club in Augusta, Georgia. It was a welcome break.

With the CBS Masters theme song playing in my head, I drove down the most famous driveway in golf, Magnolia Lane. Pulling up to the clubhouse and checking in, I found out that by random assignment, I would be staying in the Eisenhower Cabin.

Ike's Cabin, near the tenth tee and the start of the most celebrated back nine in golf, is one of ten cabins on the golf course and was built especially for President Eisenhower and his family to use on his frequent visits to Augusta, where the president pursued his passion for golf. Reagan and Bush had their ranches, but for Ike leisure time often involved golf. It was a passion I shared, and I was ecstatic to be at Augusta, and even happier to be bunking in Ike's Cabin. To be accurate, it isn't actually a cabin, in the normal sense of the word. It's a three-story white house (the basement floor was used by the Secret Service during Ike's presidency), with spacious, well-appointed rooms, on an idyllic setting with back views of the legendary par-three course. Surrounded by the most manicured grounds in the country, this was Ike's Augusta White House. A gold eagle sits above the front porch.

Ike's influence is on display everywhere at Augusta. In the pro shop stands an old-fashioned, highly polished cracker barrel, a gift to Ike from his Treasury secretary George Humphrey in honor of the many discussions they had about life and national affairs at the golf course. Humphrey told the president their talks reminded him of the old days, when men sat talking around a potbelly stove with a cracker barrel nearby, from which they would grab handfuls of soda crackers for sustenance. Thereafter, while Ike was president, the cracker barrel at Augusta was fully stocked.

This homey quality, with the ghosts of the past in the air, was resonant in Ike's Cabin. Restless and more than a little awestruck to spend the night there, I poured a glass of wine in the evening and began to wander around the house. I could feel Ike's presence in the cozy, lived-in quality of the place, the personal artifacts and books still on the shelves, and a painting by the president, an amateur artist, that hung above the fireplace, depicting the sixteenth hole—a par-three where more than one Masters had taken a thrilling turn: Jack Nicklaus drained a forty-foot putt there in 1975 on his way to a win over Tom Weiskopf and Johnny Miller; Nicklaus stuffed a five-iron to within two feet in 1986 en route to another birdie and his sixth win; Seve Ballesteros four-putted the sixteenth green in 1988 in a failed bid for a green jacket; and perhaps the most famous shot of all at 16 came from Tiger Woods in 2005, when he holed a seemingly impossible chip shot from well off the green while CBS announcer Verne Lundquist made the call as the ball rolled toward the cup, hung on the edge, and then dropped into the hole—"Here it comes . . . Oh My Goodness . . . Oh WOW! In your life have you seen anything like that!?"

I know my Masters history, but what I came to realize that night was how much I didn't understand about President Eisenhower. Soon I found myself totally immersed in what I can only describe as the spirit of Ike. This was new for me. Born a decade after Eisenhower left office, I had never given his administration a lot of consideration. Like most of my generation, I thought the world skipped a beat during Ike's years, in its eagerness to move on—accepting JFK's claim of the torch having been passed. By the time I came along, we had turned yet another page and were well into Nixon's first term.

My night at the Eisenhower Cabin changed that. It was ironic it happened on a golf course, really *the* golf course, given all the jokes about Ike's devotion to and even obsession with the sport. What *wasn't* surprising was that a television news anchor would be drawn to the original "broadcast president." Eisenhower held the first televised news conference in 1955 and was the first president to be videotaped and broadcast in color, in 1958.

Thinking about Ike, I sensed there was an untapped well-spring behind the façade. So there I was, getting ready to play what was for me a historic round of golf, where each shot on the course triggered a replay inside my head of a Masters gone by, and I was steeped in another history from more than fifty years ago. I knew there was more to be mined; I just didn't know what.

As I played, I admired the "Eisenhower Tree," a sixty-five-foot loblolly pine located on the seventeenth hole. Ike hated that tree because he hit it so many times while playing. He even proposed that it be cut down, a suggestion that horrified the club chairman. Nature eventually did the job for him. Nearly a year after my visit, an ice storm damaged the tree so badly it had to be taken down. Today, a beautiful, glass-encased cross section stands in the lobby of the Eisenhower Library, and another at the members' guest area at Augusta National.

I left Augusta full of questions, curious about the way our national narrative seemed to slide past Ike, as if he was a mere caretaker in a line of great doers. A cursory review showed that Ike's presidency was actually full of drama in the early years of the Cold War, and the decisions he made affect us even now. I was interested in finding out more, so soon after my trip to Augusta I traveled to Abilene, Kansas, to visit the Eisenhower Presidential Library, Museum, and Boyhood Home. It is a beautiful and even majestic setting, surrounded by fields of grain and alive with Eisenhower's historic contributions—from his commanding role in the Allied victory over Hitler to his decisive management of Cold War threats during the Soviet rise. The library and museum are built on the site of Ike's childhood home, which sits fully intact on its original lot—a typical modest turn-of-the-century house where you could pile in six boys, with beds squeezed into every corner, while still leaving space for a piano.

The archivists at the library told me that if I wanted to learn more about Eisenhower, there were millions of pages of documents and hundreds of thousands of feet of original film—some of it still unread and unseen. There was even a locked vault containing thousands of pages of material still classified after all these years. Now my reporter's curiosity was *really* piqued. Although the library hosts some two hundred thousand visitors a year, coming from across America and around the world, most Americans will never physically visit the heartland site. I wanted to bring it to them.

As I dug through the files, combed through the oral histories, listened to the tapes, and read the books about Eisenhower's presidency, one reality stood out for me: here was a man on a mission to save America, who largely succeeded in that endeavor. His was not the dramatic leadership of an era with bombs bursting in midair, but the wise course of a military strategist who rescued the world from that inevitability. He was a leader, in the truest sense of the word, and from my perch in the twenty-first century I was drawn to the question of what made him great.

The historian Jon Meacham made an observation that hit the mark. Referring to FDR and Churchill, he said, "One of the mysteries of history is why is it that certain moments produce exactly the right human beings?" I came to see that Eisenhower, our thirty-fourth president, was such a man. He was the buried treasure of the past century—his influence underappreciated in the clamor of great individuals jockeying for recognition. We easily speak of men like FDR, who led us through a great world war, or Ronald Reagan, who faced off with the Soviet leader Mikhail Gorbachev to help wind down the Cold War. But we dismiss the man whose epic presidency saved the world from nuclear disaster, and in the process created a new narrative about how we can use our power for the greater good. This was the centerpiece of Ike's farewell address, delivered on January 17, 1961, three days before John F. Kennedy assumed office.

The contrast between the two men was striking—Eisenhower, a man of seventy born in the previous century, now at the end of an illustrious career; and Kennedy, forty-four, the vigorous spokesman of the next generation. The American people, weary of the world they knew, were captivated by the idea of a different path.

Genial, golf-playing Ike became emblematic of the sleepy 1950s, while the 1960s were all about a tanned, urbane, matinee-idol president, with his gorgeous wife, Jackie, and two adorable children—tailor-made for the new American marquee. The Kennedys embodied the way America wanted to see itself—young, worldly, smart, and educated. Cool. Ike's acolyte, Richard Nixon, only four years Kennedy's senior, was dismissed in the 1960 election as being part of the old order. Ironically, the healthy Nixon was more vigorous than the ailing Kennedy, who we later found out was being assisted in looking strong and healthy for the cameras by a regimen of drugs and a back brace.

Yet the media storm around Kennedy was so effusive, so packaged for adulation that it swept the general public up in its wave. People were persuaded that Ike was nothing more than a historical artifact, clutching his golf club and warming his chair, while the heady drama of a new world swirled around him.

But as is so often the case with shorthand narratives, a much more complex truth lay beneath. For starters, the 1950s weren't so sleepy after all. With the world still struggling to reorder itself after the upheaval of World War II, the Soviet Union and China expanding their influence, and the Korean conflict no closer to being settled, Eisenhower took office at one of the most dangerous times in our history. The choices he made in those crucial years might well have saved us from nuclear war.

On the other hand, Kennedy's New Frontier would prove to be rocky territory—something Ike predicted. His warning, delivered in personal meetings with Kennedy and in his farewell address to the nation, was his final mission, an effort to draw a road map for the future and protect the investment he had made in peace. *Three Days in January* goes behind the scenes to detail those final days, in the process taking a measure of the man who made such a difference to the life of the nation.

In describing Ike's life and final mission, we are inescapably drawn to a central question of our era as well—that is, How should we use our military might in the world? Never before or since has any president been as confident of the answer as Eisenhower—or as willing to articulate a daring and controversial philosophy. To Ike, who knew well the cost of war and was clear-eyed about the cataclysmic potential of nuclear weapons, it was critical that we use our exceptional position in the world to create a lasting bulwark of peace. This warning was at the heart of his farewell address.

For decades historians and politicians have studied the address for clues about the man and his vision. Peace advocacy groups have gladly worn his warning about the military-industrial complex as a cloak of affirmation and used it to justify their ideologies. But Eisenhower, a military man to the core, had never shied away from a necessary use of force. So what was his true purpose in uttering those words? In *Three Days in January* we investigate and seek to pin down what Eisenhower really meant—and what it means to us.

In these pages, we'll confront the modern stirrings of issues eerily reminiscent of those that commanded the nation's attention on the brink of the 1960s—our relationship with Cuba, the broken pledges ramping up the Israeli conflict, and the posturing of Vladimir Putin, which mirrors the bullish energy of one of his predecessors, Nikita Khrushchev. Each of these conflicts is enhanced by the infectious strains of radical Islamic terrorism, which make our world a more dangerous place. The public has been searching for leadership and wisdom on how best to extinguish these troubles. In this moment, Eisenhower, the general and president from almost six decades ago, speaks with clarity and wisdom that many Americans say they are searching for in the current political debate.

The subject of Eisenhower's life has been tackled by many leading historians. I don't presume to stand shoulder to shoulder with them. I come to this story as a journalist, using a reporter's perspective. My task is to report on what I see and to offer a window into the past that might speak to issues we're facing today. As a reporter, I am in a dialogue with the reader, saying in effect, here's what I see—what's your view? (I report, you decide—pretty catchy.)

Since I work in a visual medium, I can easily picture the scenes—the barefoot boy; the general, head in hands, preparing to make the critical decision about D-Day; the grinning candidate America liked; the living-room president, who spoke regularly on the small screen, glasses slipping down his nose; the confident commander in chief, standing toe-to-toe with Khrushchev. In particular, I can imagine the purposeful elder, preparing for his final mission in January 1961. I have chosen to focus on the critical days in the transition of power from Eisenhower to Kennedy, because sometimes the truth we are looking for is easier to find when we narrow our view.

It turns out my timing coincided with a renaissance of sorts in the public perception of Eisenhower. In a 1962 poll of presidential scholars ranking the presidents, Ike scored a dismal twenty-two out of thirty-four. In 2014, the scholars placed him at number seven, behind Lincoln, Washington, Teddy Roosevelt, FDR, Jefferson, and Truman. Kennedy ranked fourteenth.

Three Days in January reached its final stages in 2016. In the background, as I wrote, America was engaged in a tumultuous election year when once again the question was being asked: Who is the right leader for our precarious times? As the chief political anchor for Fox News, the future of the presidency is my daily fare. So during this election season I was compelled to compare and contrast the visions offered by modern candidates with the powerful words and actions of a leader from a half-century ago.

The pendulum of our public life can swing widely at times; we are constantly in search of change and betterment. There are always new frontiers, and election years are usually the times we most eagerly explore them. But it is our task not just to seek change but to harness it, and the fateful transition between Eisenhower and Kennedy vividly demonstrates the significance of this balancing act. *Three Days in January* is both a cautionary tale and a hopeful one. As Eisenhower said in his first inaugural address, "Whatever America hopes to bring to pass in the world must first come to pass in the heart of America." Ike—a man from Abilene, Kansas—was from the heart of America and his presidency is worth a fresh look, especially now.

—Bret Baier
   January 2017

THREE DAYS IN JANUARY

PROLOGUE

THE VISIT

December 6, 1960
9:00 A.M.
The White House

Kennedy came alone, stepping out of his Lincoln at the North Portico of the White House to the flash of press cameras and a rousing chorus of "Stars and Stripes Forever" by the Marine Band, which Ike had ordered up for the occasion. Contingents from the Army, Navy, Air Force, and Marines lined the driveway in a respectful flourish—also Ike's idea. No entourage accompanied the young president-elect to his first meeting with Eisenhower, and Ike was happy to see it. Spectacle always seemed to follow Kennedy, but that day was to be a private meeting of two minds.

Such a seminar had been sadly lacking in Ike's own transition to the presidency in 1953. Although Truman and Eisenhower had once been close, and in many ways were cut from the same homespun cloth (growing up only 150 miles from each other), the rhetoric of the campaign obliterated any civility between them.

"The general doesn't know any more about politics than a pig knows about Sunday," Truman griped, ignoring the fact that he himself had once urged Eisenhower to run for president, before he learned Ike was a Republican. Truman was surly in his leave-taking, unable to forgive Ike for his campaign critiques and move on. Although Eisenhower was invited to the White House to confer with Truman after the election, the meeting was chilly. Looking ahead to the inauguration, Eisenhower grumbled, "I wonder if I can stand sitting next to him." By inauguration day, things deteriorated to the degree that Truman even took umbrage at Ike's choice of a homburg over a top hat—a deliberate act of rebellion on Ike's part that shocked the protocol mavens. For their part, the Eisenhowers had refused to enter the White House for a pre-inauguration cup of coffee, choosing instead to wait in the car that would take both the president and president-elect to the ceremony. At least Ike didn't meet Truman at the Capitol steps, as he'd threatened. But it was a very uncomfortable car ride. "I'm glad I wasn't in that car," head White House usher J. B. West said.

Now Ike was determined to do things differently. Out of a sense of patriotism and purpose, he wanted to orchestrate the transition, to put his stamp on it and, in the process, on the future. It wasn't a game to him. Nor was it about personalities or, God forbid, *politics*. The respect he gave Kennedy was a kind of hopeful bet on the future. His soldier's heart was steady in its desire to see Kennedy succeed. Ike understood that legacy was made not just by the actions of an administration while it was in office, but also by the way the narrative continued to unfold once the torch was passed. In that sense, his own legacy was in the hands of this young man.

Although Kennedy had been serving in the U.S. Senate during Eisenhower's entire eight years in office, the two didn't really know each other well. Kennedy hadn't particularly distinguished himself as a senator, but almost from the start he'd seemed to be in thrall to his wealthy father's vision of higher office, lobbying for (though not winning) the vice presidential slot on the Democratic ticket in 1956. Most of Eisenhower's impressions of him had been formed during the 1960 campaign. Vice President Richard Nixon, JFK's Republican opponent, often complained about the breathless press coverage that virtually elevated the Kennedys to American royalty, and although Ike was clear about his VP's personal deficiencies, he figured Dick had a point.

Ike had been depressed by Nixon's loss, considering it the biggest defeat of his life. He had essentially trained Nixon to be an able shepherd of his well-crafted strategies, and he trusted his vice president's acumen in foreign policy. He felt guilty that he had not campaigned harder for Nixon, and the press had picked up that theme, making it appear that Ike was less than enthusiastic about Nixon's candidacy. What no one fully appreciated was that it had been Nixon's choice to keep Ike out of it, preferring to run as his own man. He didn't want to be seen as "Ike's boy." Nixon also wildly underestimated the challenge Kennedy presented. He was thrilled when Kennedy was nominated, beating out the more formidable Hubert Humphrey. Nixon was confident that he could whip this Senate lightweight. He even believed—or was deluded—that his running mate, Henry Cabot Lodge Jr., whom Kennedy had defeated to win his Massachusetts U.S. Senate seat in 1952, might help Nixon take his opponent's home state.

While overconfidence surely played a role in Nixon's decision to sideline the president, Ike also had a nagging feeling that Nixon didn't fully trust him to be on his side, owing to an incident that occurred at the end of his first term. As Ike was planning his campaign for reelection, he'd called Nixon into the Oval Office. He told him that he wasn't sure the vice presidency was the best platform from which to start a successful presidential campaign—if that's what Nixon wanted to do in 1960. He suggested an alternative—a cabinet post that might be a better launchpad.

Nixon was shocked—and suspicious. Was Ike trying to dump him from the ticket?

The president was adamant that this was not his wish. He was merely offering Nixon a choice in plotting his future. It was entirely up to him.

Nixon quickly decided to stick with the vice presidency, but Ike felt he never quite got over his suspicions. So when 1960 rolled around, Nixon kept Eisenhower on the sidelines, even though the president's popularity was quite high. He didn't bring him into the campaign, and when Ike tried to advise him not to do a televised debate with Kennedy, he didn't listen—to his peril. Ike was traveling, and didn't see or hear the debate until later; then he was disheartened by what he saw. The debate was so devastating for Nixon that JFK's mother, Rose Kennedy, said she felt sorry for Nixon's mother and briefly wondered if she should call her to offer condolences.

When Eisenhower finally took to the trail in the desperate last week of the campaign, as the polls showed the candidates running neck and neck, he was disheartened to see signs at his rallies: WE LIKE IKE BUT WE BACK JACK.

At large rallies Ike attacked the Kennedy "clique of young, so-called brilliant men" and said he was "terribly tired of hearing America run down by them, of hearing their brassy and boastful words and watching their bumbling actions."

Ike was so effective on the stump that Kennedy grew worried. "With every word he utters, I can feel the votes leaving me," he told his friend Paul "Red" Fay. "It's like standing on a mound of sand with the tide running out. If the election were held tomorrow, I'd win easily, but six days from now, it's up for grabs."

Now, with the election over, Ike was left to ponder the impact of the loss, and he was a bit annoyed at his vice president, who took a little too long, he thought, to concede. Upon Kennedy's victory, Ike had immediately sent a congratulatory telegram, and then had been forced to have his press secretary, Jim Hagerty, call the Kennedy people and ask them to withdraw it and not say anything about it because Nixon hadn't yet conceded. A replacement telegram was sent the following day.

In defeat, Ike wasn't interested in wallowing in personal resentments. That had never been his way. He understood campaign rhetoric. If he was offended by the characterization of Kennedy as a fresh exemplar of "the New Frontier," and of himself as a doddering relic of the past, he kept it to himself. The question was, how much of Kennedy's campaign talk represented his true sentiments? Did he really believe that the United States was experiencing a decline in its vitality and prestige, as he'd stated, and if so, what was he planning to do about it?

Of greatest concern was the substance of Kennedy's platform, particularly his reckless charge that the "missile gap" was growing under Eisenhower. Ike suspected this was a blatant political play; still, he was angry when he heard it, erupting in a brief fit of temper to exclaim, "That's damn wrong!" He'd made sure that Kennedy received detailed briefings by CIA director Allen Dulles and his national security team during the campaign to show him otherwise, but Kennedy kept making the claim: "We are facing a gap on which we are gambling with our survival."

Most worrisome was the idea that Kennedy might actually believe his own sloganeering, having bought hook, line, and sinker Khrushchev's claim that he was churning out missiles like sausages. In truth, if there was any missile gap, it was in favor of the United States.

Eisenhower felt Kennedy had won the election in large part by portraying his administration as weak in the face of the Soviet threat. A shrewd strategist at heart, and intimately familiar with Khrushchev's ploys, Ike worried that such statements played into the Soviet leader's hands. He could well imagine Khrushchev gleefully rubbing his palms together in anticipation of toying with a naïve young president.

As he prepared to meet with Kennedy, Ike felt a sense of urgency to fully communicate the exact nature of the threat they faced, one that could not be captured in stump rhetoric. He thought Kennedy had glibly made many promises during the campaign that seemed to be empty and even callous. Now Ike was intent on getting the true measure of the man. Would he establish a closed political cadre, as Roosevelt had, and draw his authority from appeals to traditional Democratic audiences, or would he sincerely strive to be president of all the people and in the process further strengthen America's position in the world?

KENNEDY BOUNDED UP THE portico steps and firmly shook Ike's hand. "Mr. President, it's good to be here," he said, and Ike flashed him a genuine smile. The cameras clicked, and then they were walking into the White House. Once in the Oval Office they settled in for a private conversation. Kennedy, looking around, admired Ike's Spartan style, with his neat, polished desk (the Theodore Roosevelt mahogany desk, which Truman had repurposed), and the soothing landscape paintings adorning the walls. Kennedy charmingly laughed that his own office was a good deal messier—with piles of briefing books attesting to the scope of his learning curve.

Honestly, Eisenhower hadn't known what to expect from the man he'd once referred to in a moment of pique as a whippersnapper, but he would later acknowledge that from the first minute they sat across from each other there was a sense of ease. They weren't opponents or sparring partners, but two men who faced a unique weight and shared a common commitment—just the mood Ike wanted to create.

For his part, Kennedy seemed newly sober and respectful once the full seriousness of the moment struck him. The man who liked to joke about Ike with his friends now wanted very much to hear what the older man had to say. Ike found his attitude to be that of a "serious, earnest seeker for information."

Again, Ike recalled his own transition meeting with Truman, a twenty-minute uncomfortable, uncharitable session in which he learned very little. Rather than receiving wisdom and vital information, Ike had a strong feeling that Truman was out to get him. He didn't trust Truman—thought he might be trying to set a partisan trap for him—and without trust little could be accomplished. He sought a different spirit with Kennedy.

Kennedy was very interested in the White House—the administrative organization, the cabinet, and the national security establishment. But as Ike described in detail the complex national security apparatus and the vital importance of regular National Security Council meetings, he could tell that Kennedy wasn't convinced of their necessity. Kennedy seemed to regard the decision-making process as more informal. Not exactly seat-of-the-pants, but close to it. In press interviews he'd shown a level of confidence that could seem foolishly boastful, once saying, "Sure it's a big job, but I don't know anybody who can do it better than I can." Bluster, Ike figured. But now, looking at the man himself, who seemed smaller and more studious, Ike tried to impress upon him how much he needed this well-organized security consult. Suspecting that Kennedy was intent on tearing the whole apparatus apart, Ike, while appreciating the impulse to discard the old, urged him to leave the system in place for a time—to avoid reorganization until he was intimately familiar with the problems. Bear in mind, he told the dubious Kennedy, this present organization has been developed over eight years of patient study and long negotiations with Congress and the armed services. He hoped Kennedy took his point, but he thought the president-elect viewed the presidency as "an institution that one man could handle with an assistant here and another there."

The two men discussed the most pressing foreign policy issues, and Ike spoke at length about Vietnam and Southeast Asia, where six hundred American advisors were stationed. In addition, Berlin was a looming problem for the new president. Since 1958, when Khrushchev ordered a withdrawal from the city by Western powers, Eisenhower had been working feverishly to resolve the conflict, which many believed could trigger a nuclear war. Ike had resisted engaging the Soviets in a limited battle for the city, repeating his philosophy that we should not engage in wars we cannot win (and resorting to the use of nuclear weapons would be no victory at all).

On the matter of Cuba, Kennedy had already been briefed by the CIA on a plan under way to train Cuban exiles for a mission that would lead to the overthrow of the Castro regime. Kennedy was in favor of the plan. In fact, he had made a campaign speech in October calling for the Cuban people to resist their government. Now he asked what Ike thought of taking on Castro in this way. Ike was generally supportive, but it was still in the planning stages. The ultimate decision would be up to Kennedy.

Eisenhower addressed the issue of missiles head-on, describing the administration's efforts to work through NATO to form what would amount to a missile alliance that would strengthen both the United States and its allies. NATO is the greatest alliance to which we belong, he told Kennedy. Its maintenance and strength is vital to our own national security. The question of whether it was the vehicle for such a multilateral missile alliance would be among the most difficult issues Kennedy faced.

Kennedy asked if he ought to plan a personal visit with Khrushchev early in his term. Ike advised him to wait until his presidency was more firmly established. He was intimately familiar with the different sides of Khrushchev, and how seamlessly he could pass from one to the other. In his 1959 U.S. visit, Khrushchev had been the avuncular figure when, following a meeting at Camp David, he had accepted Eisenhower's invitation to join him at his farm in Gettysburg, Pennsylvania. There he charmed Ike's grandchildren with twinkling eyes and gently subversive gifts, such as a Christmas tree ornament that depicted a tiny Russian spacecraft headed for a dangling moon. But more recently Ike had seen the callous Cold Warrior face of Khrushchev following the downing of a U.S. spy plane in Soviet airspace. And he had seen the raging, shoe-thumping Khrushchev on his visit to the States only a couple of months earlier.

Khrushchev was sly; he had an agenda. But more to the point, he was answerable to the Politburo, so although Eisenhower found Khrushchev sometimes personally reasonable, and believed the Soviet leader lacked an appetite for war with the United States, he realized that Khrushchev wasn't entirely his own man. He was bound by his hard-liners. His standing as a leader was dependent on him outmaneuvering the Americans, and the president had to be careful not to be caught in the middle.

Watching Kennedy closely, Ike was surprised to find himself impressed by the man. This was not the glib politician from the campaign, but rather here was a more thoughtful person—earnest in his desire to learn the business of the office and do it well. Before, Ike had been frankly perplexed that the American people had chosen such a callow fellow over the skilled and experienced Nixon. Now he realized that perhaps the people had seen this inner quality in Kennedy—that somehow it had shone through on the trail. Their conversation was so lively and engaging that time passed well beyond the allotted hour.

Afterward the two men went to the Cabinet Room, where the secretaries of state, defense, and the Treasury were prepared for a briefing. Also present were Kennedy's advisor Clark Clifford and Ike's chief of staff, Wilton "Jerry" Persons, who had been tasked with coordinating the transition. (Kindly, Persons would call Clifford later that day to mention how impressed his boss was with Kennedy's seriousness and depth of knowledge—a gesture that went a long way toward inspiring cooperation between the two teams.)

Ike could not emphasize enough to Kennedy the importance of the cabinet, which he used as a high-level study group—an invaluable resource, with which he played rigorous games of logic: *If A is true and B is true, then C cannot be true.* It was crucial to get the most and best out of people, and to Ike that meant employing a style of leadership that was not top-down. Outsiders might have assumed that a former Army commander was accustomed to ruling the roost, but Ike's military experience taught him the opposite—to build up the members of the team so they could shine. Why have a cabinet, why have advisors, if not to listen to them?

In the Cabinet Room, as Kennedy could see, Ike was in his element. The president hid a smile as he considered the way he'd been portrayed as out of touch. To the contrary, he'd always been adept at keeping the tiger by the tail, and took great pleasure in maintaining a firm hand on things.

But Eisenhower also understood that leadership was about more than dominating a room. Leadership, he'd learned on the lonely field of war, was not only about inspiring people to do what needed to be done, but to let them inspire you, too. He'd carried that lesson into the White House, knowing that the practice of such humility found expression in a collaborative spirit.

Ike was a "leavener," as his former chief of staff Sherman Adams had once put it. Some people saw that quality and called him remote, unengaged, dispassionate, but he was quite skilled at keeping the storm troopers in his own administration at bay—to force calm in the face of threatened eruptions that might lead to disastrous decisions.

The times demanded a thoughtful leadership, a steady hand on the tiller. Ike believed that the only way to win World War III was to prevent it—that arms alone were not a guarantee of peace or even security. The president of the United States had the nuclear bomb sitting on his shoulder, whispering in his dreams. The idea of setting in motion a nuclear war—the futility of it for the human race—was a heavy burden. And yet a president must be stalwart. Under Ike's watch the nuclear arsenal had grown substantially, leaving no doubt of our ability to wield horror, but he viewed these weapons as a costly insurance policy on a catastrophe that must be prevented. The president himself was not the only player in this drama. While he might be the one with a finger on the button, the swelling military apparatus and the accompanying industrial power could overwhelm and force that finger down.

In the final moments of his presidency, Ike was not the sleepy elder, ready to go home to the farm. He was more sharply focused than ever, aware of the obligation to history that he still had a few weeks to cement. And as he looked on his young successor—bright, energetic, eager to do the right thing—he saw a looming shadow that Kennedy could not see. In this first meeting, Ike hadn't fully expressed his deepest worries about the future—the grave concern that had kept him awake at night scribbling his thoughts on notepads. His agile mind, his length and depth of experience, and his talent for isolating and cooling the hot ember of every threat gave him a sense of urgency about what lay ahead. And he had one more arrow in his quiver.

As he ushered Kennedy out of the White House after three hours and forty minutes, warmly taking his arm, Kennedy asked if he might call on Eisenhower in the future if he needed his service. Of course, Ike said with a disarming grin, reminding Kennedy to consider his age and well-earned retirement.

In reality, Ike wasn't thinking about retirement. He was thinking about the present. As he walked back to his office, his heart was pumping. He felt wound up. He had six weeks to make his final move, and he was determined to do it. In a dramatic speech, which he had mapped with the foresight and care of a military maneuver, Ike intended to pull all the fragments of the recent past and prospective future together in what he hoped would be a world-changing message. Rather than tottering meekly into the night, he was still very much ready to engage, believing that he could set a course for the fate of the civilized world and his beloved country. His plan would come to fruition over three critical days in January 1961.

PART ONE

THE SETTING

CHAPTER 1

THE MEASURE OF IKE

It is a striking fact that the nation's most famous soldier was born to parents whose religion preached ardent conscientious objection to all mortal wars. But the truth of a life is never contained in its summarizing labels; the influences that shaped our thirty-fourth president were deeper, wider, and more idiosyncratic. As Ike himself acknowledged, he wasn't an exceptional student or a particularly promising military candidate. He once told his wife, Mamie, "If I'm lucky, I'll be a colonel." His ambitions didn't reach farther than that. Yet he went on to become Supreme Allied Commander, assemble the greatest fighting force in the history of mankind, defeat Adolf Hitler's war machine, save Western civilization from fascism, and manage to get elected president twice by decisive majorities. He had never dreamed of being a general, much less president of the United States, but that's where life took him.

As a boy he was taught to be honest, humble, and hardworking—in the telling his upbringing can take on the reflective glow of a Lincolnesque story. Many have rushed to make direct links between Ike's heartland childhood, grounded in faith and work ethic, and the measure of the man he ultimately became. And that's a piece of the story. The rest—Ike's exceptional intuition, savant-like strategic intellect, and warm and open personality—were part nature and part nurture, a mysterious brew that set him apart from his brothers in significant ways.

With Ike it can be hard to differentiate the man from the myth. His achievements are monumental, his personality seemingly so transparently expressed in the blazing ear-to-ear smile, that the underlying truth goes unexamined. A White House aide once described how his friends would say, "Well, wasn't it wonderful? I bet he slapped you on the back and he had that big grin." Not so. "He didn't slap people on the back. He didn't congratulate people particularly," the aide said. "What he did was to make people feel that what he was doing had some transcendent significance." The grinning visage stamped on American minds glossed over Ike's more substantive quality—the ability to inspire and elevate those who worked under his leadership.

Dwight David Eisenhower—who would become "little Ike" and then "Ike" in childhood—was born in Denison, Texas, on October 14, 1890, to David and Ida Stover Eisenhower. He was the third of seven brothers (the fifth dying of diphtheria as an infant). Oddly, all of the boys would carry the nickname "Ike," derived from their last name, at one point or another, although Dwight was the only one for whom it became permanent.

David and Ida had met while students at a religious school, Lane University in Lecompton, Kansas, run by the Church of the United Brethren in Christ. Being a college student set Ida apart in an era when few women sought higher education, but it had always been her dream. Although she dropped out of school to marry, her lifetime love of learning was passed on to her sons, and their home was full of books. Ida was bright, forceful, and high-spirited—"a pistol in a petticoat," as her great-granddaughter Mary Jean would put it.

As newlyweds David and Ida received a gift of farmland

from David's parents, but David did not want to be a farmer. Mortgaging the land to his brother-in-law, he opened a retail store in Hope, Kansas, with the proceeds. Unfortunately, the business was plagued by misfortune as his farmer customers fell on hard times and could not pay down their credit. When David's partner stole their last remaining funds, the venture collapsed. David never got over his disappointment, but by then he had two additional mouths to feed and he needed a job. He found one four hundred miles south in the railroad town of Denison. Ike and his brother Roy were born there before the family returned to Kansas, settling in Abilene, where David got a job as an engineer at the Belle Springs Creamery. They would never leave. Abilene became the source of Ike's most folksy anecdotes. Later, it was chosen as the site of his presidential library, and the location of his burial plot.

The Eisenhower household was a striving mixture of religious fundamentalism and the all-American ethos of individualism and work ethic. Religious faith and practice was baked into the Eisenhower family life. Both the Eisenhowers and the Stovers first came to the United States from Germany in the 1740s, settling in Pennsylvania and Virginia, respectively. David's family was affiliated with the River Brethren, an offshoot of the Mennonites, while Ida was raised Lutheran and later joined David's religion. Eisenhowers were among the pioneering families to move to Kansas in 1878. Some within the group banded together to form the Belle Springs Creamery in Abilene, where Ike's father worked as a mechanical engineer, putting in twelve-hour days, six days a week.

When Ike was five, his parents became involved in the Jehovah's Witnesses. They joined the religion in the wake of their son Paul's death, comforted by the belief that death was only a state of sleeping, and they would be reunited with him soon, as the end of the world was upon them. David and Ida weren't flashy about their religion, but at home they were deeply devout, studying the Bible and abiding by the simple principles of the faith.

The Eisenhowers' religion isn't always clearly identified in historical writings, which sometimes identify them as River Brethren. When Ike's life became public he mostly avoided talking about his parents' faith, perhaps because it was unconventional, or maybe because was it opposed not only to war but also to politics and government. Followers did not believe in saluting the flag. Most people at the time viewed Jehovah's Witnesses as a proselytizing religion. There is no indication Ike's parents did any proselytizing, but they did practice a prayerful life, grounded in the Bible. Ida used the Bible as a primary source of instruction—she'd won a competition as a girl by memorizing 1,365 verses in six months. Ike's greatest speeches included passages from the Bible, and he often spoke of the power of faith in the matters of man. Uncomfortable with institutional religion as an adult, his faith was not always front and center in discussions, yet it was ever present. During Eisenhower's administration "under God" was added to the Pledge of Allegiance, and he signed the law making "In God We Trust" the national motto. He initiated the White House Prayer Breakfast and the National Day of Prayer—although he spent the first Day of Prayer fishing, golfing, and playing bridge. However, he was baptized only after being elected president, joining the National Presbyterian Church in Washington, D.C. It was supposed to be a secret baptism, but the minister had prepared handouts for the press describing the scene. Ike was so peeved he threatened to choose another church.

As important as religion, Ike's small-town roots had a lasting influence on him and cemented his image as a child of the heartland. (His 1952 presidential campaign depicted him as "the man from Abilene," in the same way that Truman was "the man from Independence" and later campaigns would promote Carter as "the man from Plains," and Clinton as "the man from Hope.")

Abilene in the late 1800s was known primarily as the end of the road—the final destination for cattle drives moving north from Texas on the celebrated Chisholm Trail. An honest-to-goodness rough-and-tumble western town of Wild West legend, Abilene was also known for its flamboyant characters, such as Wild Bill Hickok, who served for a time as the city's marshal, and for the gunfights that erupted when heavily lubricated cowboys blew off steam after months on the trail. Living right across the street from the Eisenhowers was a man named Dudley, who boasted he had served as a deputy of Wild Bill, and he regaled Ike and his brothers with stories of Hickok's dexterity with a gun. Although Abilene was no longer the wild cow town of that era, it was easy for young boys like Ike, born in 1890, to imagine it and be proud of the way such a famous gunman once tamed their town. When the popular television series *Gunsmoke* first aired in the 1950s—dramatizing the adventures of Marshal Dillon, Chester, and Miss Kitty, who fended off the coarse interlopers in Dodge City, Kansas, in the 1870s—it isn't surprising that Ike watched right along with the rest of the country when he was home in Gettysburg, eating dinner on a TV tray as he enjoyed the depiction of a world that felt emotionally familiar.

"I was raised in a little town of which most of you have never heard," Ike said in a speech in 1953. "But in the West it is a famous place. It is called Abilene, Kansas. We had as our marshal for a long time a man named Wild Bill Hickok. If you don't know anything about him, read your Westerns more. Now that town had a code, and I was raised as a boy to prize that code. It was: meet anyone face to face with whom you disagree. You could not sneak up on him from behind, or do any damage to him, without suffering the penalty of an outraged citizenry. If you met him face to face and took the same risks he did, you could get away with almost anything, as long as the bullet was in the front." That Ike followed this model of behavior is evidenced throughout his life. It's one reason he despised politics. He hated underhandedness and fakery, and his leadership style, whether in war or in peace, was based on a rare frankness, an effort to impart "what you see is what you get."

Ike relished the rural life, and between the ages of eight and sixteen he often accompanied another family friend, Bob Davis, on hunting and fishing trips. Weekends on the river also involved lessons in poker, played with "a greasy pack of nicked cards" that had seen better days. In Davis, Ike learned to value other forms of intelligence than just book smarts, seeing that it was possible to be both functionally illiterate (Davis couldn't read or write) and still be razor sharp, competent, and a damn good poker player. River sojourns with Davis were rugged, nurturing confidence and self-sufficiency. (The trips also left Ike with a lifelong love of fresh-caught fish cooked over a campfire. In later years Ike was famous in the family for his facility at the barbecue pit—his specialty being the thick western beef steaks that he loved.)

Ike's first encounter with politics came when he was six years old. In 1896, William McKinley, the Republican presidential candidate, visited Abilene. There was much excitement among the children when the town officials decided to throw McKinley a torchlight parade. Unfortunately, not enough adults gathered to carry the torches. The Eisenhower boys, Arthur, Edgar, and little Ike, standing at the origin point, were handed torches, and Ike serendipitously ended up leading the parade. The torches were homemade affairs—just a stick with a can of flammable liquid and a wick at the top—and when lit they gave off a smoky flame. Ike was delighted to march in the parade and relieved to get through it without singeing his hair. He later wrote about the incident, noting that it was one of his "few brushes with political life" until he ran for president in 1952.

The character of Ike's family, and the division of parental responsibility, was very clear: "Father was the breadwinner, Supreme Court and Lord High Executioner," he recalled. "The application of stick to skin was a routine affair. Mother was tutor and manager of our household. She was by far the greatest personal influence in our lives." That gentle influence created a foundation from which he built a life of substance. But inner discipline was developed over time and hard to come by.

Ike always admitted he was something of a scamp as a kid— and he had a temper. A favorite story involved an incident on Halloween when he was ten. Arthur and Edgar were allowed to go trick-or-treating, but his parents decided Ike was too young to go. Ike thought it was terribly unfair, especially since Edgar was only a year and nine months older. He was furious, and argued fiercely for permission to go. When his pleas failed and his brothers happily headed off into the night without him, he lost his temper. Rushing into the yard, he smashed his fists repeatedly into the trunk of an apple tree until they bled, stopping only when his father dragged him back into the house, giving him a few extra whacks with a hickory stick in the process. He was sent to bed, where he lay sobbing, full of humiliation, disappointment, and frustration.

After about an hour, Ike's mother entered his room quietly and sat beside his bed. She knew how easily little boys could be crushed by feelings of helplessness, and how the outlet of rage could seem the only way for them to assert themselves in a world where they had no control. As she ministered to his bleeding hands, she spoke softly to Ike about this very fact, telling him how mastering his temper was the task of growing up. Referring to a biblical passage, she said, "He that conquereth his own soul is greater than he who taketh a city."

Half a century later, Ike recalled her advice, noting that it marked a change in his life. "Hating was a futile sort of thing, she said, because hating anyone or anything meant that there was little to be gained. The person who had incurred my displeasure probably didn't care, possibly didn't even know, and the only person injured was myself. . . . I have always looked back on that conversation as one of the most valuable moments of my life." And indeed, in his life and career, although Ike could display a blistering temper on rare occasions, he became far better known for his calm strength under pressure. He developed a simple method for handling rage, an "anger drawer" in his desk into which he dropped slips of paper with the names of people he was angry at. Once in the drawer, the grievance was banished from thought.

THE EISENHOWER HOMESTEAD ON Fourth Street, purchased in 1898 when Ike was eight for $3,500, was literally on the "wrong" side of the tracks, with the train tracks running both in front of and behind the house. The hissing sound of the steam engine and the clanging of the bell were the audible backdrop to Ike's childhood. The house was humble, but included a large orchard, a robust vegetable garden, and an alfalfa field. There were chickens, a cow, and a horse. When the chores were divvied up among the six boys, their least favorite was working inside the house, with so much going on outdoors. And the best chore of all—which all of the brothers vied for—was being allowed to go to the store and bring the groceries home. What attracted the boys was a "dill pickle jar that you could dive into, sometimes arm deep almost, and try to get one," making the trip worthwhile.

"In retrospect," Ike once said, "I realize that we might have been classified as being poor, but we didn't know it." He added this willful ignorance was part of the glory of America. "All that we knew was that our parents—of great courage—could say to us, 'Opportunity is all about you. Reach out and take it.' "

Sometimes the duties involved watching the baby if there was one in the house, which there often was. When Ike had the chore of watching baby Milton in his carriage, he'd lie on his back reading a book, while rocking the carriage with his foot until the baby fell asleep.

Ike was easily distracted from daily life by reading. Inspired by his mother, he was a voracious consumer of histories—to the point where he neglected his homework and chores. The worst punishment his mother could inflict was to take away his books, which she did when she saw Ike was not studying his lessons or completing his chores. She placed them in a cabinet under lock and key. Ike dutifully hunkered down, but one day he found the key and was filled with a sense of victory. Whenever his mother went shopping or was out working in the vegetable garden, he'd open the cabinet and liberate his precious books.

His heroes were Hannibal, Caesar, Pericles, and Socrates—the ancient stories spoke to him even more deeply than the more recent western heroes. He also idolized George Washington; his study of Washington's speeches would be instrumental when he wrote his own.

He loved reading about the Civil War—not long in the past—but he never saw his reading as anything more than pure enjoyment. He was unconscious of building a foundation or of gaining any lessons for the future. Had anyone suggested he would one day visit the battlefield at Gettysburg, much less build a home on its edges, he would have responded skeptically. Lofty aspirations were far from his mind, and as a boy his restless nature was reined in, he later said, by a sense that "life was a flat plateau of assigned tasks, unchanging in monotony and injustice." This surprisingly grim view was born out of the Eisenhowers' hardscrabble existence on the central Great Plains.

Hard work, study, faith, and discipline were taken for granted: you did your chores, prepared your lessons for school, and took responsibility. But lest anyone would assume in a high-minded way those strict bedrock values were the sturdy foundation of his success, Ike would tell you that the singular factor that formed his nature was the love in the Eisenhower household—between his parents and their children. And second to love was the willingness of David and Ida to let their children self-actualize—be themselves, achieve a level of independence in thought and deed, and pursue their own dreams. As he wrote in *At Ease,* "ambition without arrogance was quietly instilled in us by both parents. Part of that ambition was self-dependence. . . . Whenever any of us expressed a wish for something that seemed far beyond our reach, my mother often said, 'Sink or swim,' or 'Survive or perish.'"

Ike described himself as being "gangly and awkward" in his young years, although that description discounts his athleticism. He was passionate about sports—baseball and football in particular. But an accident when he was a freshman in high school threatened his athletic career. One day, while running with friends, Ike slipped and fell, scraping his knee. He didn't think much of it at first, except for the disappointment of ruining a new pair of trousers. But by the second day, he was feeling ill, and he lay on the sofa, feverish and delirious with infection. His parents called a doctor, who tried to treat the wound and infection to no avail. Slipping in and out of consciousness, Ike, half-conscious, heard the doctor use the word *amputation*. Suddenly he was wide awake. When his brother Edgar came home, Ike called him over. "I'd rather be dead than crippled and not be able to play ball," Ike told him urgently. Remarkably, Ike's parents supported his refusal to have an amputation, even as his condition grew more dire. Other methods were tried— including painting carbolic acid around his body. Eventually he recovered, but Ike remained out of school for the rest of the year.

Undoubtedly this experience was often on his mind later as he comforted the men under his command who suffered grievous wounds and amputations. Not surprisingly, the story of Ike's near-death experience was sometimes enhanced in future writings to include a picture of his devout parents on their knees praying by his bedside night and day. He scoffed at the characterization. "This is ridiculous," he wrote. "My parents were devout Christians and there is no doubt that they prayed for my recovery, but they did it in their morning and evening prayers. They did not believe in 'faith healing.'"

As a result of his missed schooling, Ike graduated from high school behind his peers. Then it was a question of what to do with the rest of his life. Ike's road to West Point and the military career that later defined him was more happenstance than aspirational. After high school, with no money for college, Ike was working at the creamery, unsure of what he would do. The answer came thanks to his close friend Ed "Swede" Hazlett, who had attended a private military high school. He planted the idea in Ike that an appointment to a military academy would mean a free education and—just as important—a chance to play sports.

To be sure, Ike was a lover of military history, but he had yet to apply it to his own life. His concerns at the time were far more practical. He feared he would never be able to afford college on his own.

On August 20, 1910, Ike sent a letter to Kansas U.S. senator Joseph Bristow. "Dear Sir," he wrote in a boyish scrawl, "I would very much like to enter either the school at Annapolis, or the one at West Point. In order to do this, I must have an appointment to one of these places, and so I am writing to you in order to secure the same. . . . If you find it possible to appoint me to one of these schools, your kindness will certainly be appreciated by me."

Attached to his earnest letter was a batch of testimonial letters from influential men in Abilene, who praised Ike's father and family and vouched for his character.

Ike was rejected by the U.S. Naval Academy, in Annapolis, Maryland, because of his age—remember, he was a year older than his peers from being held back in school—but he scored in second place on the qualification exam for West Point. After a short time in limbo, he moved into the first-place slot after the other candidate failed the height requirement. A second entrance examination sealed his acceptance, and he was instructed to report to the U.S. Military Academy at West Point on June 14, 1911.

As strict conscientious objectors, Ike's parents hated war and might have been troubled by his choice of West Point. But they never betrayed their feelings. They believed firmly that one's destiny was one's own affair, and Ike, like their other children, had a right to choose as he saw fit. They never said a word against it. Their consciences might have been eased by the fact there was no war on the immediate horizon.

Milton, who was twelve at the time, remembered the day

his older brother left for West Point: "Dad was at work when Ike left. I went out on the west porch with mother as Ike started uptown, carrying his suitcase, to take the train. Mother stood there like a stone statue, and I stood right by her until Ike was out of sight. Then she came in and went to her room and bawled like a baby. I was the only person home. Oh, of course I cried too."

On June 14, Ike arrived at West Point, located fifty miles north of New York City. Its stunning vistas above the Hudson River had inspired young men since Thomas Jefferson was president. As Ike raised his hand to be sworn in as a cadet, he was jarred by the realization that from that moment on—at least for the foreseeable future—he would be in service to the United States of America above self and family. Entering West Point was like embarking on a journey to a place that, while strange, contained familiar signposts—these being discipline, moral character, physical and mental toughness, and obedience to a higher purpose. But these attributes were not entirely clear to Ike. At the time what most inspired his passion was the chance to play sports in one of the nation's best settings.

In his early weeks at West Point, Ike spent his recreation periods on the baseball field, mindful as he practiced that the baseball coach had his eye out for promising candidates. Ike really wanted to make the baseball team—he'd been a pretty fair center fielder in high school and in a Kansas league after graduation. The coach told Ike he was impressed with his fielding but didn't think much of his hitting style. "Practice hitting my way for a year, and you'll be on my squad next spring," he said. But Ike was too impatient for that. Denied an immediate place on the baseball squad, he tried out for football and was delighted to make the team as a linebacker. He played with passion. Of his football days at West Point, he wrote, "It would be difficult to overemphasize the importance I attached to participation in sports. I so loved the fierce bodily contact of football that I suppose my enthusiasm made up somewhat for my lack of size." Perhaps the highlight of his career was a 1912 game between West Point and the famed Carlisle Indians, whose star player, Jim Thorpe, was fresh from winning Olympic gold medals in the pentathlon and the decathlon at the Stockholm Games. The Indians won, and soon after Ike suffered a knee injury in a game with Tufts that ended his football playing days. "Homer and his legendary birthplaces cannot hold a candle to the number of Tufts men who say they caused the original injury," he wrote later in life. He recalled how over the years he heard from two or three dozen of them claiming to be the one, and joked it must have been quite a crowded field.

Ike's class at West Point—the class of 1915—would come to be known as "the class the stars fell upon" because of the number of graduates who went on to earn stars—two five-star generals (Ike and Omar Bradley), two four-star generals, seven three-star lieutenant generals, twenty-four two-star major generals, and twenty-four one-star brigadier generals.

Ike, who would reach the pinnacle of military success, was at the time a somewhat lackluster student with frequent ruptures in discipline—not a rising star, as one might expect. That's not to say he lacked intellect, but he always tended to downplay his smarts in favor of appearing to be one of the guys—a quality that would win him equal measures of praise and scorn throughout his life. More than anything, he despised pretentiousness, so he was regularly underestimated. As he approached graduation in 1915, there was even a question about whether he'd receive a commission. Out of 164 graduates, he ranked 61st academically and number 125 in discipline. His disciplinary infractions, which fill a lengthy list in his record,

included dancing—a repeat offense—lateness, and general slop-
piness, among others:

Absent at 8 A.M. drill formation. 3 demerits.
Dirty gun and collar not properly adjusted at parade.
    4 demerits.
Late at chapel. 1 demerit.
Room in disorder after inspection. 2 demerits.
Soiled waist belt at inspection. 2 demerits.
Late at drill, 15th instant. 1 demerit.
Wearing very white dirty trousers about 9:99 A.M.
    2 demerits.

It goes on like this for several pages. But in large part due
to his sheer likability—and the judgments of those who were
keen enough to recognize the intellectual light he hid behind
an affable smile—he skated through and was assigned, at age
twenty-five, as a second lieutenant to Fort Sam Houston in San
Antonio, Texas, for the princely pay of $141.67 a month. He
was disappointed. He'd originally requested duty in the Philippines, and been so confident of getting his wish he'd purchased
tropical khakis and whites. Now he was in hock for more uni-
forms, a worrying matter until a particularly fortuitous poker
game allowed him to pay his debt.

Ike arrived at Fort Sam Houston on September 13, 1915,
tasked with training enlisted men—although the United States
was determined to stay out of the war in Europe, which had
been raging for more than a year. Many people, Ike included,
believed that America would eventually join the war effort, but
that reality was years away. Meanwhile, Ike practiced becoming
a reliable team player and a good soldier. He later wrote that
he tried to do a good job and not obsess about promotions—to

make every boss sorry to see him go. In this way he made a good impression on his superiors fairly quickly.

In San Antonio he met the woman who would become his love, his lifelong companion, and his North Star.

Eighteen-year-old Mamie Doud from Denver was wintering in San Antonio with her wealthy parents when she met Ike serendipitously. As officer of the day he was making his rounds on the base when one of the wives called him over to meet some visitors.

"Sorry, Mrs. Harris," he called back, "I'm on guard and have to start an inspection trip."

"We didn't ask you to come over to stay," she insisted. "Just come over and meet these friends of mine."

His acquiescence was rewarded when Mrs. Harris introduced him to the Douds—especially their daughter. Mamie, attractive and "saucy," appealed to him instantly. He asked if she'd like to accompany him on his rounds, and she said yes. They never looked back, dating steadily for months, until they became engaged on Valentine's Day. Mamie was in love, but she was young and had lived a pampered life. Her father was extremely protective of her, and he only agreed to the engagement if they waited to marry until the end of the year.

Ike was soon to find out exactly how much control Mr. Doud exerted over his daughter's life. At the time Ike was enamored with the idea of joining the Aviation Section and becoming a pilot. The day he was accepted, he was elated, and hurried to tell Mamie and her family—certain that his new responsibility, which came with a substantial bump in pay, would please them.

Instead, Mr. Doud was furious. He lectured Ike, stating that until that point they'd been happy to have him in the family, but were prepared to withdraw their approval if he went ahead with the crazy scheme to fly. He wasn't wrong to be concerned. Flying itself was only a decade old, and fighter pilots from the

Royal Flying Corps, chasing the Germans in the skies over Europe, had an average survival period of eleven days.

After much soul-searching, love apparently won out and Ike announced he would not join the Aviation Section after all. The marriage was on. (As a side note, weddings were commonplace for those stationed at Fort Sam Houston. According to biographer Merle Miller, "So many young officers got married while they were stationed at Fort Sam that everyone in the army called it 'the mother-in-law of the army.' ")

Ike and Mamie were married in Denver on July 1, 1916. Ike got a special ten-day leave for the wedding. Traveling back to San Antonio by train after the wedding, they made a side trip to Abilene. Arriving at 3 A.M., they found Ike's father waiting at the station and Ida at home preparing a massive fried chicken "breakfast." This was Mamie's first encounter with Ike's family and hometown, and she was pleased by the warm welcome. It would set the stage for a close relationship, especially between Mamie and Ida—helpful because there were many changes in store for Mamie. Suddenly she went from being a pampered upper-class girl to an Army wife. But she adapted well— probably not fully realizing she was setting off on a life course of frequent upheavals, with no home to call her own until late in life, when the Eisenhowers finally bought property at Gettysburg.

When the United States finally declared war on Germany and joined the war effort on April 6, 1917, Ike longed to head overseas to lead a platoon. Instead, he was kept at home in his training capacity. Until the very end of World War I he expected to ship out, but it never happened. Later, people would marvel how the man chosen to direct the course of the next world war had never seen a day of combat.

His major joy during that period was Mamie's pregnancy. But four days before their child was born, Ike was uprooted and sent to Fort Oglethorpe in Georgia to train officer candidates. He was not present for the birth of their son, Doud Dwight (who would be nicknamed "Icky"). Hearing the news, he wrote excitedly to Mamie, "I understand that Mr. Ike Jr. has my feet, hands, and shoulders. . . . Just wait until I come home, if we don't have more fun with that boy than with a barrel full of monkeys. . . ."

After the war, in the fall of 1919, Ike was assigned to Camp Meade in Maryland, where he became friendly with a World War I hero named George Patton. Temperamentally, they were an unlikely pair. Patton could be profane and unpredictable, with a grandiose style, and he was five years Ike's senior. But they bonded over their shared passion for the mechanics of military maneuvers—specifically, the development of a better-equipped tank fleet. Although their ideas met with resistance from the high command, their friendship lasted. Born to a wealthy family, Patton didn't need to be a soldier, but in his heart he could be nothing else until the day he died, which was in a car accident in Germany following the end of World War II. According to Mamie, the Pattons lived as humbly on base as everyone else. It would certainly have surprised Ike early on that he would one day be Patton's commander during World War II—and that the war years would cement their relationship.

Ike's future rise to power and greatness was still not evident. On one occasion, President Woodrow Wilson and Secretary of War Newton Baker were on an inspection tour of Camp Meade when they wandered over to the housing area to greet some Army wives—including Mamie. Baker asked her, "What does your husband do best?" and Mamie replied quickly, "He plays a good hand of poker."

AN UNTHINKABLE TRAGEDY STRUCK the Eisenhowers while at Camp Meade. Their adored son Icky, only three, contracted scarlet fever and died on January 2, 1921. Ike called it "a tragedy from which we never recovered." Throughout his life, he regularly expressed a deep grief over the loss, as if it were still fresh, even many decades later. His White House secretary Ann Whitman recalled walking into the Oval Office one day to find him staring off into space. He told her he was thinking of his little boy. Every year on Icky's birthday, Ike sent Mamie yellow roses, which he claimed were Icky's favorite.

Ike was in a daze during the months after Icky's death. Everything was rendered a somber gray by the loss. Ambition seemed meaningless, plans on hold. So it was with some surprise that Ike learned that a requested transfer to Panama, which had earlier been denied, was now being approved, at the request of Major General Fox Conner. Conner, who had served under General John J. Pershing as operations officer for the American Expeditionary Forces in France during World War I, seemed to be just the father figure and mentor Ike needed during this troubling period in his life. Ike would always say that Conner taught him the most about military principles. He'd never met a man so steeped in knowledge of military history. But what most impressed him was Conner's nimble mind, the way he questioned history in the context of current action, frequently asking Ike to consider what *he* would do if faced with similar circumstances. Their long talks elevated the experience—for Panama, with its damp heat and moldy, bug-infested living quarters, was a difficult posting.

WITHIN A YEAR OF Icky's death, Mamie became pregnant again, and they were elated. The baby was due in August, and because the climate and conditions in Panama were so harsh, Mamie flew home to Denver in the final months of her pregnancy. Ike joined her there in time to see his son born on August 3, 1922. John Sheldon Doud Eisenhower would be the couple's only living child.

Perhaps because he was born in the shadow of his brother's death, and perhaps too because Ike was a strict, unbending, and often absent father, John struggled for much of his life to achieve a loving rapport with Ike—which he revealed with the opening words of his memoir: "I am certain I was born standing at attention." John would follow Ike to West Point and into a military career, work for him at the White House, and be his companion on some of his most historic trips. He also gave him four grandchildren, whom Ike would unabashedly adore in a way he could not fully manage with his son.

AFTER TWO YEARS IN Panama, Ike embarked on a series of postings that appeared to be grooming him with the kind of comprehensive command knowledge that would set him up for future elevation. He didn't always see it that way, however; nor did Mamie with the wearying hopscotch of postings—from Colorado to Kansas to Washington, D.C. But in 1933 Ike received an assignment that would mark a solid shift in his trajectory as a leader. He joined the staff of Douglas MacArthur, the Army's chief of staff.

The economy was in a state of crisis as Franklin D. Roosevelt took office on March 4. The nation was consumed with the economic plight, and in MacArthur's office the concern was with the fate of the military budget. (As a precursor to his later coinage of *military-industrial complex,* one of Ike's jobs was planning the industrial mobilization for war.)

It was not a particularly happy time for Ike, who felt side-lined and was only earning three thousand dollars a year. However, he recognized a clear opportunity in working for General MacArthur and being able to learn from him. He had never known such a person: forceful, personable, and demanding, with a brilliant, encyclopedic knowledge of the military, politics, and history—but incredibly imperious. MacArthur had a habit of referring to himself in the third person, a trait that struck Ike as peculiar. The general often regaled his staff with lengthy monologues about the state of the world as the listeners sat silent. Ike found it quite amusing when another officer told him MacArthur thought Ike was a great conversationalist—considering he rarely got in a word edgewise.

Ike's sour mood began to change as he immersed himself in a great challenge. In 1935, the newly established Philippine Commonwealth, under President Manuel Quezón, needed a strong defense program, and putting money worries aside, Ike committed himself to the task of drawing up such a plan. He was elated when he was chosen to accompany MacArthur to the Philippines—finally securing the posting he had long ago desired—to help put his plans into effect with the Filipino army. Mamie stayed behind in Washington with John, and Ike checked into a hotel in Manila until they joined him the following year.

Although MacArthur was in charge, increasingly Ike became the "go-to" man for Quezón and the others—in part because MacArthur kept short hours, often not reaching his desk until 11 A.M. and retiring after a late lunch. Ike was the man on the scene for long hours each day, and he began to take on the manner of a commander.

Ike's devotion and abilities didn't go unnoticed by his superior. "This is the best officer in the army," MacArthur wrote of Ike. "When the next war comes, he should go right to the top."

But the seven years Ike spent under MacArthur's command—first in Washington and then in the Philippines—were not smooth. Ike mostly kept his opinions to his diary, but he found MacArthur capricious, arrogant, and often unwilling to face facts. He had heated disagreements with the general, which did not do him much good.

The two men had different views of leadership. For MacArthur it was about being authoritarian and issuing commands—often in an arrogant and even brutal manner. For Ike it was about study, listening, and reflection. He said, "You do not lead by hitting people over the head. That's assault, not leadership." At the core of this sentiment is the idea that leadership isn't about simply pushing your own ideas. It's about a conversation that demands mutual respect—"the art of getting someone else to do something you want done because he wants to do it."

Although he had tremendous respect for MacArthur's intellect, commitment, and military acumen, he also observed a crucial flaw in his character, saying, "MacArthur could never see another sun, or even a moon for that matter, in the heavens, as long as he was the sun."

MacArthur's analysis of Ike was more effusive. In an efficiency report of his time in Panama, MacArthur wrote Ike was "[a]n officer of the most superior professional qualifications as well as of the soundest basic character. Distinguished by force, judgment and willingness to accept responsibility."

These qualities would soon be put to the test as the world entered another war. On September 1, 1939, Hitler invaded Poland, and Britain and France declared war on Germany. Even as the United States resisted engagement, the War Department wanted Ike back home as an instructor for enlisted men. He was assigned to Fort Lewis in Washington State to begin his

THE MEASURE OF IKE   37

new mission as chief of staff of the Third Army. He was at that posting for less than a year before being assigned to Fort Sam Houston—the place his military career had begun—in the same role.

IKE AND MAMIE ARRIVED in San Antonio in the summer of 1941. Once again Mamie was busy settling into another new household. John was at West Point, and they were looking forward to visiting him there over Christmas. Their son's decision to go to West Point had been a sobering one for Ike and Mamie. Not only did they know too well the hardships of military life, they were also aware the peacetime years they had enjoyed were coming to an end. To become a cadet with the world at war—if not yet the United States—was risky. Ike felt certain the day would come. He spoke long and seriously with John, trying to show him the advantages of a civilian education, but John would not be deterred from his desire to go to West Point. He turned the conversation around on Ike, reminding his father it was he who had spoken so glowingly of the satisfaction he'd experienced in the military, especially the pride he'd felt at being associated with men of character. John said, "If I can say the same thing when I've finished my Army career, I'll care no more about promotions than you did."

On December 7, 1941, Ike was napping when Mamie heard the news of the Pearl Harbor attack over the radio. "I immediately went and wakened up my soldier," she recalled, "because I knew he'd want to know right away."

Five days later, Ike received a message from Washington, at the request of Army Chief of Staff General George C. Marshall: "The Chief says for you to hop a plane and get up here right away."

Unfortunately, bad weather had halted plane flights, and the last train had already left San Antonio. So Ike finagled a pilot at Brooks Field to take him on a white-knuckle flight to Houston, where he boarded the train. It was packed, with not a seat to be had. Ike, who was in uniform, hunkered down on top of his suitcase and was found there by Sid Richardson, a wealthy Texas businessman who would later become one of Eisenhower's key supporters. He invited Ike to join him in his drawing room and they played poker on the ride to Washington. As the train made its way to Washington, Ike played cards and distracted himself from the deep disappointment he felt at once again being left behind. Thoughts of the battlefield consumed his dreams, but it did not seem to be his destiny.

Mamie spent Christmas alone with John before joining Ike in the capital and renting an apartment in the Wardman Park Hotel, where she remained throughout the war.

One bright spot of his new job was the opportunity to work under General George Marshall. Ike recalled his old mentor Fox Conner often telling him that Marshall was a genius with the ability to see the big picture and transcend nationalistic considerations. Conner said if Ike ever had a chance to work for Marshall he should jump at it.

Ike soon saw why. Marshall could not have been more different than MacArthur. From the start Ike noticed that the general's leadership style was clear: he did not tolerate self-seekers, one-man shows, those who sought the limelight, or pessimists. Ike shared this attitude and knew they would get along just fine. He would come to grow very fond of Marshall, although it wasn't the general's way to be overly warm and informal. He was one of the rare people who didn't use Ike's nickname, always calling him Eisenhower.

Ike found the War Department in chaos. "Tempers are

short," he wrote in his diary. "There are a lot of amateur strategists on the job, and prima donnas everywhere." He was also concerned that a certain complacency had set in. There was no sense of urgency. "Some of the officers," he wrote, "had worn for themselves deep ruts of professional routine within which they were sheltered from vexing new ideas and troublesome problems."

Initially, General Marshall sought out Ike for his experience in the Philippines, and Marshall was impressed by his plan to defend the Philippines, which had been invaded by the Japanese only hours after Pearl Harbor. But as America engaged in the war in Europe, a strategic plan was needed for that vast enterprise as well. Ike could see there was no clear strategy—or even a solid idea about which countries would be involved. He set himself to the task of sorting out a strategic plan, working long hours, with little time for rest.

The news from overseas was discouraging, as the Axis powers advanced across Europe and into Russia and North Africa, tearing up the map as they sought broader domination. Noting that "brainpower is always in far shorter supply than manpower," Ike concentrated on defining and shaping the missions that would make the greatest impact. In particular he focused on what would become known as Operation Torch, an Allied assault against the Axis powers in North Africa, which would serve as a beachhead in the war effort. But he was also consumed with the larger picture—how to put all the pieces together in a coordinated Allied effort.

During his rare breaks Ike began playing golf in earnest, chipping balls on a field behind the Old Soldiers Home, which stood on a hill three miles from the White House. His son, John, later recalled the scene: "Dad would make a tee out of wet sand, and then take a big, powerful swing that produced a horrendous slice. Often, at this point, the air would be punctuated with expletives." Perhaps Ike was taking out his famous temper on the ball, as an expression of his frustration at being stuck in Washington while the world was at war overseas.

On March 10, 1942, Eisenhower was crushed to hear that his father had died, and he could do no more than wire his regrets. Lonely and bereaved, he wrote in his diary, "I should like so much to be with my Mother these few days. But we're at war. And war is not soft, it has no time to indulge even the deepest and most sacred emotions. . . . I'm quitting work now, 7:30 P.M. I haven't the heart to go on tonight."

The day his father was buried, Ike closed himself off for thirty minutes at the hour of the funeral to reflect and think of him. Like so many sons, he regretted most of all that his father had never known the depth of Ike's love for him. Four years later he lost his mother, who died quietly at eighty-four. Although Ike and his siblings had arranged for a full-time companion in her final years, and tried to pamper her, she refused to be pampered, saving her money and living as frugally as ever. Ike visited her as often as possible after the war, saying, "The sight of my mother was one of the rewards of peace." Her death left him without the woman who had anchored his life for fifty-six years.

On June 8, 1942, Ike presented a draft of his report, "Directive for the Commanding General European Theater of Operations," presenting a plan for a unified command. He mentioned to Marshall that this was one document he should read carefully, because Ike believed it was a blueprint for the course of the war.

"I certainly do want to read it," Marshall said. "You may be the man who executes it. If that's the case, when can you leave?"

It was Ike's first hint that he might be headed overseas, and the assignment was made permanent three days later. At last! After more than twenty-five years in the Army, dutifully taking on every task assigned to him, Eisenhower was going to war.

Ike traveled to West Point and took John out for a boat ride. He broke the news he was going to England.

"What's your job going to be over there?" John asked.

"Well, I'm going to be the boss."

John was puzzled. What did that mean?

"I'm going to be the commanding general," his dad told him.

"My God!" John exclaimed, realizing the enormity of the situation.

Not only was his father finally going to war; he was going to be the man leading the charge.

CHAPTER 2

IKE IN COMMAND

On June 24, 1942, Ike flew to London to take command. Suddenly he was the man of the hour, hounded by the press and booked solid with meetings and greetings. "Darling," he wrote Mamie, "in a place like this the commanding general must be a bit of a diplomat, lawyer, promoter, social hound, liar, at least to get out of social affairs, and, incidentally—sometimes I think most damnably—a soldier."

The social side was a problem for Ike. He simply didn't like it and felt he had far too much to do to attend dinner parties. On one occasion early on, he was pressured to attend a high-level military dinner on the invitation of Ambassador John Winant. He arrived, sat down, and lit a cigarette. The next day the ambassador came to see him, and delicately informed him one did not smoke before the toast to the king.

"Well, this is very bad, Mr. Ambassador, for me," Ike said mischievously. "But it does let me out of one thing, and that is out of dinners."

Ike saw these public commitments as a sideshow to his true purpose, which in the immediate future involved planning the operation in North Africa. There wasn't a moment to lose. The invasion was slated to occur in November. The strategic importance of Operation Torch, the Algeria-Morocco campaign, was clear. Rather than an immediate assault on the heart of Europe, the plan was to open up a pathway—from North Africa to Sicily, to mainland Italy and onward through Europe. Not only would it be Ike's first field command, but it would be his first experience in actual warfare.

He battled loneliness, and at the end of long days would often write to Mamie. He could not share many details of his life, but he empathized with her, knowing she was lonely, too. On September 15, 1942, before Operation Torch, he wrote:

> Your letters often give me some hint of your loneliness, your bewilderment and your worries in carrying on your own part in this emergency. Don't ever think that I do not understand or that I am not truly sympathetic to the lost feeling you must so often have. Just please remember that no matter how short my notes I love you—I could never be in love with anyone else—and that you fill my thoughts and hopes for the future always. You never seen quite to comprehend how deeply I depend upon you and need you. So when you're lonely, try to remember that I'd rather be by your side than anywhere else in the world.

The chief stumbling block to the Algeria-Morocco push was that the region was under control of Vichy France, which was sympathetic to Hitler. The success of the campaign depended on the French forces not opposing the American and British troops launching the attack. Ike's first "political" problem was how to bring the French into alignment with Allied goals. It meant making a critical decision: the Algerian French forces would agree to an armistice only if their chosen representative, Admiral Darlan, a member of the Vichy French and a reported

Nazi collaborator, was appointed. After much soul-searching Ike agreed, knowing full well he might pay a political price. He was more determined than ever to expedite the offensive quickly and put all fears to rest. Ultimately Operation Torch would go forward with the uneasy awareness that the Vichy French forces might be more foe than friend. (Darlan would not survive the year. In December he would be killed by an anti-Vichy assassin in Algeria.)

With the task of leading a joint force, Ike made it clear he would not tolerate any dissent between British and American soldiers. "I will clamp down on anyone who tries to start any trouble between the Americans and British under my command," he said. "There will be neither praise nor blame for the British as British or the Americans as Americans. We are in this together as Allies. We will fight it shoulder to shoulder. Men will be praised or blamed for what they do, not for their nationality."

The operation would be coordinated from Gibraltar, a longtime British beachhead in Spain that was uniquely situated in the region for the oversight and control of sea vessels. Inside the Rock of Gibraltar was a virtual city of tunnels, rooms, and working areas, and in this underground staging area, Eisenhower set up his command center on November 5, three days before the invasion. It was a dark and gloomy place. "Damp, cold air in block-long passages was heavy with stagnation and did not noticeably respond to the clattering efforts of electric fans," Ike wrote in his war memoir. "Through the arched ceilings came a constant drip, drip, drip of surface water that faithfully but drearily ticked off the seconds of the interminable, almost unendurable, wait which always occurs between completion of a military plan and the moment action begins."

In the desolate environment, Ike understood most vividly

that leadership involved portraying an attitude of optimism and confidence in victory, even in the darkest circumstances, and he always strived to impart that positive attitude to the men in his command.

Three landings, at Casablanca, Oran, and Algiers, were planned for 1 A.M. on November 8. As massive convoys of warships and cargo ships made their way to the area from England, Ireland, and America, Ike waited for news of the landings, barely sleeping.

The most difficult of the three landings would be at Casablanca. At Ike's request his old friend George Patton was leading the landing. Many in the high command were put off by Patton, disliking his penchant for melodrama. But for Ike what Patton lacked in emotional intelligence he more than compensated for by his brilliance in battle and his dogged determination to win at all costs. Ike's confidence in Patton would be well rewarded when he succeeded against great odds at Casablanca.

The waiting period as the invasions began was absolutely brutal. In the tomblike catacombs of his Gibraltar headquarters, Ike had no way of knowing the full extent of the German response—whether the ships passing through the narrow Strait of Gibraltar would be bombarded, sunk, or set aflame at sea, spilling thousands of his Navy and Army men into the deep, cold waters of the strait. And more troublesome, it was an open question whether the Vichy French forces would decide to respond to the invasion forces and try to repel them, or mount any kind of fight at all.

As it turned out, all three landings were successful, with only minor Vichy resistance and very few Allied casualties. With a foothold firmly in hand in North Africa, the Allies began quickly offloading troops, transports, and supplies, resolutely advancing across the span of North Africa and eventually

onward and into Italy. As they moved forward, there were many
hard-fought battles, but Ike's first major success strengthened
his conviction that with the correct strategies, troops willing to
fight as smart and as savagely as the Germans, and continuous
support from open supply lines, the Nazis would be defeated
and the war could be won.

In the course of the war Mamie forged the resolve common
to military spouses. It took some effort. "I worried like all the
rest of the wives," she acknowledged. "I worried and stewed
and fretted . . . and finally, I thought, well, this is absolutely ridiculous. There's nothing I can do about it. And so one time, I
just sat down and I thought this thing out." Placing her trust in
God, she came to the conclusion that He had important work
for her husband.

"Ike depended a great deal on the Man above," Mamie
said, "and I think that's what carried him through so many
things." He memorized and recited the prayer of St. Francis of
Assisi—"Lord, make me an instrument of thy peace. . . ." For
Ike, peace, not war, was always the point.

HAVING SUCCEEDED IN THE first line of attack through North
Africa and across Italy, it was now time to plan the most critical
maneuver of all—a direct invasion of France dubbed Operation Overlord. In December 1943, while Ike was in Tunis, he
received word from General Marshall that President Roosevelt
would be traveling through the area and wanted to meet with
him to discuss a change in assignment. When FDR arrived and
Ike joined him in his car, the president got straight to the point:
"Well, Ike," he said, "you are going to command Overlord."

Ike might have been surprised by the assignment. The obvious choice for such a role would have been Marshall, but Roosevelt needed him in Washington, providing advice, keeping

lines of communication open with the other general officers as well as Congress, and helping the commander in chief devise carefully crafted and appropriate strategic responses. "FDR also liked Ike," wrote historian Jean Edward Smith. "Not only was he easy to get along with, but he exhibited none of the posturing that often accompanies high rank."

Of course, the choice of Ike had not been made lightly—it was in fact a carefully calculated decision, one based on the very different personalities of all of the major officers capable of such a command. And of course Ike's masterful work with the successful North African invasion, Operation Torch, was taken into consideration. It had been decided that of all the commanding generals in play, Ike was the one with the most egalitarian method of command, both naturally respectful of those with whom he worked and a synergistic collaborator; he was capable of changing a fixed position if a better option was presented to him. And although Ike thought the title "supreme commander" was ostentatious—kind of like *sultan*—he was pleased to have the job. He was convinced that Marshall had a strong hand in the decision.

"Mr. President, I realize that such an appointment involved difficult decisions," Ike said candidly. "I hope you will not be disappointed."

THE WAR EFFORT WAS a study in male ego. The looming figures of the Allied front included the powerful troika of Winston Churchill, Charles de Gaulle, and FDR, supported by imposing military brass at home and abroad—George Marshall, Omar Bradley, Bernard Montgomery, and George Patton, with King George VI hovering in the background, often wishing he were not king so he could join the fight.

It might have been a disaster of clashing egos were it not for the mutual decision to stand behind the leadership of General Eisenhower.

It was in Ike's hands to mold the disparate forces to form a cohesive strategy, to tamp down the errant wills and explosive personalities of men accustomed to power. In this role Ike defied stereotype. He did not have the conceit of MacArthur, the unruly temperament of Patton, or the swagger of British general Montgomery. He had a confident presence that made him seem larger than his height of five feet ten and a half inches. Unlike Patton, he did not relish war. He was not a bull charging into battle, but a strategist whose field was the map room and the conference table. Ike compared his role as supreme commander to chairman of the board—responsible yet a hair removed from the daily tasks. There was a loneliness at the core of such power—a constant worry his failure would have catastrophic consequences.

Even Montgomery, who was one of Ike's greatest critics, acknowledged his persuasive power: "He's not the greatest soldier in the world. His real strength lies in his human qualities. He has the power of drawing the hearts of men toward him as a magnet attracts a bit of metal. He merely has to smile at you and you trust him at once."

But it wasn't just personality. Ike had a talent for seeing the big picture and for moving the pieces on a complex chessboard to his advantage. And in the spring of 1944, that chessboard involved Operation Overlord. To this day, even people born decades after the war will shiver imagining the implications of a German victory. But with Nazi Germany in control of most of Western Europe, a daring plan was necessary to shake loose the Nazi grip.

Operation Overlord (D-Day in the popular lexicon) was a staggering enterprise, whose risk-reward ratio was incalculable. The Allied planners knew going in that the casualties would be large, and perhaps thousands of men would be sacrificed on the desolate shores to a greater purpose. Yet they must try. With the hindsight of history, we can conclude that without success on D-Day, the war might have been lost. But in the war room leading up to the decision, the script would need to be written nearly from scratch, based on only the thinnest orders from the Combined Chiefs of Staff: "You will enter the continent of Europe and, in conjunction with the other Allied nations, undertake operations aimed at the heart of Germany and the destruction of her Armed Forces."

The devil, of course, was in the details. By May, under Ike's direction and after lengthy discussions, the plan was set:

1. Land on the Normandy coast.
2. Build up the resources needed for a decisive battle in the Normandy-Brittany region.
3. Pursue on a broad front with two army groups—one to gain necessary ports and reach the boundaries of Germany and threaten the Ruhr, and the other to link up with forces to invade France from the south.
4. Secure ports in Belgium, Brittany, and the Mediterranean and build up a base along the western border of Germany.
5. While building up forces, keep up an unrelenting offensive to wear down the enemy and gain advantages for the final fight.
6. Complete the destruction of enemy forces west of the Rhine, while constantly seeking beachheads across the river.
7. Launch the final attack as a double envelopment of the Ruhr, and follow up with an immediate thrust through Germany.
8. Clean out the remainder of Germany.

As Ike wrote long after the war, "This general plan, carefully outlined at staff meetings before D-Day, was never abandoned, even momentarily, throughout the campaign."

For Assaulting Army Commander of Operation Overlord, Ike chose his old West Point classmate Omar Bradley, whose leadership in North Africa he had come to admire. He found Bradley to be an emotionally centered and strong leader, and a keen judge of the men in his command. Ike also wanted Patton on board, and hoped he wouldn't balk to being second to Bradley as an Army commander. He needn't have worried. Patton was happy with his assignment.

Unfortunately, once Patton arrived in London, his tendency to shoot off his mouth got him into trouble almost immediately. At a British gathering he held forth that after the war America and Great Britain should combine forces to rule the world. Meant to be private, his words leaked out, and once they hit the press there was a huge outcry and Ike feared he might have to relieve Patton of command.

Ashamed and demoralized, his own victim, Patton came to Ike to face the music. He immediately offered to resign. But by then Ike, who had weighed the advantage of Patton's battlefield skill against the disadvantage of his imprudence, had already decided to keep him on. There were times, Ike thought, when deportment alone was not disqualifying, and this was one of them. Nearly in tears, Patton thanked Ike and apologized repeatedly. Ike laughed off his show of gratitude and countered Patton's thanks with, "You owe us some victories; pay off and the world will deem me a wise man."

The scale of the invasion was great: 5,000 sea vessels, 13,000 aircraft, and more than 160,000 men all poised to sweep down on the beaches of Normandy. More than 16,000 staff were involved in the planning. At Ike's insistence, this was a far larger force than had originally been planned for. He felt strongly that overwhelming force was the key to success. And it all had to be done in secret because the element of surprise was also crucial. The invasion was scheduled for June 5, 1944, when the moon would be full to guide the way and the tides low enough to support a landing.

IN FREQUENT CONVERSATIONS WITH Ike, Churchill expressed his deepest reservations. "When I think of the beaches of Normandy choked with the flower of American and British youth, and when, in my mind's eye, I see the tides running red with their blood, I have my doubts . . . I have my doubts." Ike had his fears, too, because the ultimate result and the cost in lives were essentially unknowable.

Although staff meetings consumed most of his waking hours, Ike made a point of visiting the troops. In the months leading up to D-Day he personally visited twenty-six divisions, twenty-four airfields, five ships of war, and many other installations. His purpose was twofold: to keep a close eye on preparations and to lift morale. He instructed his commanders to do likewise. "Soldiers like to see the men who are directing operations," he wrote. "They properly resent any indication of neglect or indifference to them on the part of their commanders and invariably interpret a visit, even a brief one, as evidence of the commander's concern for them."

Operation Overlord was considered so significant and potentially decisive, Churchill and King George hatched a plan to watch the invasion from a cruiser off the coast, a scheme that so alarmed the British government it was immediately rejected. Disappointed at once more being relegated to the sidelines, the king wrote to Churchill, "The right thing to do is what normally falls to those at the top on such occasions, namely to remain at home and wait."

At Southwick House, the invasion headquarters in the southern English town of Portsmouth, Ike and the core group of invasion strategists pored over the plans, looking for any flaws in the invasion strategy. The invasion plan was nothing short of balletic, an intricate choreography in which each new arm of force was slated to enter into the order of battle at its precisely designated time: paratroopers would drop from the skies in the dark early hours of June 6; air assaults would commence on the surrounding bridges; transport planes would drop men and supplies along the beaches; and finally, at dawn, troops would begin landing on the beaches. It was a well-designed plan.

But as the saying goes, "Man plans, God laughs," for the biggest fate-determining issue became the weather.

Weather on the English Channel was unpredictable in the best of times, and while the prospect of perfectly serene seas was certainly unrealistic, a stormy forecast would make the invasion impossible. So it was very bad news on June 4 when British group captain J. M. Stagg, the chief meteorologist of Operation Overlord, told Ike about the forecast for the next day. A storm was rolling in across the Channel, and he urged Ike to delay the invasion by a day.

But would a day be enough? Meteorologists in 1944 had none of the sophisticated equipment we use today to predict the weather. There was little surety that June 6 would be a safe bet. But what was the alternative?

"How long can you keep this invasion on the end of a limb and let it hang there?" Ike asked. The answer, it seemed, was not long. If they waited two weeks for another window in the tides and weather, the cloak of secrecy would almost surely have been lifted. Meanwhile, thousands of men would be held in suspended animation, weakening strength and resolve. If the invasion didn't happen on June 6 the chance might be lost forever.

Ike slumped in his chair, bowing his head in thought. He didn't really see another way but to invade on June 6, but he decided to table the discussion for a few hours and sleep on it—though it is hard to imagine anyone in the room, least of all Ike, actually slept.

At 3:30 A.M. on June 5 Ike gathered his team together for a final decision. He asked each man for his opinion, and as he listened he paced the room. Captain Stagg had cautiously better news. He thought there might be a clearing. Ike felt a little bit better, but the weight of the fateful decision belonged solely to him. Finally he made it:

"Okay, we'll go."

It was on.

The order of the day, which Ike had been drafting for weeks, was distributed to the forces:

Soldiers, Sailors and Airmen of the Allied Expeditionary Forces:

You are about to embark upon the Great Crusade, toward which we have striven these many months. The eyes of the world are upon you. The hopes and prayers of liberty-loving people everywhere march with you. In company with our brave Allies and brothers-in-arms on other Fronts you will bring about the destruction of the German war machine, the elimination of Nazi tyranny over oppressed peoples of Europe, and security for ourselves in a free world. . . . Good Luck! And let us all beseech the blessing of Almighty God upon this great and noble undertaking.

That day, in a moment of privacy, Ike scribbled a note, which he placed in his wallet. He was compelled to record a statement in the event the invasion failed, and his words on that piece of paper startle the modern mind into contemplation of what might have been. They also depict a man of great humility who knew that while he had done the best he could do, he did not possess godly power:

> Our landings in the Cherbourg-Havre area have failed to gain a satisfactory foothold and I have withdrawn the troops. My decision to attack at this time and place was based upon the best information available. The troops, the air, and the navy did all that Bravery and devotion to duty could do. If any blame or fault attaches to the attempt it is mine alone.

In the evening, Ike drove some fifty miles to Newbury, where the 101st Airborne Division was preparing to take flight. Captain Harry C. Butcher, who had been by Eisenhower's side for years, wrote movingly of the scene: "We saw hundreds of paratroopers with blackened and grotesque faces, packing up for the big hop and jump. Ike wandered through them, stepping over packs, guns, and a variety of equipment such as only paratroop people can devise, chinning with this and that one. All were put at ease. He was promised a job after the war by a Texan who said he roped, not dallied, his cows, and at least there was enough to eat in the work. Ike has developed or disclosed an informality and friendliness with troopers that almost amazed me."

Ike's feeling for his troops was always plain to see and completely heartfelt. In an affecting personal account for the *Chicago Tribune*, correspondent John Thompson wrote of how urgently Ike wanted to communicate what they were experiencing to the ordinary people back home, quoting Ike: "[Does the citizen] realize just exactly what these people are doing and how they are performing? Does he realize it as well as the feats of the big bombers or of one of our destroyers carrying out a gallant mission to Taranto? This is something I've felt for a long time, and I don't know whether there is much to do about it, but it is from the heart and I believe it."

Ike's own recollection of meeting the paratroopers on June 5 was soldierly: "I found the men in fine fettle, many of them joshingly admonishing me that I had no cause for worry, since the 101st was on the job, and everything would be taken care of in fine shape. I stayed with them until the last of them were in the air, somewhere about midnight. After a two hour trip back to my own camp, I had only a short time to wait until the first news should come in."

That news was good in that the mission succeeded, but the loss was horrendous. In the end, nearly 4,500 men died that day; thousands more were wounded. But the Allies gained a crucial foothold that ultimately saved the war.

As it turned out, had Eisenhower chosen to delay the invasion for two weeks, the weather would have been even worse. "I thank the Gods of war we went when we did," he wrote. As it was, the weather was certainly not ideal on June 6, the choppy seas spitting out the landing parties in waves so fierce many men drowned before they reached the beaches. Ironically, one factor in the success of the landings was the conviction of the German command that the Allies would not dare such a venture in the prevailing weather conditions.

Ike never bragged about the accomplishments of D-Day. For him it was simply a matter of duty—and nerves. "Honey," Mamie always asked him, "how in the world did you have the nerve to do this?" He would reply simply, "I had to." He might have been afraid, but he told her, "If I let anybody, any of my commanders, think that maybe things weren't going to work out, that I was afraid, they'd be afraid, too. I didn't dare. I had to have the confidence."

THE STORY OF WAR is often told through its major operations, and although D-Day was certainly decisive in the ultimate Allied victory, it was followed by nearly a year of the most brutal battles of the war. The Germans never let up, determined to maintain their grip on every territory as Allied forces advanced. The most vicious German response came on December 16, 1944, as the Allies moved into Belgium. In a surprise attack in the forested land of the Ardennes region, more than 250,000 German forces overwhelmed 80,000 American forces in what would become known as the Battle of the Bulge. Terrible weather made an American air assault impossible, and the forces were stranded and surrounded. In many respects it was Hitler's last stand in a war that hadn't been going his way.

Ike acted quickly to arrange for reinforcements, and called Generals Bradley, Patton, and Jacob Devers (Commander of the Sixth Army) to his headquarters for a meeting. When they gathered around a long table, Ike said to them, "The present situation is to be regarded as an opportunity for us and not a disaster. There will be only cheerful faces at this table." It was a hard order to follow. With defeat a clear possibility, the men mapped out a strategy that would overwhelm and surround the Germans, while praying the heavy fog would lift to allow for the much-needed air support.

Ike knew that in the face of such a pounding assault the most confident men could easily suffer panic or discouragement—

and those same plights could beset commanders as well. To inspire confidence he wrote one of his rare orders of the day:

> By rushing out from his fixed defenses the enemy may give us the chance to turn his great gamble into his worst defeat. So I call upon every man, of all the Allies, to rise now to new heights of courage, of resolution and of effort. Let everyone hold before him a single thought—to destroy the enemy on the ground, in the air, everywhere—destroy him! United in this determination and with unshakeable faith in the cause for which we fight, we will, with God's help, go forward to our greatest victory.

The Germans had moved fifty miles beyond the American line before Patton's Third Army checked their advance. Simultaneously, the weather cleared and an aggressive bombardment from the skies ended the German effort. But the casualties were high—more than 20,000 Americans killed, 43,000 wounded, and another 23,000 captured or missing.

It was the final major assault of the war. Within months the Allied victory was complete—VE Day (Victory in Europe Day) was celebrated on May 8, 1945. President Roosevelt had died suddenly in April, and in July, Ike met President Harry Truman for the first time when he was in Germany for the Potsdam Conference. There Truman joined Joseph Stalin and Winston Churchill to hammer out the details of the war's end. Ike and the president were driving and talking about what came next when Truman said, "General, there is nothing that you may want that I won't try to help you get. That definitely and specifically includes the presidency in 1948."

Ike, who felt "suddenly struck in his emotional vitals,"

laughed at the idea and assured Truman he had no interest.
Years later, after the fissures developed in their relationship,
Truman would deny he'd said any such thing, although records
and recollections of others tell us he said it on more than one
occasion.

Ike had graver matters on his mind during the Potsdam
Conference. Earlier, Secretary of War Henry Stimson had come
to see him at his headquarters in Germany to deliver the news
the United States was planning to drop an atomic bomb on
Japanese cities. The idea sickened Ike. He recalled, "During his
recitation of the relevant facts, I had been conscious of a feeling
of depression and so I voiced to him my grave misgivings, first
on the basis of my belief that Japan was already defeated and
that dropping the bomb was completely unnecessary, and sec-
ondly because I thought that our country should avoid shocking
world opinion by the use of a weapon whose employment was,
I thought, no longer mandatory as a measure to save American
lives. It was my belief that Japan was, at that very moment,
seeking some way to surrender with a minimum loss of face.
The Secretary was deeply perturbed by my attitude. . . ." Now,
with Truman in front of him, Ike once again expressed his
strong disagreement with the plan. Most likely Ike didn't know
Truman had already confided in Churchill and Stalin that the
bomb would be dropped. (According to Churchill, writing in
his diary, Stalin's reaction to the news was chilling: "He seemed
to be delighted. A new bomb! Of extraordinary power! Probably decisive on the whole Japanese war! What a bit of luck!")

Ike's reservations about using such a drastic weapon against
an enemy that was all but defeated remained unacknowledged,
and the bombs, one on Hiroshima and a second on Nagasaki,
fell within a week of the Potsdam Conference. The sad truth
was, it all might have been avoided had not Truman insisted on

unconditional surrender. Given a chance to save face, the Japanese might have come to the table. The use of atomic bombs haunted Ike's thoughts throughout his presidency, right to the moment of his final address. He once scoffed at the naïve ideas people held about the aftermath of a nuclear war. "If we have a nuclear exchange, we're not going to be talking about reestablishing the dollar," he warned. "We're going to be talking about grubbing for worms."

In August Ike accepted an invitation to visit Russia for the Physical Culture Parade. There he received a huge reception. Georgy Zhukov, an officer in the Red Army who was Ike's new Soviet counterpart in postwar operations, invited him to attend a soccer match with him, and when they entered the stadium the crowd roared. Ike reached out and put an arm around Zhukov, and the crowd roared louder. Ike and Zhukov spent time reminiscing about their experiences at war. Zhukov, like Ike, was a soldier's soldier, who was instrumental in waging the Battle of Berlin. Remarking about the strategic difficulty of maneuvering through minefields, Ike asked Zhukov how he protected his men when they encountered them. Zhukov told him he just walked his division straight through. Ike reflected to himself on the critical difference between the nations in how they valued the lives of their soldiers.

This was the honeymoon period between the United States and Russia. Russia had been an ally during the war, and though Ike knew political rumblings were threatening to crack the relationship between the two nations, on that visit he and Zhukov were just old soldiers together—and they would become friends.

Later, in a visit to the victorious General MacArthur in Tokyo, he found the ebullient general wanting to talk politics. MacArthur boasted that as the two conquerors, either he or Eisenhower would surely become president of the United States.

Noting that he was getting on in years—MacArthur had a decade on Ike—it should be Ike who stepped up.

The last thing Ike was thinking about was political capital, and he found the conversation distasteful. General Marshall had always impressed upon him that the military and politics existed in separate spheres. Neither Marshall nor Ike had ever voted in a presidential election. Ike told MacArthur he subscribed to Marshall's view that a military officer should not get involved in politics. As for accolades, he felt America had already given him all the recognition he could possibly deserve or want.

MacArthur leaned over and patted Ike's knee paternally. "That's all right, Ike. If you go on like that you'll get it for sure."

Ike left the encounter red-faced and angry. He couldn't care less about politics.

CHAPTER 3

A NONPOLITICIAN IN THE POLITICAL ARENA

Ike returned to the United States and a ticker-tape parade in New York City, with millions in attendance. He was on everyone's mind at that moment. Seated next to Ike on the dais at a dinner following the parade, New York governor Thomas Dewey, meeting the general for the first time, recalled being impressed with Ike. As Dewey came to know him better, he grew certain Ike possessed all the qualities needed for the presidency. Years later, after Dewey's own presidential aspirations were thwarted by an indifferent Republican electorate, he became even more convinced the party was in great need of reform, and in Ike he saw a vision of how they might be. "I felt that the Republican Party was weak with the electorate," he explained, "and that a new style of candidate was the only sure way to win, and I was confident that General Eisenhower would win—and I wasn't confident that anybody else would."

Dewey's reasoning was clear and on point: "In the first place, he was not handicapped—if it is a handicap—with the label of 'politician.' He had a personality which projected as far as he could be seen. He could be a mile away and you could see the enormous charm and attractiveness of that smile. He had equal capacity to charm people in private. His standing in the world was at the very pinnacle. The confidence of the American people in him at the moment was at the pinnacle." In other words, he had it all.

The postwar drumbeat for Eisenhower to run for president refused to let up—despite the fact that he had never revealed a political party affiliation. In 1947 Truman again encouraged Ike, saying he'd consider not running for reelection in 1948 if the general would carry the Democratic banner. Truman assumed Ike was a Democrat in the Roosevelt-Truman mode, and he promised to virtually deliver him the nomination of the party. In one letter, Truman wrote he should let him know his plans because he was afraid of the isolationist movement in the country, and Ike's decision might affect his plans. He was saying, in effect, that if Ike didn't run, he would. Eisenhower politely declined—and kept doing so.

AFTER THE WAR, EISENHOWER had an important role as Army chief of staff, a job he didn't like, and in 1948 his career took a new turn when he accepted a position as president of Columbia University. He didn't fully retire from the Army at that point, only from active service, but he was testing the idea of a postmilitary career. When the Columbia board of trustees approached him about the university presidency, he told them they were talking to the wrong Eisenhower; surely his brother Milton, then president of Kansas State University, was much more qualified for the job. Ike thought the presidency of such an esteemed institution was out of his league, more suited to a scholar, which he was certainly not. But no, they wanted Ike—no doubt for the cachet and fund-raising ability of the beloved general. For his part, when Ike finally got his mind around the idea, he was intrigued with the thought of how he could make a difference for the students. Once in the position, he was disappointed to discover he would have little direct interaction with them. His administrative and fund-raising duties were all-encompassing.

Ike and Mamie did enjoy their life in Morningside Heights in northern Manhattan, though. The accommodations were far more elegant than they were used to, and the pace was less frenzied than it had been in the military—although Ike was soon drawn in to a military advisory role, often returning to Washington as a consultant to the Joint Chiefs of Staff. He also wrote a well-received autobiography of his war years, *Crusade in Europe*.

In 1950 the nation was on war footing once again. Since the end of World War II, an upheaval had been threatening on the Korean Peninsula. The United States and the Soviet Union had divided Korea, formerly under Japanese rule, after the war, with the Soviets taking the North and the United States the South. From the outset tensions were high between the Soviet-backed People's Republic of Korea and the Western-supported regime of South Korea. Then on May 25, 1950, in the first aggression of the Cold War, troops from the North invaded South Korea with the goal of unifying the country under communist rule. After a United Nations resolution calling on the support of member nations, sixteen countries sent troops to support South Korea, with the bulk of them being American soldiers under the leadership of General MacArthur.

Ike was not involved in the Korean conflict. In fact, President Truman had another job in mind for him. In October 1950, Ike was in Chicago on university business when he received a message stating that Truman wanted to speak with him. He returned the call and the president asked him to come to Washington. A few days later Ike flew on a military plane to the capital, where the president informed him he was needed to take command of the NATO forces in Paris. It had been unanimously decided that the commander should be an American—and it should be Ike.

Truman made it clear that he considered it a request, not an order, but Ike accepted, although he worried about putting Mamie's life in disarray once more. But as Mamie put it most succinctly, "He was a soldier." He went when called.

In February 1951, Ike and Mamie sailed to Europe on the *Queen Elizabeth*. They chose a house at Marnes-la-Coquette, a suburb of Paris, and they were happy there. It was a challenging job. But NATO, whose treaty extended only to direct attacks on member states, played no role in the Korean War, putting Ike on the sidelines of the conflict.

As the war in Korea grew larger and more complex, with China engaging on the side of North Korea, Ike was aware of a bitter feud raging between President Truman and General MacArthur. MacArthur was on a tear, publicly challenging Truman on the war and calling him timid. In MacArthur's view, nothing short of an all-out attack on China was called for—a strategy Truman feared would start World War III.

MacArthur's greatest sin, in Truman's view, was to behave as if he, not the president, were the commander in chief. America's core principle of civilian control of the military was at stake. Truman fired MacArthur—an action not popular with the public, who revered the general. He then made matters worse with a spiteful quip, which managed to insult not only MacArthur but all generals: "I fired him because he wouldn't respect the authority of the president. I didn't fire him because he was a dumb son of a bitch, although he was, but that's not against the law for generals."

MacArthur did not go quietly. At Senate hearings on his dismissal, held within days of his return to the United States, he spoke for six hours—disparaging the president and calling him an appeaser. He ended with words of farewell, promising that like the old soldier of the popular ballad, he would just fade away. And for the most part he did. Although history seems to support Truman's decision not to escalate the war into China, MacArthur's popularity remained strong, and he is still considered one of the greatest modern generals.

BY 1951, WITH THE calls growing louder from both parties, Ike was still resisting a presidential run, writing in October, "I am amused to note that even good friends finally fall prey to the idea that anyone would want to be president. Not me." When the public discussion of his candidacy would not let up, he joked he would like to say, as William Tecumseh Sherman famously did, "If nominated I will not run; if elected I will not serve."

The pressure continued throughout Ike's time at NATO, and it came from both parties, but Republican politicians back home were particularly aggressive. Massachusetts senator Henry Cabot Lodge Jr. spearheaded the campaign for an Eisenhower candidacy, often visiting Ike at NATO headquarters. Dewey told him his own narrow loss to Truman in 1948 "now makes it mandatory for you to run."

The savvy politicians saw in Ike an antidote to the malaise falling over the nation after long years of war and Democratic control. Ike represented a new, much-needed change in the character of politics. He was an intuitive strategist without being politically calculating. Americans loved him. He was not imperious, but had an endearing personal touch. Most of all, people felt they *knew* him. He was the supreme commander, the hero of their youth, and for those coming out of the military, he was their *actual* commander—or "Boss," as even his own son called him.

Ike began to soften to the idea when he considered the stakes. During his time as military commander of NATO, he grew increasingly convinced of the necessity of America playing a vital role in global affairs. Perhaps the turning point came in 1951, when he had a confidential conversation with Senator Robert A. Taft of Ohio, the Republican Party's leading candidate for the presidential nomination. As the two men talked about domestic policy, Ike was pleased to see that they were mostly in agreement. But when the discussion turned to foreign policy, Ike recoiled at the isolationist streak in Taft's soul. Taft had been one of the loudest voices in protest of America's entry into the war against Nazism, and he was an opponent of NATO. He continued to preach a philosophy of America as separate and not beholden to the world at large. In their meeting Taft refused to commit to a system of mutual security—especially for Europe, but in other locations as well.

Ike's resistance to running weakened. "He was absolutely devoted to doing anything he could to bring us a little closer to peace in the world," his brother Milton said, an accurate description of Ike's thinking. Ike didn't have the mentality of a politician who was always weighing the odds on a scale of potential votes, but rather of a soldier accepting his next mission. The politicians urging him were consumed with their belief that Ike could win and was therefore desirable. Ike was more focused on whether he could make a difference if he won.

Sherman Adams, the governor of New Hampshire, began to see the groundswell, as influential Republicans returned from meetings with Ike in Paris, filled with glowing reports. He was everything they wanted in a candidate—his wonderful personality, his forcefulness, his remarkable comprehension of world problems. What he lacked in practical knowledge of the intricacies of American politics was more than compensated for by his unparalleled understanding of America's place in the world. Ike was, they told Adams, right for the time. With the quagmire in Korea threatening to go on indefinitely—and perhaps even turn into a third world war—here was a man who could be trusted with America's security. Adams agreed, but getting there was difficult. "You know, Governor," Ike said when Adams raised the matter, "there isn't anything this country can give me that it hasn't given me. I've had the greatest opportunity of any citizen in history in respect to the things I've been engaged in. I have no interest in politics. In fact, it nauseates me." Adams saw something Ike could not yet see. Breaking with the pro-Taft conservative forces in his state, he endorsed Ike, and he and Lodge put his name on the ballot in the New Hampshire primary without his permission, creating a momentum that never waned.

In February 1952, a Draft Eisenhower rally at New York's Madison Square Garden drew twenty-five thousand people. A few days later, Jacqueline Cochran, a famed aviator and cosmetics executive, who had initiated and headed the Women's Flying Training Detachment during the war, brought a film of the event to Eisenhower in Paris. Watching it, Ike's eyes filled with tears. He later wrote in his diary, "Viewing it [the film] finally developed into a real emotional experience for Mamie and me. I've not been so upset in years. Clearly to be seen is the mass longing of America for some kind of reasonable solution for her nagging, persistent, and almost terrifying problems. It's a real experience to realize that one could become a symbol for many thousands of the hope they have."

Simply put, people liked Ike—more than that, they trusted him. "They knew that he was honest," said Milton. "They knew he was a man of integrity. They knew that he was working not for a single selfish group in this country, but working for the welfare of all the people. He was an attractive man with a great personality. He won friends very easily." Ike held the belief that the office should seek the man, not the man the office—and that's essentially what was happening. Gradually, too, the political views of a man who had lived apolitically came into focus. In finally announcing his candidacy, Ike also revealed something few people knew until then—he had been a lifelong Republican. Many within the Democratic Party were bitterly disappointed to learn Ike wouldn't be their man.

Ike was not naïve about the ephemeral nature of public support. He knew how quickly praise could turn to scorn. He often referred to a letter written by George Washington when he was facing exactly that situation in 1789: "Though I flatter myself the world will do me the justice to believe that at my time of life and in my circumstances, nothing but a conviction of duty could have induced me to depart from my resolution of remaining in retirement; yet I greatly apprehend that my countrymen will expect too much from me. I fear if the issue of public measure should not correspond to their sanguine expectations, they will turn the extravagant (and I may say undue) praises that they are heaping upon me at this moment into equally extravagant (though I will finally hope unmerited) censures." Studying Washington helped Ike keep public adoration in perspective.

Ike's mother was also helpful in that regard. At a big parade and rally for Ike in Abilene after the war, Ida sat proudly on the reviewing stand. But when asked, "Aren't you proud of your boy?" she replied, "Which one?" There was no favoritism—or swelled heads—allowed in the Eisenhower family.

Ike's politics, previously under wraps, were a revelation when he finally came forward, but it's easy to surmise how he came to his political philosophy. Although his parents were not politically partisan when he was growing up, Kansas was a conservative state, and as adults all of his brothers and many of his friends were Republican. But at heart, Ike's philosophy—and therefore choice of party—probably grew from his belief in being "middle of the road," what today we call moderate, and his insistence on not trying to categorize people as liberal and conservative. "I'm not going to accept headline designations," Ike told Milton. "I want to know where a man stands on the twenty or thirty most important issues before the American people, and I will judge him on the basis of what his knowledge is and his judgments may be on these." More pragmatically, after two decades of Democratic governance, Ike was of the strong opinion that the nation would be best served by a change of party.

IKE MADE HIS DECISION to run for president in March 1952 and immediately resigned his position as NATO commander, highly sensitive about any mix of politics and military. He also formally retired from the Army. He delivered the announcement in Abilene in the midst of a driving rain, with his pants rolled up to keep them out of the mud. Then Ike and Mamie traveled to New York City, where their Columbia house was awaiting them, and they began planning for a new life on the road.

Before traveling to Abilene to make his announcement, Ike huddled with Milton, James Hagerty, and trusted aide Lucius Clay in a suite at the Statler Hotel, poring over questions and answers on all the big issues of the day—although Hagerty admitted that he didn't dare question him about Europe, since Ike knew more than anyone in the room on that topic. Perhaps his smartest decision was tapping political operative and former Dewey campaign manager Herbert Brownell to run his campaign.

Ike was not a natural politician. Hagerty once observed, "If he had a weakness during his years in the presidency, it probably was this—he hated and despised the smallness and pettiness of everyday politics." Nor did campaigning come naturally to him, although his open, guileless face, with its signature broad grin, was completely authentic.

In historical hindsight, it might seem that with all the clamor for Ike, he was a shoo-in to win the nomination. That was far from the case. In fact, the nomination was won through rules challenges and convention delegate sleight of hand.

Going into the convention in Chicago, not only did Robert Taft have the lead, but he'd done some groundwork in sewing up delegate votes that left the latecomer Ike with a definite disadvantage. On the eve of the convention, the Associated Press reported that of the 604 delegates needed for nomination, Taft had 530 and Ike had 427. Two favorite sons held the remaining delegates—California governor (and future chief justice of the Supreme Court) Earl Warren had 76, and former governor of Minnesota Harold Stassen had 25.

Taft, a seasoned politician and the son of a president (the twenty-seventh, William Howard Taft), was a favorite among the party elite, one might even say the heir apparent, with special strength in the East and Midwest. He also represented the conservative wing of the party, the anti-Dewey wing, which was tired of losing with moderate candidates. But with Ike in the race, Taft's beachhead was crumbling, since many forecasters believed, ideology be damned, that Ike could *win* in November. Ike had the media behind him, and even the *New York Times* argued against Taft on the grounds Republicans needed to spread a wider net—to include Democrats and independents—to win back the White House, which had been in Democratic hands since 1933. Many people agreed Ike could build a broader coalition. Democrats were deeply disappointed Ike had not chosen their party; they would have loved to see him at the lead, and they feared his candidacy on the other side, believing he would be more difficult to defeat than Taft.

But to have a chance at the nomination, Ike's forces would have to tackle a delegate map favoring Taft. Ike's people aggressively challenged pro-Taft delegates in several states, claiming there had been shenanigans preventing Eisenhower voters from getting fair treatment. They then put forth a rules challenge called the "Fair Play" rule, stating these challenged delegates should not be allowed to participate in roll call votes.

Ike wasn't on the floor during the wrangling. He was closeted at his hotel with a bad stomachache, which could have been the ileitis that plagued him, or, as one aide suggested, just a result of poor eating habits. Mamie, also ill, spent most of the convention in bed. The image of a bedridden Mamie and nauseous Ike waiting for reports from the convention might have given the delegates pause. But of course no one knew.

After a heated debate, the contested delegates broke for Ike, and voting on the first ballot showed him falling just short of the magic number, with 595 votes. In a dramatic move, Stassen rose to announce Minnesota would switch its votes to Eisenhower, and others followed. In the end, Ike won a decisive victory, with 845 votes to Taft's 280.

Ike's first act was to embrace his chief rival—rushing across the street as soon as he was nominated to speak to Taft. As he left his hotel in a hurry, his hat askew, everyone called, "Where are you going?"

"Where am I going? I'm going across the street and say hello to Mr. Taft. I just called him and asked if I could come over."

Taft swallowed his disappointment—and probably shock—to appear jointly with the nominee in an appeal to party unity. Later, historians would favorably compare Ike's efforts toward healing divisions with Barry Goldwater's complete indifference to the concerns of dissenting factions after he was nominated in 1964. Taft returned to the senate, and he and Ike became friends and golfing partners, in spite of their political differences, which led to heated debates.

In the selection of a vice president, Ike listened to advisors. He didn't know Senator Richard Nixon well but liked his youthful exuberance—Nixon was thirty-nine at the time—and appreciated that he hailed from the state of California. But basically his advisors suggested Nixon and Ike said, "All right with me"—a casual response for what would become a historic decision.

Two weeks later, the Democrats would gather in the same location to nominate Illinois governor Adlai Stevenson. Stevenson was a popular governor, but he had a weakness on the international stage that Ike could exploit. He was also virtually unknown outside his home state, while Ike's name recognition was nearly unparalleled.

Ike was not a traditional politician—a fact that appealed to his supporters. He often chafed at the bureaucracies of the campaign trail. Before a trip to Philadelphia, he was astounded to be handed a thirty-five-page set of logistics. He looked it over and then started to laugh. "Politics is a funny thing," he said. "Thirty-five pages to get me into Philadelphia. The invasion of Normandy was on five pages."

Ike's inexperience as a candidate often could be a plus, in that he rejected being roped into certain rigid conventions. For example, it had been long understood that the South "belonged" to the Democrats and he should just write it off. However, when told by his advisors, "Of course you're not going into the South," he bristled.

"What do you mean I'm not going into the South? I'm running for president of all the country, aren't I?" In his best general's voice, he declared, "I'll tell you, gentlemen, I'm going to go into the South right after Labor Day." And he did, traveling to Atlanta, Birmingham, Little Rock, Tampa, and other southern locales. Hagerty recalled there were big crowds at every stop, and the local Republican officeholders in attendance sat in the audience with dropped jaws at the sight of a Republican nominee entering their territory. It ended up being a masterful play because the Democrats hadn't planned on having to do much in the South, and with Ike nipping at his heels, Stevenson was forced to devote more time there than he'd wanted to. So in doing the right thing, Ike also made a *politically* astute choice. It was a different kind of campaign than anyone was used to.

On the other hand, Ike's political inexperience was perhaps responsible for one of the most unsavory episodes on the campaign trail. In 1952 Joseph McCarthy's communist witch-hunt was reaching full steam, and one of his targets was none other than Ike's old boss, General George Marshall, who had gone on to serve as secretary of state and secretary of defense in the Truman administration and was the author of the Marshall Plan, the economic aid program that rebuilt Western Europe after the war. In his accusations against Marshall, McCarthy said the Marshall Plan aided America's enemies and Marshall was "eager to play the role of a front man to traitors." He accused him of being in bed with Stalin—part of "a conspiracy on a scale so immense as to dwarf any previous such venture in the history of man."

Truman, of course, was enraged by the accusation, and so was Ike. On a campaign trip to Wisconsin, McCarthy's home state, Ike planned to give a speech in which he included a paragraph praising Marshall as a patriot. McCarthy, who was running for reelection, was expected to be in the audience in

Milwaukee that night. But shortly before giving the speech Ike was accosted by state Republican leaders on his campaign train. They settled in for a private conversation, urging him not to take on McCarthy in Wisconsin, as they feared battling him on his home turf would harm Ike in the state. When he emerged from the meeting, one of his aides noticed Ike "was purple down to the roots of his neck. He was glowering." He abruptly ordered the paragraph about General Marshall removed from the speech.

Truman launched an immediate and vicious attack, charging that Ike of all people should be willing to openly defend Marshall. "I had never thought the man who is now the Republican candidate would stoop so low," he said bitterly. "A man who betrays his friends in such a fashion is not to be trusted with the great office of President of the United States." (Truman later boasted about his remark, saying, "I skinned old Ike from the top of his bald head to his backside.") Privately, Ike agonized over what he considered to be a mistake. But hindsight didn't account for the fact that in 1952 the "Red Scare" was a visceral panic. In this instance, political expediency trumped true belief, and it was a rare stain on Ike's record of authenticity. McCarthy won his reelection and continued to be, as Dewey put it, "a real hair shirt."

It wasn't just the McCarthy incident that riled Truman. He was reeling with the sense of betrayal he felt watching his golden boy aggressively campaign against his administration. He was unable to accept that by its nature a political campaign was an argument against what *is* and a promise of what will be. He took it personally. As John Eisenhower observed, "Truman is a man who thinks in extremes. You've either got a hell of a white hat or you've got a hell of a black one, at any given time. He's a very kind man, [with] kind instincts. But Truman has a small mind."

The hostility began almost immediately because of the nature of a political campaign. When Stevenson declared, "I will clean up the mess in Washington," Ike delightedly seized on the line, noting the two sides had that much in common. At the White House, Truman seethed.

Another incident that could have stalled Ike's advance was a scandal involving Nixon. On the campaign train from Des Moines to Kansas City, where he would deliver a speech on honesty in government, the news broke about what came to be known as the Nixon Fund. It was reported that Nixon had used campaign funds for personal expenses.

Ike held his fire until he knew all of the details, but he was privately very worried, since integrity was an absolute for him. He ignored the cries to "throw him off the ticket" and waited to hear the facts. "There was a great deal of hue and cry about Nixon resigning from the ticket," Sherman Adams recalled. "Eisenhower took all of this advice, the messages and the importuning that he got from all over the country in a rather reflective mode," even telling Adams, "Well, if Nixon has to resign, we can't possibly win the election."

In a career-salvaging television speech, Nixon defended his honesty and spoke of his middle American values, referring to his wife's simple "Republican cloth coat." The winning remark was his vow the family would not give up their beloved dog, Checkers, a gift to his children—thus the label the "Checkers Speech." It worked, but Ike never quite felt at ease with Nixon, whom he deemed "too political."

Perhaps the speeches on the trail that mattered most were the short local addresses—sometimes as many as twelve a day—given from the caboose platform of Ike's campaign train as it powered across America. Here he tried to meet the public as fellow citizens, using words of personal meaning and endearment. He also enjoyed using props to demonstrate the inefficiency of the federal government. One of these was a piece of lumber about four feet long, sawed almost completely through in two places. He'd hold up the wood and tell the crowd how in a previous time they could buy this strip of lumber for 25 cents. Then he'd break it over his knee at the first sawed place and hold it up again, saying, this was how much you could buy for 25 cents a few years earlier. Finally, he'd break it a third time and hold up the result, announcing this was what 25 cents would buy you in 1952. It was a huge crowd-pleaser—a simple and effective way of demonstrating an economic fact everyone could relate to. His campaign staff was kept busy stocking precut lumber on the train.

Trying to run a political campaign without being a political man could be difficult. Ike's aide Gabriel Hauge recalled a typical incident while in Indianapolis. Senator William Jenner, a right-wing Republican who had been very critical of General Marshall, and, for that matter, Ike, saw an opportunity to gain from Ike's reflected glow. He got on the platform with Ike, grabbed his hand, and yanked their arms together in the air. Afterward, Ike let Hauge know he was enraged by having been taken advantage of in this way. Apparently, he and Jenner had agreed to meet *privately,* but Jenner just took over the show.

Wanting to bring new voters into the fold, Ike made sure many of his rallies were managed by Citizens for Eisenhower, organized outside of Republican officialdom. That way people didn't have to "sign on" as Republicans. They could just be fully for the candidate. Ike had an abiding faith in the American people, and he didn't want the party to stand in the way of them forming a full relationship. Despite being sixty-two, Ike had tremendous appeal to young people, and his formal rallies usually featured large trailer trucks festooned with balloons, manned by young men and women. Although Ike favored older, more experienced people to do the heavy lifting, he was energized by being around the younger generation. His love of people and his respect for them shined through. "He could have been elected on a Chinese laundry ticket," Hagerty put it—a bit inelegantly. Once, driving through Carmel, California, Ike noticed a group of nuns standing on the curb waving to him. He stood up in the car and bowed to them, explaining, "When I consider the dedication of those people, the least I can do is pay my respects."

Irving Berlin penned a campaign song, "I Like Ike," whose lyrics touched the public imagination:

> I like Ike
> I'll shout it over a mike
> Or a phone
> Or from the highest steeple
> I like Ike
> And Ike is easy to like
> Stands alone
> The choice of "We the People"

The song was used with different lyrics in an animated campaign ad produced by the Walt Disney studio. The catchy tune and eye-grabbing animation struck a cheerful embracing note, the kind of tune that sticks in people's heads—even to this day—like a popular commercial jingle:

> You like Ike
> I like Ike
> Everybody likes Ike for president
> Hang out the banner
> Beat the drums
> Let's take Ike to Washington

Already thinking ahead, Ike confided to Hagerty two days after the convention about his determination to end the war in Korea. "If we don't get some settlement before I become president, I'm going to go over to Korea," he said, adding, "Just keep that quiet." And so, in October, he dramatically announced, "I shall go to Korea," putting a finishing touch on a very successful campaign while further enraging Truman. Here his status as a famed and revered general was in his favor. One cannot imagine Adlai Stevenson declaring, "I shall go to Korea," and having any credibility. But the public faith that Ike was capable of doing the impossible in times of war inspired hope in the midst of a crippling standoff.

The 1948 election had been a squeaker, leaving Truman with no mandate. The 1952 election didn't feel like a slam dunk to Ike, who had little trust in polls. Writing to his son, John, who was stationed in Korea, Ike took a philosophical view of the campaign. The last thing he wanted was for his son to be concerned. "Now don't worry about the election," he wrote. "We're having fun and we're doing our best, and if we don't get elected it's not going to kill Mamie and me."

ON ELECTION EVE, NOVEMBER 3, an hour-long television program, sponsored by the Republican National Committee and the Citizens Committee for Eisenhower and Nixon, aired. It was stylistically different than anything viewers had seen before, opening with an attempt at coziness in a living room–style scene of Ike and Mamie with Dick and Pat Nixon seated around a television set themselves. Of the four, only Ike looked comfortable, smiling into the camera and telling viewers that the four of them didn't know anything about the program but were going to watch along with the American public. What followed was a love letter to Ike, as ordinary citizens and campaign workers from across the country praised the general and spoke of their hopes for the future. At the end of the program, a giant cake was wheeled into the room, with seven lit candles, but it was not a birthday celebration. The candles, it was explained, depicted Ike's lucky number.

A few more words were spoken into the camera, and then Mamie said, "Now let's get home to our ranch." To which Ike replied, "I'm all for that. As is proper, the lady has the last word."

But first a photo op. During the evening a photographer had an idea that, while corny, appealed to Ike. He arranged for the candidates to stand under a giant clock, and he'd shoot the picture as soon as the clock struck midnight—signaling the end of the campaign and the start of voting. The problem was the clock wasn't well mounted, and when midnight fell and the photographer began to snap his picture, the clock slipped loose and landed on Ike's head. As blood flowed, he feared his unlucky start to Election Day might be an omen—but he was gracious enough to mop his bald head and allow the photographer to remount the clock and get his shot.

November 4, 1952, was the first nationally televised coverage of election returns. When you consider the technology employed today that is capable of giving instant results based on fragments of the vote, the process of getting to a result was once far more laborious. But as Walter Cronkite anchored election night coverage on CBS, it was revealed that a computer called Univac would be calculating the results. Cronkite didn't trust the computer, and when very early in the evening it predicted an Eisenhower landslide, he held back the results, not believing them. But when the results were tallied later that night, the computer turned out to be right. Eisenhower won a solid victory with 55 percent of the popular vote and a landslide in the Electoral College, with 442 votes to Stevenson's 89. He even scored well in the South, taking a larger percentage of the popular vote than any previous Republican candidate and capturing Virginia, Florida, Tennessee, and Texas. Ike had not written an acceptance or a concession speech, and he hastily cobbled together a few short words when victory became apparent.

The election was a referendum on the Democratic Party, which had been in power for a long time; it was a "change" election that handed control of Congress to the Republicans as well—albeit by slim margins. Eisenhower's coattails were just long enough to achieve small majorities in the House and Senate. In Massachusetts, Henry Cabot Lodge Jr. lost his Senate seat to John F. Kennedy. Not only did Kennedy prove adept at retail politics, but the lingering animus of the pro-Taft forces hurt Lodge among conservative Republicans.

The day after the election, Ike headed to Augusta for a thirteen-day visit. He spent the mornings working with his transition team and in the afternoons he played golf. He was joined on the course by a series of friends—some of them golf luminaries, including PGA great Byron Nelson. Mindful that he was now playing with the president-elect, not just an ordinary civilian, Nelson was rattled when Ike—nimble "like a cricket"—jumped out of the golf cart before it stopped moving. Finally, he implored him, "Mr. President, I would feel a lot better if you would wait until I stopped the cart before you get out, because it is going to make great headlines if Byron Nelson throws the president of the United States out of a golf cart and breaks his leg."

Back in Washington, President Truman penned a cool note of congratulations, adding, "The presidential plane *Independence* will be at your disposal if you still desire to go to Korea."

According to the savvy reporter Drew Pearson, this seemingly gracious offer was actually an insult, contained in the word *if*. Ike was offended and determined that *when* he went to Korea, he would fly on an ordinary military plane.

Before that trip the two men met at the White House for a perfunctory meeting that did nothing to heal the acrimony. Afterward, Truman would make some mischief in a speech before the CIA, characterizing Ike as "rather appalled at all that the president needs to know in order to reach decisions"—hardly a credible description for a man of Ike's stature and experience.

The women were warmer. Bess Truman invited Mamie to the White House to look around, and she accepted. Bess greeted her excitedly. "Oh, Mrs. Eisenhower," she said, "I want to show you—I picked out the most wonderful suite for the grandchildren!" And the two women went off to explore, Mamie feeling very touched by the thoughtful gesture. It turned out Bess Truman had read Mamie's mind, for the one concern she had about the White House was that it be a welcoming place for her grandchildren.

Used to traveling as he pleased, Ike didn't know the extent he would be hamstrung by the Secret Service until he arranged the trip to Korea. Without consulting them, he had his aide Jerry Persons arrange the trip in secret. He was brought up short in this effort when the head of the Secret Service called him on the carpet. Did Persons know, he demanded, that by law the Secret Service was required to be with the president-elect at all times? Obviously not. Persons relayed the information to Ike, who reluctantly agreed to have one agent on the plane with him, with others traveling on a second plane.

One dustup further cemented the troubles with Truman. Hearing that MacArthur had said in a speech he had a "clear and definite solution to the Korean conflict" and had offered to tell Ike privately, Ike thought, Why not? He wanted to hear what MacArthur had to say. If he had a good idea, all the better. Ike sent a message: "I appreciate your announced readiness to discuss these matters with me and assure you I am looking forward to informal meetings in which my associates and I may obtain the full benefit of your thinking and experience."

MacArthur responded gratefully, writing, "This is the first time that the slightest official interest in my counsel has been evidenced since my return."

Ike wasn't interested in keeping the communications private, so he released them to the press, predictably incurring Truman's anger. At a press conference the president lashed out at both Eisenhower and MacArthur, saying that if MacArthur had a plan for ending the war, he had a duty to present it to the president. In the process Truman also denigrated Ike's Korea trip as a political stunt, which in turn angered Ike.

The mismanagement of the Korean War further infuriated the president-elect. More than two years in, with negotiation attempts at a standstill, Ike believed the parents and families of the boys fighting would be sickened to hear exactly how powerless and vulnerable their sons and brothers and husbands were in the face of fresh onslaughts from the North. But only on his visit did he see the full indignity of the situation. It was a very hard trip, involving traveling many miles by jeep and riding aboard scary puddle-jumper planes in freezing weather. But by being close to the action, Ike learned the truth of the war. Visiting the First Marine Division at Panmunjom, just outside the Panmunjom Circle—the ten-mile area where lackluster and ineffectual talks were going on—he was outraged to find that as the North Koreans, now supported by the Chinese, shelled the troops regularly each day, American soldiers were under orders not to fire back.

Eisenhower was president-elect, but in Korea everyone saw him as General Eisenhower. They were transported back in time to when he had last defeated a monstrous enemy. Ike's warnings were not bluster, and he had the reputation to pull it off. He warned that unless there was an agreement to sit down at Panmunjom and work out an immediate truce, the war would resume full throttle. "They knew he wasn't kidding," said Hagerty. "The word was sent . . . you either sit down and settle this, or there's going to be no imaginary line at the Yalu River, there's going to be hot pursuit of your planes regardless of where they come from, and we're going to end it."

The commanders on the ground favored a full-throttle approach, but Ike, the old general, wanted to see the fight come to an end. And he succeeded, within six months of taking office. After the Korean War, only one known military death (in Vietnam) occurred during his administration.

Moved by what he saw in Korea, and determined to put an end to the war once he assumed office, Ike returned to the United States to prepare for the inauguration.

CHAPTER 4

IKE'S HIDDEN CARD

January 20, 1953

The mood inside the limousine carrying President Harry Truman and Eisenhower to the inauguration was tense and just short of hostile. As they neared the Capitol, Ike finally broke the stony silence by asking Truman who had ordered his son, John, an Army major, home from Korea for the inauguration. Of course he was delighted to have his son there, safe for the moment, but he worried it would appear as favoritism and wound the hearts of all the mothers and fathers who did not have the joy and privilege of having their soldier sons by their sides. John felt the same way and had originally protested the order to return.

"I did," Truman told him curtly, and Ike thanked him sincerely. As Truman wrote in his memoir, Ike then tried another topic. He mentioned that in 1948 he had chosen not to attend the inauguration, not wanting to distract from Truman's moment, to which Truman replied that he had not been there because he hadn't been asked. "If I'd told you to come, you would have been there." The rest of the ride continued without conversation. And so Ike began one of the most significant days of his life sparring with his predecessor. But he was used to fragile egos, and he didn't think much of it. His mind was on his speech.

Arriving at the Capitol, Eisenhower and Truman exited the car and walked through the Rotunda to the east front, onto the inaugural platform. The sun had miraculously broken through minutes earlier.

At noon, Eisenhower took the oath of office flanked by two past presidents, the people who loved him, and those who would carry his vision forward. Chief Justice Fred Vinson, an old political crony of Truman who had been elevated to the bench in 1946, swore in the thirty-fourth president of the United States. Ike placed his hand atop two Bibles—the one his mother had given him when he graduated from West Point, and the Bible George Washington used for his oath as the first president. When he was finished, he turned and kissed Mamie, the first inaugural kiss in history.

Richard Nixon, who took the vice presidential oath immediately before the new president, flubbed it a bit by leaving out the word *support* in the line promising to "support and defend the Constitution of the United States." Nobody cared, much less suggested his oath was invalid, as would occur in 2008 when Chief Justice John Roberts mixed up the words in Barack Obama's oath, leading the men to redo the ceremony privately the next day, just to be on the safe side.

Seated to Ike's left was a tight-lipped Harry Truman and an elderly Herbert Hoover, now seventy-eight, the last Republican to occupy the White House, twenty years earlier. Hoover, a one-term president who suffered the 1929 stock market crash on his watch, had been a fervent Taft supporter in 1952, and he and Ike didn't have much of a relationship—and never would. Hoover was, however, quite close to Truman, despite the latter having served in the administration of Franklin Roosevelt, the man who had denied Hoover a second term in 1932. After Roosevelt's postelection visit to the White House, during which Hoover lectured FDR on the gold standard, Hoover called his successor "very badly informed and of comparably little vision." Roosevelt cared little about the opinion of the man who had overseen the destruction of the economy, and the two traded insults throughout Roosevelt's presidency. But in Truman, Hoover found a president who was willing to give him the respect he felt he was due, and the two men spoke frequently. Hoover never developed a particularly warm relationship with Ike, and one can imagine Hoover and Truman rocking on the porch and discussing the inadequacies of the successor neither of them cared for. (One of the realities of politics and the presidency is that one person's bragging rights is another's judgment of failure—until the more objective verdict of "history" is made.) Nor was Truman, though loyal to the party, shy about expressing his dislike of FDR, who had not treated him well in their brief time together. They had only two private meetings before Roosevelt died, and the president never told Truman about the plans under way for the atom bomb.

Ike's inauguration, just the second to be televised, drew 29 million viewers, remarkable ratings for the time, although the following day 44 million people watched Lucy Ricardo (Lucille Ball) give birth to little Ricky on *I Love Lucy*.

As Ike stepped to the podium to deliver his inaugural address, he looked out on the crowds and hoped to speak to them from the heart. Writing the speech was a task he had undertaken with extreme care. He'd wanted to communicate a clear and central idea—a simple matter, he thought ruefully, until the speechwriters got involved. His speechwriter Emmet John Hughes seemed more interested in words than ideas. Hughes loved the lofty turn of phrase—not at all Ike's style. (Speechwriter and political scientist Malcolm Moos would later describe Hughes's florid style as "belching smokestacks.") Ike didn't like words to call attention to themselves—a difficult concept for a speechwriter to grasp—but rather to reach out to the average citizen with a message that would ring true, creating a bond of shared resolve across the miles.

Dissatisfied with Hughes's draft, which Ike had labored over for days, the president-elect scribbled and deleted—in one case writing, "I *hate* this sentence." Finally, three days before the inauguration, he called C. D. Jackson, his campaign speech-writer, and asked him to craft a new draft from start to finish. Jackson's overnight draft was a mess. Reading it, Ike's heart sank. "It sounds like I'm giving a sermon," he complained.

A flurry of drafts and redrafts ensued. At one point, he gathered his staff together at the Hotel Commodore, where they were doing the transition work, and told them he wanted to read them a new draft of the address. Like a general consulting his staff about battle plans, he made it very clear he expected them to get out their blue pencils—he wasn't seeking praise but hard criticism. "Here is this thing going out to probably one of the greatest audiences that has ever heard a speech," he told them, highlighting the stakes. "You want every person there to carry home with him a conviction that he can do something."

But it was on Inauguration Day itself that Ike came up with a new idea—an unexpected opening. He still resisted the appearance of sermonizing. But at church that morning he began to reflect on how much religion meant to him—how a deep faith in the beneficence of the Almighty had been embedded in him in childhood by his devout and loving mother. So he began his address by asking everyone to bow their heads while he offered a little prayer of his own:

Almighty God, as we stand here at this moment, my future associates in the executive branch of government join me in beseeching that Thou will make full and complete our dedication to the service of the people in this throng, and their fellow citizens everywhere.

Give us, we pray, the power to discern clearly right from wrong, and allow all our words and actions to be governed thereby, and by the laws of this land. Especially we pray that our concern shall be for all the people regardless of station, race, or calling.

May cooperation be permitted and be the mutual aim of those who, under the concepts of our Constitution, hold to differing political faiths; so that all may work for the good of our beloved country and Thy glory. Amen.

Mindful of the men still losing their lives in Korea, he returned to the topic of faith in the body of the speech:

At such a time in history, we who are free must proclaim anew our faith. This faith is the abiding creed of our fathers. It is our faith in the deathless dignity of man, governed by eternal moral and natural laws.

This was a message that fit the moment—not just rhetoric, but an appeal to the heart. A humble call to faith and action, sincerely offered to a nation receptive to the message.

After the ceremony, the Trumans took a short ride to Union Station for the train journey home to Independence, Missouri. Union Station was still in a state of disrepair. Five days earlier a runaway train from Boston had plowed into it, injuring eighty-seven people and collapsing part of the structure. The body of the train was still wedged in the basement, and with tens of thousands of people expected for the inauguration, hasty repair efforts had made the station barely operable.

Before the inauguration, Ike had written to the president, offering him the use of the presidential plane to make the trip, rather than enduring an uncomfortable train ride. Truman never bothered to respond. So off he and Bess went in the humblest manner, saying goodbye to their Secret Service agents before they boarded the train. In those days former presidents did not receive Secret Service protection.

Meanwhile, Ike and Mamie attended a congressional luncheon before the parade. It was the first time such a luncheon, sponsored by the Congressional Committee on Inaugural Ceremonies and held in the Old Senate Chamber, was held; after that it became a tradition. Ike had worried about stopping to dine on a multicourse meal—Gulf shrimp, creamed chicken, potato puffs, ham, ice-cream sundaes—while the parade participants stood in the cold. "Speaking as one who has marched in one of the blankety-blank things and had to wait an hour on Pennsylvania Avenue while someone went up to lunch, I would very much like to help out several thousand people who will be waiting in the cold." He kept harping on the matter, suggesting they could essentially eat and run—he didn't see why the lunch should take more than fifteen minutes.

Afterward, the presidential couple rode down Pennsylvania Avenue in a white Cadillac convertible. An estimated 750,000 people jammed the parade route between the Capitol and the White House, hoping to get a glimpse of Ike and Mamie. Decamping to the viewing stand in front of the White House, they settled in with family and friends for a long afternoon of parade watching. President Hoover sat next to Ike for the entire time, a warming blanket on his lap. They watched parade floats from fifty states, dozens of musical acts, hundred of horses, and three elephants—in homage to the Republican symbol. Approximately 22,000 servicemen marched in the parade, and more than 60,000 people paid between three and fifteen dollars to watch from grandstand seats. There were also live acts. One, a rodeo cowboy named Montie Montana, rode his horse right up to the viewing stand and lassoed the president, startling Hoover, who ducked, and jangling everyone's nerves. (Needless to say, such a moment would be unthinkable today.) The inaugural parade, at four and a half hours long, tested the mettle of the viewers and didn't end until the skies had darkened and the lights had switched on along Pennsylvania Avenue. Then an exhausted Ike and Mamie left to prepare for two lavish inaugural balls at the National Guard Armory and Georgetown University. Originally, there had only been one ball planned, but the demand for tickets was so great a second had been added. It was a far cry from later inaugural balls: fourteen for Clinton in 1997 (the high point), nine for George W. Bush in 2005, and ten for Obama in 2009—although the number was reduced to two in 2013.

Once all the hoopla of the parties was over, Ike put on his old brown bathrobe and spent his first night in the White House talking to his son, John. They conferred together in Ike's bedroom long into the night. Truman had not given Eisenhower a tour before the inauguration, and unlike many newly elected presidents, Ike didn't wander around the place marveling at the famous rooms—in fact, he had to be shown where his office was the next morning. He was content to spend his first night as president just being a father, holding close the son who would soon return to a war he was committed to ending.

———————

TRUMAN FAMOUSLY HAD A plaque reading THE BUCK STOPS HERE on his Oval Office desk. Less known is that Ike had a paperweight, with words etched in Latin: *Suaviter in modo, fortiter in re*: "Gently in manner, strong in deed." Those words sum up Eisenhower's core philosophy. He came into power seeking to be a calming influence in a volatile world. He worked hard to discipline his temper, and was not one to rage and pound his desk. "He had this vein in his temple and sometimes it would throb," reported his secretary, Ann Whitman, describing his occasional flare-ups of anger. She herself recalled very few arguments with Ike, although she was by his side for eight years. (One outburst involved the squirrels on the White House lawn. Ike hated them—he liked to hit golf balls on the South Lawn and they got in the way. Ann defended the squirrels, saying they had a perfect right to be there. One night Ike had them rounded up and taken to Rock Creek Park, where they would be out of range of his swing.)

Administratively, Ike favored practical tacticians, sometimes choosing people outside the political class. For him it was a matter of getting people who could *do* things, not just rewarding political operatives. He liked to tell a story that illustrated his philosophy of a strong team, which also happened to be a lesson in leadership. It involved a general inspecting paratroopers. He asked each of them, "Do you like jumping?" One after the other they replied, "Oh, yes, sir." At last he came to the final paratrooper, who responded to the question, "Oh, no." The general was perplexed. "Then what are you doing in a paratroop regiment?" The man replied, "I like to be around people who like to jump." For Ike the story had a simple message: surround yourself with the best people and you'll be better for it.

Ike's choices were not from the usual suspects of the political stable. Richard Stout made a joke in the *New Republic* that stuck: "Ike has picked a cabinet of eight millionaires and a plumber"—the "plumber" being Secretary of Labor Martin Durkin, head of the Journeymen Plumbers and Steamfitters Union. And, by the way, a Democrat.

A perfect example of Ike's unconventional selections was Charlie Wilson—"Engine Charlie" as he was known—the former CEO of General Motors, as his secretary of defense. From long experience Ike believed the Pentagon was mired in waste and made sluggish by size and inefficiency. He thought a man of Wilson's organizational skills and strong personality could bring about a streamlined, more effective force. Wilson's famous statement, delivered during his confirmation hearings, has often been misquoted. Asked whether he would be capable of making a decision that conflicted with GM's interests, he replied that he could, "because for years I thought what was good for the country was good for General Motors and vice versa." (The misquoted version, "What's good for General Motors is good for America," is precisely the opposite sentiment.) Adlai Stevenson joked, "the New Dealers have all left town to make way for the car dealers."

In the same way, Ike's choice of George Humphrey as secretary of the Treasury was pragmatic. Humphrey, a prominent businessman and chairman of the M. A. Hanna steelworks company, was tapped to oversee the economic direction of the administration. The new administration had inherited a $9 billion budget deficit and a fragile economy, and Ike felt confident in handing over these challenges to the mild-mannered Midwesterner, who was a no-nonsense believer in the edict that people—including the government—had to live within their means.

Ike had an eye for the doers, even if, like his choice for secretary of state, John Foster Dulles, they were not the most outgoing or popular. He had great admiration for Dulles, although the two men were never friendly—Dulles could be something of a stuffy Calvinist, cold as the icy waters of Lake Ontario, where he enjoyed taking swims. But few questioned his penetrating clarity or experience, and he remained Ike's right hand until he was forced to resign in 1959 due to advancing colon cancer, which killed him months later.

Secretary Dulles has been called the "bellicose counterpart" to Ike's foreign policy, and the two men were often at odds. But from the start, Ike made it clear who was boss and sought to moderate Dulles's approach. He even reviewed his secretary of state's speeches before they were delivered. In September 1953, before Dulles delivered a speech to the United Nations, Ike offered a gentle suggestion, aimed at blunting the secretary's sharp elbows: "I rather feel that it would be well to state flatly in the beginning . . . that your purpose is to advance the cause of conciliation and understanding and not to be concerned merely with excoriation."

Ike's choice of Herbert Brownell for attorney general surprised many, and might have seemed like a political favor to his campaign manager were it not for Brownell's natural abilities. Ike found much to like about Brownell—and indeed his warm personality, unassailable character, and sharp intellect made him a very effective attorney general. He also had a gift for empathy and would shepherd into law the first civil rights advances in eighty years.

Recognizing the importance of including women in leadership positions within his administration, he appointed Oveta Culp Hobby, who had founded the Women's Auxiliary Corps (WAC) in World War II, as the head of the Federal Security Agency. It was not a cabinet position, but nonetheless she sat in on cabinet meetings. In 1955 she became the secretary of the

newly formed Department of Health, Education and Welfare—
becoming the first woman to sit on a presidential cabinet. (Kay
Bailey Hutchison, the Republican senator from Texas for twenty
years, credits Hobby for providing her first professional opportunity as a reporter at Hobby's television station in Houston.)

Ike felt especially close to Jim Hagerty and wanted him for
press secretary. He presented Hagerty with the offer while they
were in Denver after the nomination. One day Ike came strolling
into Hagerty's office and said, "Come on, Jim, we're going to go
out and play golf at Cherry Hill." That's when Hagerty got an
inside view of the way Ike worked. "We got into a golf cart, and
while he hit the ball around for eighteen holes, during the two
and a half hours we were on the golf course, we worked out our
working relationship, on how I would do my job, how he would
keep me informed. That never changed one iota from that day
through the next eight and a half years I worked for him."

Sherman Adams was chosen for the most intimate position
of all—chief of staff to the president. It was for all intents a new
role, created by Ike, who had relied so closely on a staff assistant in the military. He considered appointing a military officer
but feared it would look as if he were trying to set up a military
operation. Instead he chose Adams, once referred to as a New
Hampshire "chunk of granite." Jerry Persons, who had served
as a special assistant to Eisenhower at NATO, was appointed as
Adams's deputy.

"Every president has to have an official SOB, and Sherman
Adams was the president's official SOB," Hagerty said. Adams
was loyal, tough, and, occasionally, diabolical. He had a reputation for being aloof, humorless, and also fiercely protective
of Ike. He had a habit of speaking as if he were channeling
the president, with forceful declarations that never betrayed
any doubts. Decades later, in the aftermath of Watergate, Bryce

Harlow, who was a congressional liaison in Ike's White House, drew a comparison with Nixon's infamous aides: "Governor Adams was a combination of Haldeman and Ehrlichman and bigger than either as a result."

The cabinet meetings themselves were a study in collaboration. "It was an education in working together with big men, all of whom were prima donnas and were accustomed to going off on their own," said Maxwell Raab, the first secretary of the cabinet. Everyone had to be ready to explain and defend their opinions. The meetings were not taped; Ike didn't want cabinet members posturing for history. He insisted they be allowed to speak freely. Ike's management style was very informal, and he always made time for people who wanted to see him. The routine was simple: Saunter in to the appointment secretary. Ask, "Is there anyone in with the Old Man?" Get a response. If yes, leave a request to be called when he was free. If no, go right in. But anyone in their right mind would not dream of doing so unless the matter at hand was both important and well thought out. Ike insisted on being fully informed, whether the news was pleasant or unpleasant. "Frankly," said Persons, "there were times when you wondered when something pleasant could come up so you could tell him that for a change."

The open-door policy seemed sacrosanct, but some gatekeeping had to take place. In this regard, Adams played the bad cop. He'd sometimes hesitate when people asked for appointments, and they'd take umbrage. "Are you telling me I can't see the President?" He'd lay it on the line: "You know better than to ask me that. The President has made it clear that if you request the appointment, you get it. But I have to tell you that if I wanted to see the President on the matter that you have in mind, I wouldn't ask for the time."

Eisenhower expected his staff and cabinet to be disciplined.

That Ike had rock-ribbed discipline should have surprised no one, given his military history. Adams, knowing Ike had been a chain smoker during the war, once asked him how he ever gave it up. Ike replied, "The only way to stop is to stop, and I stopped."

Adams persisted. "Didn't you have quite a lot of battle with yourself when you gave up a habit that you liked and lived with so long?"

He told Adams, "If you have anything like that to disturb you, put it out of your mind. Don't think about it." That was pretty much the way Ike handled most difficulties, compartmentalizing them so he could focus on important matters at hand.

EISENHOWER OFTEN JOKED—ALTHOUGH ONLY half in jest—that he considered the ability to play bridge a key qualification for any of his top aides and confidants. Bridge is a game of secrets and strategy, and it's not surprising Ike was a skilled player. He steadied his nerves in the run-up to D-Day playing bridge with his closest advisors.

The aspect of Ike's character that allowed him to excel at bridge, in war, and in government has been called the "hidden hand," a term coined by political scientist Fred I. Greenstein. Greenstein wrote of Ike's ability to strategically mask his underlying intentions. He described five ways Ike achieved this: First, he downplayed his skills as a politician, found surrogates to do the dirty work, and convinced Americans he was above politics. Second, he used ambiguous language. Third, he never attacked people personally and maintained his public image as a likable, goodhearted person. Fourth, he always tried to put himself in the other person's shoes. And fifth, he gave his subordinates important assignments but never lost control of policy.

The hidden-hand approach, while often effective, could have a downside, especially when circumstances seemed to call for more dramatic action. At those times Ike's circumspection could make him look indecisive and weak instead of cautious and thoughtful.

According to Greenstein, the most significant early example of a "hidden hand" in Ike's presidency—and the one that gave his critics the most ammunition—was the matter of Wisconsin senator Joseph McCarthy. Since his awkward handling of McCarthy during the campaign, Ike had continued to be haunted by McCarthy's antics in the Senate. In 1954, as McCarthy doubled down on trying to root out communists in Ike's beloved Army, things were reaching a crescendo. Ike was growing increasingly alarmed. "It's his Army and he doesn't like McCarthy's tactics at all," Hagerty noted.

Specifically, McCarthy was targeting Dr. Irving Peress, an Army dentist stationed at Fort Monmouth, New Jersey. The case displayed all the madness of a campaign ruled by innuendo and slurs. When Peress received a seemingly routine promotion from captain to major, McCarthy lit upon it as a favor given to communist sympathizers, crowing that the promotion was the work of a "silent master who decreed special treatment for Communists." He called Peress the "pink dentist," and the unhinged implication was clear: communists were pulling the strings in the Army.

Called to testify before McCarthy's Senate subcommittee, Peress invoked the Fifth Amendment, which only inflamed McCarthy further. The senator was now prepared to march on into higher echelons, calling on Brigadier General Ralph Zwicker to testify in the Peress case. Zwicker was a high-profile target, an enormously respected officer, and veteran of World War II, whose decorations included the Silver Star, the Bronze Star, the Legion of Merit badge, and the British Distinguished Service

Order. As the commanding officer of Camp Kilmer, he was Peress's boss. Sitting under McCarthy's hot lights, Zwicker endured being called a perjurer, "unfit to wear the uniform," and a person who lacked "the brains of a five-year-old" by the senator.

All of this enraged Ike—so why not launch a counterattack? Ike's supporters were begging him to take on McCarthy, and they couldn't understand why he was so reluctant to do so. Was he indifferent? Was he afraid? Was he lending tacit support? None of the above: Ike despised McCarthy and felt he was a danger to the nation. "You can't defeat Communism by destroying America," he said, but he refused to "get down in the gutter with that guy."

Among Ike's harshest critics over his reluctance to speak out was his brother Milton. "McCarthy was such an evil and penetrating force in our society that I wanted the president, in the strongest possible language, to repudiate him," he said later. But Ike believed by remaining silent he might starve McCarthy of the publicity he craved. As Hagerty put it, "Do you take a junior senator from Wisconsin and elevate him to the level of the president in public debate? Or, what is worse, do you have the president come down to the level of a junior senator from the state of Wisconsin? Both those answers in his own mind were: hell no!"

Ike remained cautious. Although the president did not like to play politics, he knew knocking out McCarthy might put the Republican majority in jeopardy. And the "Red Scare" had some momentum with the public. So it was a tricky matter. Still, McCarthy was getting to be too much for Ike to endure, and he began a steady backroom campaign against him. In a phone call to Leonard Hall, the RNC chairman, he called McCarthy a pimple on the path of progress and urged him to use his influence to stop the abuse of power. In a meeting with the legislative leadership, Ike urged them to rein McCarthy in. Privately, the president was in a rage. Pacing angrily in his office, he exploded to Hagerty, calling McCarthy's actions "the most disloyal" ever seen by anyone in the government of the United States. Appalled by McCarthy's assault on Zwicker, Army Secretary Robert Stevens ordered Zwicker to refuse to testify further, but in a meeting with McCarthy Stevens inexplicably then signed an agreement reversing himself and opening the door to further investigations of the Army. This ultimately led to Stevens himself being called before the committee and launched the Army-McCarthy Hearings, which began on April 22, 1954. Joseph Welch, special counsel to the Army, took on McCarthy in weeks of hearings, often sending the senator into a rage of vitriol.

At the White House Ike was still holding his fire. But in a speech at Columbia University's Bicentennial Dinner on May 31, he spoke plainly about those who would confuse "honest dissent with disloyal subversion." He never mentioned McCarthy's name, but the audience, interrupting the speech frequently with loud applause, got the point. "Through knowledge and understanding we will drive from the temple of freedom all those who seek to establish over us thought control," Ike said as the crowd cheered, "whether they be agents of a foreign state or demagogues thirsty for personal power and public notice." There was no doubt who he was talking about.

Things came to a head in the Army-McCarthy Hearings on June 9 when a sputtering McCarthy named a young man in Welch's office as having communist affiliations. The moment broke a years-long spell when Welch responded in quiet but burning anger, calling out McCarthy's tactics with words that would echo down through the decades: "Until this moment,

Senator, I think I never really gauged your cruelty or your reck-
lessness. Have you no sense of decency, sir?" The hearing room
erupted in cheers.

History has deemed Welch's rebuke as the moment that
brought McCarthy down. It is less certain of Ike's role. While
it is probably true the president's behind-the-scenes efforts hastened McCarthy's demise, to those who were hunted and ru-
ined by his demagoguery, in hindsight it was a slow death where
a more rapid and brutal end was called for.

ON FRIDAY, SEPTEMBER 23, 1955, Ike was in Denver on a
well-deserved break. After a four-day fishing trip, he was relax-
ing with Mamie at his in-laws' and trying to get some golf in
between the constant flood of calls and correspondence that followed him even on vacation. After playing golf in the morning,
he made what he would admit was a foolish choice for lunch—a
large hamburger sandwich garnished with fat slices of Bermuda
onion and a pot of coffee. He regretted it immediately, suffering
digestive pains throughout the afternoon, even though he managed a second round of golf. Blaming his lunch for the continued distress, he went to bed that night feeling unwell. When he
awoke at 1:30 A.M. with chest and stomach pains he told Mamie he needed some milk of magnesia. She was so alarmed she
called for his personal physician, Major General Howard Snyder. The doctor arrived shortly and examined his patient. He
did not immediately send Ike to the hospital. Instead, he treated
him with amyl nitrate for angina; heparin, a blood thinner, to
prevent clots; and morphine for the pain; and left him sleeping
in his own bed until 11:30 A.M. Only then, when the chest pains
persisted, did Snyder alert doctors at nearby Fitzsimons Army
Hospital and get an electrocardiogram confirming that Ike had

had a heart attack. He wasn't taken to the hospital until midafternoon.

Snyder's actions that night are shocking in retrospect, and they earned him a great deal of censure at the time. Why the twelve-hour delay? He later said he thought Ike was suffering from a chronic digestive complaint, not a heart attack, but that explanation does not account for his choice of medications, which were definitely related to a heart condition. Snyder never lived down the fact that the president might have died from his carelessness.

In Washington, Hagerty took a call on Saturday afternoon from Dr. Snyder informing him the president had suffered a heart attack and was on his way to Fitzsimons. One by one Ike's closest aides were notified, and there was shock and dismay in the White House. Ann Whitman, with the president in Denver, was crying when Hagerty reached her on the phone. "Please hurry and get out here as soon as you can," she said. "Both General Snyder and I need you out here."

Richard Nixon was home when he received word of Ike's heart attack, and he immediately sprang into action. It's interesting to note that the Twenty-Fifth Amendment, outlining the succession of powers if a president is unfit for office, was not ratified until 1967. So while Nixon readily took on responsibilities during Ike's recuperation, he did not assume the power of the presidency. (In a different era, President George W. Bush transferred power to Vice President Dick Cheney during the single hour he was under anesthesia for a colonoscopy in 2002.)

Long before, Ike had told his staff that if he ever became ill, he wanted everything disclosed to the American public. "Tell the full medical facts to everyone," he said. He knew his history, and cited President Woodrow Wilson as an example of doing it the wrong way. After he suffered a stroke, Wilson's wife and doctor covered it up and the nation had no idea its president was out of commission. The severity of FDR's health condition was likewise kept from the public, contributing to the shock of his death in office.

Hagerty flew to Denver and spoke to the press outside the hospital. "Gentlemen," he said, "I have been given orders by the President of the United States a long time ago to give the complete and full medical reporting. These are my orders, and I expect to follow them out, and I am sure you will agree." So the nation was allowed to suffer with and root for Ike as he went through his health crisis.

Treatment for heart attacks was nothing like the standard of care today. Angioplasty and coronary artery bypass were nonexistent, and patients were prescribed several weeks of bed rest—the opposite of the *up-and-at-'em* prescription of modern cardiologists. Ike spent seven weeks in the hospital. During that time Hagerty kept the American public fully informed, relating the most minute details of the president's condition, right down to his bowel movements—a little bit too much detail, Ike thought.

Ike recovered from his heart attack, but since he had yet to announce whether or not he would run for reelection in 1956, speculation ran high that he would not. When the Newspaper Enterprise Association polled Washington correspondents, 88 percent of them were of the opinion that he would not run.

Ike, who was feeling well, was not so ready to pull the plug. In his mind it boiled down to an easy calculation: he hadn't completed the list of things he wanted to accomplish. Sherman Adams astutely observed, "There's never been a president who ever thought a successor could carry out the things he was trying to accomplish as well, if at all—also, no president ever looked at a possible successor and said, 'Well, you're as good a man as I.'" And while it wasn't Ike's style to beat his chest, he certainly believed in himself and in what he and his team could still do, especially in strengthening the nation's position in the world. At the same time, he had to weigh the desire to carry on with the effects of service on his health, the weariness of engaging in the fight day after day, the disappointment over his constant battles with Congress, and the seductive call of freedom and leisure.

As with most other important decisions, he sought counsel from those he trusted. In January 1956 he hosted a private dinner at the White House with his closest cadre—among them Milton, Jerry Persons, Herb Brownell, John Foster Dulles, Sherman Adams, James Hagerty, and Henry Cabot Lodge Jr.—and asked them to discuss, pro and con, the reasons he should or should not run. Every one of them, with the exception of Milton, who abstained, believed it was his duty to run. They argued he was the only one who could work effectively to stop a world war and build the promise of peace—and as long as his health permitted, he should do it.

John Eisenhower leaned against his father running, for health reasons, but Mamie, the person Ike cared about most, refused to weigh in. "No, I certainly am not going to say one word," she told her husband. "It's your decision. If you don't do it, and are unhappy because you didn't do it, it's got to be your unhappiness. If you do it, and it breaks your health down, it has to be your decision too."

In February Ike went to Walter Reed Hospital for tests, and on February 14 the doctors announced him well enough to take on a second term. Dr. Snyder told him, "If you run, I will vote for you."

He decided to run. Those who knew Ike best believed he would have been miserable if he hadn't taken on the challenge of a second term, when so much was left to be done. And to few observers' surprise, the popular president was easily reelected. The Democrats as good as conceded defeat by once again nominating Adlai Stevenson, who lost by a greater margin than he had in 1952. The only drama in the process was the Democratic contest for vice president. Stevenson decided to open the matter to a convention vote, and in a fierce fight, Senator Estes Kefauver defeated John F. Kennedy on the third ballot. In the process, the young Massachusetts senator achieved a national platform from which he would build a White House run four years later.

Since January 20, 1957, fell on a Sunday, it was decided Ike would take the oath in a private White House ceremony (to fulfill the constitutional requirement) and then take it again publicly the following day. The television age was in full force by then, with the networks eager to bring both the inauguration and the parade to Americans, canceling *Search for Tomorrow, Guiding Light,* and other popular programming. Cecil B. De-Mille was hired by Republicans to direct the inaugural balls. For the first time, videotape was used, allowing segments to be replayed throughout the day. Over many hours, an estimated 90 percent of Americans tuned in to see portions of the pageant.

Ike's second inaugural address was characteristically humble and full of resolve: "May we pursue the right—without self-righteousness. May we know unity—without conformity. May we grow in strength—without pride in self. May we, in our dealings with all peoples of the earth, ever speak truth and serve justice."

Ironically, almost as soon as Ike was reelected, commentators started talking about his being a "lame duck" president. The context was much different than it is today, since the Twenty-Second Amendment, setting a two-term limit for presidents, had only just been ratified in 1951. Ike thus was the first president for whom it was a certainty that he would leave the presidency after eight years. (Until that time, presidential term limits were entirely voluntary, though only FDR broke the tradition with four terms.) And yet despite the now-familiar "lame duck" pronouncements, there's often a certain freedom that emerges in that last sprint in office. Indeed, in many ways Ike's second term would be more ambitious than his first, and more fraught with global consequences. "He turned the second term, under our two term provisions now, into a term when the President of the United States can do things and is not a lame duck," said Hagerty.

IKE'S SECOND TERM FEATURED a contentious civil rights debate, culminating in groundbreaking legislation. Here, too, Ike's hidden hand was evidenced, and like the McCarthy drama, his preference for behind-the-scenes maneuvering masked his historic contribution to civil rights.

The stage had been set in his first year in office when Chief Justice Fred Vinson died and Ike appointed his longtime friend Earl Warren to his seat. Warren wasn't exactly a liberal—he had advocated for the internment of Japanese during World War II—but among party regulars he was considered left of center. The Warren Court, which would last until Warren's retirement in 1969, would be activist on many issues, but arguably its most important ruling came shortly after Warren joined the bench with the unanimous decision in *Brown v. Board of Education,* which reversed the separate-but-equal doctrine, in place since 1896, and paved the way for school desegregation.

The ruling created a storm of protest across the South, with officials refusing to accept integration as the law of the land. Progress was stymied for years by state intransigence, and Ike heard plenty of criticism, not only from Democrats, who held a stronghold in the South, but also from Republicans. A prominent Republican congressman grumbled to him, "Mr. President, maybe I shouldn't say this but I'm going to: I expected to be correcting the Supreme Court's decisions through the Congress when the Democrats were naming them all, but I never dreamed we'd have to do the same damned thing after we got a chance to appoint."

Despite resistance and long delays, the new law was finally tested in September 1957 at the Central High School in Little Rock, Arkansas, when nine black students enrolled for class. As they tried to enter the school, they were repeatedly blocked by protesters, and then by police who were acting on the order of the governor.

Ike did not use the bully pulpit to decry segregation, but rather considered it his mandate to enforce the law. The way he saw it, once the Supreme Court made its ruling and integration was settled law, it was his obligation to make sure it got done. Further, while he believed government couldn't legislate morality, he understood it *could* legislate equality. When Arkansas governor Orval Faubus mobilized the Arkansas National Guard to restore order and, in effect, prevent the students from entering the school, Ike had had enough. On vacation at the Navy base in Newport, Rhode Island, he called Faubus to a meeting. It started out cordially enough, but when Faubus asked for "breathing room" to enforce the order, the president could not agree. He reminded Faubus that desegregation was the law, and that the only legitimate use of the National Guard should be to escort the students into the school.

In separate statements released after the meeting, the two men seemed to be on the same page about enforcing *Brown v. Board of Education*. The problem was, when Faubus got back to Arkansas, he did nothing. Ike, who had believed Faubus was agreeing to comply, now saw they were back to square one. He felt tricked. He penned an immediate cease-and-desist order.

In a press briefing, reporter Merriman Smith of United Press International (UPI) asked Hagerty, "What happens if they don't obey? If the reaction of this group is not cease and desist and go home?"

"Well, Smitty," Hagerty replied wearily, "if I were you I'd be around tomorrow."

Smith nodded. "I thought so," he said.

Indeed, the cease-and-desist order was read, it was not obeyed, and the president chose to intervene federally—with the best power America had at its disposal. Troops from the 101st Airborne descended on Arkansas.

Addressing the nation from the Oval Office, Ike looked tired but resolute. "Good evening, my fellow citizens. For a few minutes this evening I want to speak to you about the serious situation that has arisen in Little Rock," he began. "In that city, under the leadership of demagogic extremists, disorderly mobs have deliberately prevented the carrying out of proper orders from a federal court." He then walked viewers through a history of the conflict, and announced his executive order directing the use of troops to "aid in the execution of federal law in Little Rock." He used an uncharacteristically emotional appeal to remind Americans of their place in the world. "Our enemies are gloating over this incident and using it everywhere to misrepresent our whole nation," he said sternly, his indignation clear. "We are portrayed as a violator of those standards of conduct which the peoples of the world united to proclaim in the Charter of the United Nations. There they affirmed faith in fundamental human rights and in the dignity and worth of the human person, and they did so without distinction as to race, sex, language or religion."

The troops did their job, the mobs faded away, and the black students entered the school and began the business of education. Interestingly, Ike's firm action didn't win him points in the civil rights community. Once again, he was harshly criticized for not being more outspoken and passionate in defense of desegregation. People were looking for the big moment, the uplifting speech, the dramatic rhetoric, and that wasn't Ike's style. Yet if you judge a man by his actions, the cause of civil rights greatly advanced on Ike's watch. At the very moment he was going head-to-head with Orval Faubus, Ike signed the Civil Rights Act of 1957—the first civil rights legislation passed by Congress since 1875—overcoming a filibuster by South Carolina senator Strom Thurmond that lasted twenty-four hours and eighteen minutes. The legislation proposed by Eisenhower put federal muscle behind the right to vote, which was regularly denied black citizens, especially in the South. Perhaps Ike suffered for not being as articulate on the issue of civil rights as others wanted him to be. But he got things done.

However, the crisis in Little Rock undoubtedly took its toll. Two months later Ike suffered a mild stroke, once again raising questions about his fitness for office. The effect of the stroke was short-lived—he wasn't even hospitalized—but it caused grave concern for a few days as his family and aides watched him stumble for words. When he insisted on attending an important NATO conference in Paris in mid-December, there was plenty of hand-wringing from his aides. But by then he was "himself" again.

SCANDAL WAS LARGELY ABSENT in Ike's White House, with the notable exception of an episode that took down one of the president's closest advisors. It all happened because of a vicuna coat. (Prized for its woolen fur and native to the South American Andes, the vicuna is a relative of the llama.) Bernard Goldfine, a textile manufacturer, gifted his close friend Sherman Adams the coat; at the same time, Goldfine was complaining about problems he was having with the Federal Trade Commission and the Securities and Exchange Commission. Adams then made what he characterized as routine calls to the two agencies about Goldfine's difficulties, although he said he hadn't tried to influence them. In the congressional investigation that ensued, Adams called his actions imprudent rather than unethical, and he disingenuously (considering he'd been a governor and political animal for decades) blamed them on "inexperience." The scandal wouldn't die, and in September 1958 Ike reluctantly decided to take action.

The call from the president came while Adams was on a fishing trip on the Miramachi River in Nova Scotia with his deputy Jerry Persons and their wives. They were miles from any telephone when the word came that Adams was wanted on a phone call with the president. They drove several miles to a place with a phone, and when Adams came out to the car afterward he reported he had to return to Washington, but told Persons to stay and fish. Persons refused and returned with Adams, at which point he learned of his boss's resignation. Suspecting he was the logical replacement, Persons went to Ike and assured him he did not want "the damn job" as chief of staff, and he gave him a list of names of possible successors to Adams. But a week later Ike called Persons. "Jerry, you'll have to take the job," he said, and the matter was final.

Those close to the president understood these decisions were not made in a callous political sense, but with a deeper judgment about the character of his administration. He might not have been successful at it 100 percent of the time, but Ike consistently tried to separate "the political" out of his decisions, much like skimming the fat from a pot of soup. "In the hierarchy of motivations for presidential action, partisan political effect was not only at the bottom of the list," Special Assistant Arthur Larson said of Eisenhower's leadership, "indeed, it did not exist as a motivation at all."

Ike remained impatient with politics, but with greater experience he also came to see it in a more nuanced manner—and to recognize his own political talents. In a conversation with UPI's Merriman Smith, he put it this way: "I have been in politics, the most active sort of politics, in the military most of my life. There is no more active political organization in the country or in the world than the armed services of the United States. As a matter of fact, I think I am a better politician than most so-called politicians . . . because I don't get as emotionally involved. I can accept a fact for what it is."

Smith had sparred with Ike on many occasions over the years, but he appreciated the complexity of a man whose "hard and stern" childhood had taught him an unearthly restraint that masked his true nature: "I don't know of a man I've ever seen in better control of his will, better control of his emotions," Smith said. "But this was the façade. Underneath was a man who could be quite, quite sensitive, and a man who did himself a disservice, in that there were aspects of his character, of his personality, which almost never surfaced."

This inner steel was in evidence after the 1958 midterm elections when the Republican Party "took a really rough shellacking," in the words of Hagerty. Ike called his staff together for an early breakfast the following day before his press conference. As they shuffled into the room, he said, "What's all the gloomy faces around here today? Pretty bad, wasn't it?" They acknowledged this fact with unhappy murmurs.

"Well, know what I'm going to do today? I'm going to go into that press conference and I'm going to relate this Democratic victory to rising cost of government and how much it's going to be in taxes for every person in the United States." He'd already added up all of the Democratic proposals, he told them, and he was ready. That's what he did, to great effect. Rather than an apologetic president, the press got a feisty one.

IN HIS FINAL WHITE House years, Ike was beginning to get a taste of what life on the other side would look like, and it had its appeal. He and Mamie had purchased a run-down farm in Gettysburg for forty thousand dollars a decade earlier, and had spent seven years on a massive renovation that when completed gave them the homey atmosphere they had missed so much during their many moves while Ike was in the military. As his second term drew to a close, Ike found himself enjoying more than ever the bucolic family life the farm provided. With John and his wife, Barbara, and the grandkids living in a house on the property, the atmosphere was happily boisterous, with children racing up and down the stairs and Mamie calling out, "Hands off the wallpaper . . . use the banister!" Simple pleasures meant everything to Ike—family barbecues, reading the Sunday paper on the porch while Mamie knit hot-water bottle covers—usually in pink—or answered correspondence. (She replied to every letter she received, by hand.) Fishing with the grandkids in the little trout pond on the property. Hitting balls on the putting green. Christmas mornings, with the gifts piled up to the sky. Ike had an unwritten rule not to discuss business and politics at home, and he mostly managed to follow it.

But the pastoral scenes at Gettysburg could not make up for the challenges in Washington—and Ike relished them until his last day. As the famed journalist Howard K. Smith, who covered Ike over the years, put it, "We have a big thirteen-ring circus going on here in Washington, and the main ring is always the presidency." Ike was happy to be in the fray.

Eisenhower was a paradox—a man of war who craved peace. Many people assume that when you put a general in the White House it elevates the military class. Yet if a single theme defined his eight-year presidency, it was the goal of keeping the world from war. As a man who knew firsthand the scourge of the battlefield, he was alert to the terrible prospect of a "battlefield" consumed in a mushroom cloud.

Part of the paradox of Eisenhower is found in his own struggle throughout his presidency to balance his quest for peace with a tough stance on the avoidance of war. "He put on a mask of ambiguity," said his valued aide Andrew Goodpaster, "in the sense that you did not show your hand to the other fellow." Arthur Larson summed up Ike's contribution to history most succinctly when he wrote, "President Eisenhower's standing in history will rest mainly on this fact: in essentially the same modern world that saw the Second World War under President Franklin D. Roosevelt, the Korean War under President Truman, the Bay of Pigs invasion under President Kennedy and the Vietnam War under President Johnson, Eisenhower closed out one war, the Korean War, and carried his country through eight difficult years without any war, large or small, and without any loss to Communist aggression." How he achieved this is a masterful hidden game.

Ike was more than anything else a problem solver. Issues mattered, not just on the surface—what today we call sound bites—but deep down in the core. He was morally consistent and thoughtful, the antithesis of the politician who finds glory in the eye of the camera.

This inveterate late bloomer who didn't take military command until he was fifty-two, or enter politics until he was sixty-two, did not dodder into old age. In spite of a heart attack, a stroke, and persistent intestinal problems, he maintained a mental vigor that, seasoned with wisdom and experience, made him an effective president for his times.

THAT INTELLECTUAL ENERGY IS the reason Ike, in his final days in office, was still producing an agenda. Specifically, three days before the inauguration of John F. Kennedy, he was determined to give the speech of his life. Far from being a one-off, the speech would be the culmination of all he had done and all he believed, taking its own prominent place in history. It would not be just another speech, much less a sentimental goodbye. Ike was staking out a position on the future. And the crucible of that position was held in the words he spoke so fervently to the American people.

PART TWO

THE SPEECH

CHAPTER 5

FAREWELL IN
BLACK AND WHITE

January 17, 1961
The Oval Office

The speech had already been sent to the mimeograph machine to be copied and distributed to reporters. But sitting at his desk in the Oval Office, the president was still rewriting. Reporters who were used to Ike's tendency to edit his speeches up until the very last minute had learned not to take the "official" version as final. Those tempted to file their stories before the actual speech risked waking up red-faced when Ike's delivery veered off in another direction.

At 8:30 P.M., millions of Americans would miss their Tuesday night episodes of *The Many Loves of Dobie Gillis, The Red Skelton Show,* or *Alfred Hitchcock Presents* to watch the president bid goodbye. Earlier, some of his friends had urged him to give the address before Congress and make a big display of it. He'd replied, "No, this is the president-elect's show. I'll just do it quietly from the White House."

Ike had been at the final editing since before eight that morning, with a strong sense of purpose. In the background he could hear pounding and hammering as the inaugural parade viewing stand was erected outside. It was, he thought, like being a condemned man in a cell listening to the scaffold going up. Now the hour was nearing when the final script would have to be handed to the technicians to set up the teleprompter. (As it turned out, he would bypass it that night, deciding at the last moment to keep a paper copy on his desk and to turn the pages as he read—while the teleprompter scrolled pointlessly along.)

Television was still a new medium, but Ike had accepted the technology even though there wasn't an ounce of Hollywood in his demeanor. He'd been the first president to approve the use of television cameras at press conferences back in 1955, believing the American people would surely benefit from seeing the president firsthand without the press filter.

Not that it didn't take some getting used to. Before the first televised press conference, Hagerty had arranged a "dummy" conference, answering questions for about ten minutes with the camera rolling. Later, Ike watched the result, gave it some consideration, and decisively told Hagerty, "Set it up." Naturally, there was a fair amount of grousing from the newspaper press, but soon everyone had accepted it. For this contribution Eisenhower became the first president to win an Emmy.

For Ike, television was no more than a necessary evil; he tolerated it. He'd never forget the time during his first presidential campaign when a representative from the Republican Party's advertising agency had approached him, quaking in his boots, to suggest that Ike use makeup on TV. His broad face and shiny bald head threw off the light, the candidate was told. Ike let him have it with colorful language, but he eventually gave in.

That first time in the barber chair with the makeup man coming at him, he was in a bad mood. "Were you in the Army?" Ike barked at him, preparing to make a remark about this sissy enterprise.

"Yes, sir," the man replied. "Hundred-and-First Airborne, General."

Ike snapped his mouth shut and never complained about the makeup again. And he made sure to have that same brave soldier do the honors for the remainder of the campaign.

Eisenhower never became the perfect messenger for the television era, but he did what he could to improve himself. His friend Robert Montgomery, an Academy Award–winning actor who was active in Republican politics, often came to the White House to coach him before a speech. His primary goal: helping Ike be Ike.

THE ORIGIN OF IKE'S farewell speech traces to a spring 1959 chat with his speechwriter Malcolm Moos in the Oval Office. Moos had joined the administration in 1957 to give a shot of fresh adrenaline to the administration's rhetoric. "Whenever you get in the sunset of an administration, these are low times always," Moos said. "You've lost that heady enthusiasm that comes on the takeoff," and you might need help communicating your vision.

Among Moos's first observations was the tendency of Ike's people to write speeches by committee—producing a jumbled mess, like "lumps of cottage cheese," as he put it. On one occasion Moos presented a speech written by committee to Ike without comment. But sensing Moos's distaste for the prose, Ike asked, "You don't think I ought to say that, do you?"

"No," admitted Moos.

"Go out and do me a speech," Ike instructed. From then on, Moos had tremendous leeway. In May 1959 Ike said to him, "I want to have something to say when I leave here. I'm not interested in capturing headlines, but I want to have a message and I want you to be thinking about it well in advance."

With a year and a half remaining in Ike's tenure, Moos promised to start "dropping ideas into a bin."

Such advance planning wasn't unusual for the president. He was determined to get his message just right. At that point, he had only an inkling of broad themes—among them the need for common sense to accommodate the broad range of beliefs in the political spectrum of America, particularly in an era when the nation had an executive of one party and a Congress of another.

As he wrote to Milton, his closest confidant, who was then president of Johns Hopkins University, "The purpose would be to emphasize a few homely truths that apply to the responsibilities and duties of a government that must be responsive to the will of majorities, even when the decisions of those majorities create apparent paradoxes."

For the next year and a half Ike and Moos worked over the idea through many drafts, most provided by Moos. Later, the themes would expand to focus on America's role in the nuclear age. Throughout the process the president was always in control. "The business of writing speeches," Bryce Harlow once observed, "is not the most enjoyable work in the world, normally, particularly if the person for whom you're writing is a skilled writer himself." This was the case with Ike. Milton had once joked that his drafts were like waving a red flag at a bull—an invitation to attack and tear apart. In fact, Milton wrote, "when he had finished [editing], one would have thought that a dozen chickens with dirty feet had found delight in scratching on every page." Ike always rewrote the speeches, infusing them with his plainspoken manner, deleting the highbrow phrases that writers liked so much. He recalled an occasion when he was invited to give a talk to some group or other and they said, "Don't worry. All you have to do is show up. We'll give you a speech. Just change it to your own words." After he finished giving the talk, the speechwriter came up to him. "I want to thank you for keeping in a few words of what I wrote," he said.

Ike smiled, a little surprised. "What were they?"

"Ladies and gentlemen."

Once, bristling at a charge he never wrote a word of his own speeches—and would, in fact, be incapable of doing so—Ike said, "You know that General MacArthur got quite a reputation as a silver-tongued speaker when he was in the Philippines. Who do you think wrote his speeches? *I* did." He was such a good writer that his war memoir, *Crusade in Europe*, was rumored to have been written by the bestselling novelist James Michener, although every word was Ike's own.

Indeed, one of the running jokes about Ike was his tendency to garble syntax. The reporter James "Scotty" Reston once wrote a whole column about it following a press conference. Hagerty called him up. "Scotty," he said, "I read your column with a great deal of interest. May I read back to you the question you asked the president, and ask you to parse it?" He did, and Reston was shocked. "My God," he said, "did I put it that way?"

"This is the text," Hagerty responded coolly.

But Robert S. Kieve, one of Ike's speechwriters during his first two years in office, said Ike appreciated the problem he had speaking extemporaneously, once saying, "I have a capacity for starting a sentence on something that's happened in my backyard, and before I put a period on the sentence I'm talking about the Normandy landing."

Reflecting on the matter in 1969, Howard K. Smith defended Ike on the question of syntax. "I think it's hard to hold syntax against a president ad-libbing. He's really walking on eggs. If he says the wrong thing, the stock market's going to go to hell, Guatemala's going to break relations, Nasser's going to seize the Suez Canal, and I think you've got to grant him a little weaving with his syntax." Smith noted that JFK, whom he had also covered, could do a bit of weaving, too, and when he faced a rough question, "it's pretty hard to find the verb sometimes."

Whatever his flaws in speaking, Ike was rigorous about speechwriting—"Absolute pedant with the English language," Kieve said. "Insufferable." If he didn't think it hit the right tone, he'd display his infamous temper. "When those explosions came, I always felt like I was being court-martialed," Moos said.

The farewell address had been rewritten almost thirty times since 1959, with Milton taking the whole thing apart and putting it back together more than once. Milton had a confidential phone line set up in his office that bypassed the Secret Service switchboard and went straight to Ike's desk, and they'd often discuss the speech. In the end Ike rewrote the opening passages in his own hand.

Finally, in early December 1960, Moos took a rough draft into the Oval Office. On such occasions, he never quite knew what to expect. Sometimes Ike would seem to like a speech but ultimately reject it, or he'd think about a subject more and change his viewpoint. In this case, Ike read it right away and said, "I think you've got something here." He slid it in his drawer to review further.

The next day he summoned Moos. "Call Milton, tell him to come over." And so a rigorous final crafting began.

In December, Ike had been mildly amused to get a call from Norman Cousins, the editor of the *Saturday Review* and an outspoken peace advocate, offering his services in helping to write a farewell speech. Ike's personal secretary, Ann Whitman, normally so unflappable, was aghast at the thought. "The idea of trying to get anyone like Norman Cousins working on it would be dreadful," she wrote to Moos. "How in the world do we diplomatically thank him, but say no?" They found a way. Later it would annoy Ike no end when he'd occasionally be asked, "Didn't Norman Cousins write that speech?"

What people expected from the farewell speech was a simple message from a retiring elder performing a traditional ritual. Sentimental farewells, heavy on bragging about accomplishments, were the standard for these addresses. Truman's goodbye was almost entirely devoted to a replay of his achievements sprinkled with homespun sentiments—"So, as I empty the drawers of this desk, and as Mrs. Truman and I leave the White House, we have no regret. We feel we have done our best in the public service."

Ike wasn't interested in bragging about his achievements, although he could have because they were substantial: an end to the Korean War, eight years of peace, the ambitious Interstate Highway System, the first civil rights legislation since Reconstruction, several balanced budgets. What his critics charged was a molasses pace was the careful administration of a serious leader who had kept America safe in a nuclear era.

The 1950s had been a time of prosperity in America, characterized by growth, stability, and promise. The economy grew by nearly 40 percent and unemployment was low. The GI Bill, giving millions of World War II veterans access to higher education and better jobs, helped create a stable middle class. It's worth recalling the context: the double stunner of the Depression followed by a second world war had left the population weary, and Ike could credibly claim he'd helped usher in a very different era. Those who complained about how dull the Eisenhower years were (especially given the more showy 1960s) had short memories, or none at all, of the unemployment lines, military funerals, rationing, and hardships of the 1930s and 1940s.

For Ike the farewell address was a moment of opportunity

to quell the sense of alarm, ramped up in the recent election, and cool the notion that the nation was slipping off its pedestal as the greatest country in the world. In three days John Kennedy would stand before the American people and offer his own vision to the nation. Before that day, Ike wanted to impress upon his countrymen in his own words a closing prophecy. The fact it had taken a year and a half to craft his words was indicative of the gravity of his message.

EISENHOWER'S MODEL IN SAYING goodbye was another old general, George Washington, whose 1797 final address set a standard. Ike must have seen in Washington a kindred spirit. Both were celebrated war heroes who had commanded their nation's armies to victory in an existential conflict, then embraced political power only reluctantly. Washington, like Ike, proved to be an underappreciated politician, whose greatest contribution to his country may have come while presiding over the Constitutional Convention, using the "hidden hand" approach to unite the fractious states behind the scenes, while Alexander Hamilton and James Madison received much of the credit for the finished Constitution. Washington's exit was particularly meaningful because before he stepped down it was unproven whether a democratic transfer of power—this election of civilian leadership and the ritual of torch passing—would work. Further, the cautions Washington expressed in his farewell address resonated with Eisenhower's own thinking—in particular the way the first president spoke of taking care to protect the precious freedom Americans had gained, using intellect, time, and a conservative frame of mind toward the Constitution:

Towards the preservation of your government, and the permanency of your present happy state, it is requisite, not only that you steadily discountenance irregular oppositions to its acknowledged authority, but also that you resist with care the spirit of innovation upon its principles, however specious the pretexts. One method of assault may be to effect, in the forms of the Constitution alterations which will impair the energy of the system, and thus to undermine what cannot be directly overthrown. In all the changes to which you may be invited, remember that time and habit are at least as necessary to fix the true character of governments as of other human institutions; that experience is the surest standard by which to test the real tendency of the existing constitution of a country.

Washington understood modernity was always beckoning—the desire for change both a blessing and a threat. He also dedicated a substantial portion of his speech, as Ike would, to the conduct of the nation toward the world at large.

As with Washington before him, Eisenhower knew war intimately and was concerned with how America used its power in the world; he was mindful that its primary obligation was to its own citizenry. Balance and good judgment were required now as then. As the careful shepherd in the fraught years after a global war—and in the first years of an unprecedented nuclear arms race—Ike was now passing the torch to a young man whose rhetoric was more bullish and whose understanding of the delicate balance of global politics was untried. The speech would become a solemn moment, offering sober warnings for a nation giddy with newfound prosperity, infatuated with youth and glamour, and aiming increasingly, it seemed, for the easy life.

Early on, a theme that would eventually become the centerpiece of Eisenhower's speech was the idea that for the first time in its history the United States of America had a permanent war-based industry.

Ike's intent was to plead for balance—to avoid the temptation to feel a spectacular and costly action could solve all of our problems. The nation was in an impatient mood. But patience was a virtue worth cherishing.

Ike believed it was possibly a warning only he—the World War II tactician, the mastermind of Hitler's defeat—could make with any level of credibility. In the nuclear age, it was unfortunately necessary to maintain a potent military apparatus as a protection against ever having to use it. But the domestic industrial partners in this endeavor were enthralled by their bombs and in service to their bottom lines, and the country must be on guard to keep the national interest first, not that of these powerful interests.

In one draft this danger was characterized as the "military-industrial-*scientific* complex," but Ike agreed to drop "scientific" on the advice of his science advisor. In another draft the danger was the "military-industrial-*congressional* complex," but Ike deleted "congressional," not wanting to seem as if his last address was a partisan harangue. In the end, the "military-industrial complex" remained; the scientists and Congress got a pass.

AS HE PICKED OVER his speech in the late afternoon light, readying it at last for the teleprompter, an overwhelming feeling fell over him. His watch was ending. He could hear the bustle of final preparations, the movers taking box after box of private belongings to the moving truck parked outside, the furious activity of his staff in a busy countdown of leave-taking. The Eisenhowers' only personal pieces of furniture—a hi-fi set and

Mamie's electric organ—had already been moved. A third item was Ike's Cabinet Room chair, which had been purchased for him from the government by cabinet members as a parting gift. Everything else would remain behind, the property of the U.S. government.

Ike wasn't an especially sentimental man. But it was hard not to reflect on the dizzying transition from commander in chief to private citizen. Undoubtedly, no president in his or her final days can be fully prepared for not being president. Relief surely mingled with regret for what remained undone, and melancholy over the end of a grand adventure.

As he prepared to leave, Eisenhower hosted a dinner party in the State Dining Room at the White House for some sixty reporters and photographers who had covered him during his presidency. He'd always received mixed reviews from the press. As the first "television president," he opened up greater access to the public, but he tended to go over and around the White House press corps when it served his purpose. And, of course, he didn't have the riveting glamour of JFK, which seduced many in the media. Most reporters respected Hagerty, though, and acknowledged that he did a masterful job of keeping them in the loop.

At the party, James E. Warner of the *New York Herald-Tribune* mentioned to Ike he'd been assigned to cover him on his trip back to Gettysburg after Kennedy's inauguration.

Ike was surprised. "Why in the world would anybody want to cover an old ex-president?" he asked.

Warner demurred. "That's my assignment, sir."

Ike laughed and pumped Warner's hand. "Well, welcome to the Old Frontier," he said, playing off JFK's famous campaign slogan.

He might also have told Warner to pack his clubs. Golf was

certainly on the schedule for Ike's postpresidency. During his presidency golf had been his regular stress reliever. He'd often worn cleats in the Oval Office, so he could quickly pop outside and hit a few balls, and a trail of cleat marks scarred the floor. He'd received a lot of ribbing for his love of golf, and his harshest critics would claim he let his aides run the place while he hit the links. During the 1956 campaign, the Democrats had produced a bumper sticker: "Ben Hogan for President: If we're going to have a golfer, let's have a good one."

But golf wasn't, as his critics suggested, a sign of a retiring man's inattention to his office. To the contrary, golf energized him. He could be dragging with pure exhaustion and he'd grab Jim Hagerty or one of the other guys and go out to Burning Tree Golf Club, just outside Washington, play a round, and return fully restored and ready to tackle anything.

Golf was also a way to grease the political wheels. "I suppose one of the greatest things in Washington, for many presidents," said Hagerty, "is for a member of the Senate or Congress to say, 'Gee, I can't accept your appointment this afternoon. I have to play a round of golf at Burning Tree with the President of the United States.'"

What he'd miss most in retirement was the camaraderie of his staff. He could not thank them enough. A few months earlier he'd said to his long-suffering chief of staff, Jerry Persons, "You've done so much for me. I'd like to do something for you, too. What would you like?"

Jerry was delighted. "Easy," he said. "I'd like a portrait."

That could be done, Ike assured him. "Just choose the pose and who you'd like to do it."

"Well, that's not so easy," Jerry said. "I want it *of* you, *by* you."

Ike's hobby as a painter stayed under the radar. He'd picked it up on the advice of Churchill, and he enjoyed painting country scenes of farms, barns, and even the house in England where they'd planned D-Day. In the White House, his "studio" was a room in the family quarters on the third floor, and he never kidded himself that his paintings were particularly good. But painting was a way to release tension and it gave him pleasure. After his heart attack, Ike's doctor had urged him to paint more. He enjoyed his hobby so much that one year he gave paint-by-numbers sets to all of his staff.

Jerry's request was completely unexpected. "You're crazy as hell," Ike said laughing, and Persons let the matter drop. But in secret Ike decided to paint the portrait, depicting himself in a relaxed posture. Persons was shocked when Ike presented it to him a few months later.

His closest advisors had become like friends, and in December he'd sent them a letter:

> During my entire life until I came back from World War II as something of a VIP, I was known by my contemporaries as Ike. Whether or not the deep friendships I enjoy have had their beginnings in the anti or postwar period, I now demand as my right that you, starting January 21, 1961, address me by that nickname. No longer do I propose to be excluded from the privileges that other friends enjoy. With warm regard, as ever—Ike

SHORTLY AFTER 8 P.M., Ike, after dining with Mamie and changing into a fresh suit, walked into the Oval Office, which had been transformed into a TV studio. The room was packed with people in busy preparations. He stepped over the tangle of electric cords, submitted to the makeup brush, straightened his tie, adjusted his suit jacket, and chatted with his aides before finally taking his place behind the desk and pulling his chair into position. The spotlight was on him, the teleprompter in front, but his notes close at hand. He looked at the page and then into the camera. The floor director counted down, "five . . . four . . . three . . . two . . ." and then motioned his hand toward the president. Ike began to speak.

"Good evening, my fellow Americans . . ."

CHAPTER 6

INTIMACY AND INTERDEPENDENCE

Our people expect their President and the Congress to find essential agreement on questions of great moment, the wise resolution of which will better shape the future of the nation. My own relations with Congress, which began on a remote and tenuous basis when, long ago, a member of the Senate appointed me to West Point, have since ranged to the intimate during the war and immediate post-war period, and finally to the mutually interdependent during these past eight years.

—From Eisenhower's farewell address

In the end, the last thing Ike wanted was to sound partisan. In fact, although his farewell address was largely about foreign affairs, the looming threats around the world, and the dangers of the military-industrial complex, the speech also revealed the president's obsession with the question of how to actually run a country across party lines and ideologies.

Writing to his brother Milton about the speech he had in mind—back in May 1959—he emphasized that he didn't want to do "anything that was partisan in character."

There's no question that for a president to hold such a passionate philosophy of bipartisanship grates on the modern nerve, where the parties have taken to their corners, forever shadowboxing in preparation for the next fight. Bipartisanship is undervalued in today's political environment, because it is viewed as the wishy-washy behavior of those who lack moral convictions. Indeed, the bases of both parties expect their representatives to be defiant in opposition of the other party. Republican obedience to the "Hastert Rule"—the (unfortunately named) principle that a bill cannot be brought to the floor unless it is supported by a majority of the majority—is complete. And while Democrats don't have an official "rule," they behaved similarly when they held the majority under Speaker Nancy Pelosi. Deliberate refusal to promote potential interests out of party loyalty would have puzzled and frustrated Ike, who did not mind pushing through his agenda with the help of moderate Democrats.

Ike's view offers a lesson for our times, but mostly it needs to be taken in the context of who he was and the way his experiences as a military commander made this approach a natural fit for him. In a sense his relationship with the Russians in World War II, through Georgy Zhukov, was a bipartisan effort on a global scale. We'll return later to the downsides of this calculation, but suffice to say that in the Second World War, the Russians sought the same result as their fellow Allies—surviving and then defeating Hitler—and indeed the Soviet people sacrificed more than their share, with an estimated 25 million combined military and civilian casualties. (The United States by comparison lost approximately 420,000 lives to the war.) Their core ideologies, of course, could not have been more different, as became apparent after the peace, when the United States sought to rebuild Europe on democratic foundations, while the Soviet Union saw an opportunity to dominate the so-called Eastern Bloc. But during the war years, Ike was able to set aside the differences for the larger goal, and he knew how to work across that massive "aisle" to win the war. By the time he reached the White House, Ike had already had experience corralling some of the biggest egos on the planet. In addition, as a military aide to General Marshall, he'd overseen relations between the Army and Congress, and he knew well that the most difficult personalities could be brought to the table if the cause was great.

An early draft of his farewell address included a passage that was something of a love letter to Congress, but it was struck from the final version. In this rejected draft, he seemed to marvel that during the six years when Congress was run by Democrats (following the 1954 midterms) "we did not fall out into bitter, irreconcilable factions which in other nations have paralyzed the democratic process." Rather, "despite our differences, we worked together, and the business of the nation went forward, and the fact that it did so is in large measure a credit to the wisdom, forbearance, and sense of duty displayed by the Congress." Apparently, even Ike thought that was a little much, and in the final version, he took it down a notch:

> In this final relationship, the Congress and the Admin-
> istration have, on most vital issues, cooperated well, to
> serve the nation well rather than mere partisanship, and
> so have assured that the business of the nation should go
> forward. So my official relationship with Congress ends
> in a feeling on my part, of gratitude that we have been
> able to do so much together.

Was Ike's "gratitude" to Congress genuine? Let's say it was complicated. Remember, Ike was, above all, a pragmatist in governing. He had always despised the craven aspects of politics, and he wasn't about to cave in to them once he became the most important politician in the land. Almost immediately upon taking office, he had an uncomfortable reality check. Assembling the Republican House and Senate leaders for the first time, he began to talk about how they would fulfill the promises of the party platform, which they'd agreed to at the party's national convention in Chicago in July 1952. The men around the table smiled indulgently. Oh, they told him, that wasn't really necessary. They "laughed off platforms as traps to catch voters," he wrote, and it shocked his sensibilities. It was an unhappy confrontation with a bitter truth—now he was entering a political world, where motivations and actions were often unrelated to rhetoric and divorced from what needed to be done. Having spent several months on the trail telling the American people what he and his party were going to do, he was now expected to put that aside and get down to the *real* business of governing.

If Ike was shocked by his encounter with the "practical politicians" on Capitol Hill, they weren't quite sure what to do with him, either. Given that he was the first president since Ulysses Grant who had not previously been a member of Congress, a governor, or in a president's cabinet, they were worried Ike didn't know the rules or understand how the game was played. The concern came not just from Republicans, but from Democrats, too. "Good man, but wrong business," said Speaker of the House Sam Rayburn when Ike was elected in 1952. Rayburn, arguably the most powerful legislator in Washington at the time, served as Speaker from 1940 until his death in November 1961, with the exception of a pair of two-year gaps when the Democrats were out of control, 1947–49 and, after the election cycle that swept Eisenhower into office, 1953–55. The Texan would loom large over Ike's administration.

The jealous guardians of the House and Senate, including

those from both parties who had already staked out their oppositional positions to Ike—conservatives on the right and liberals
on the left—might well have agreed with Rayburn. When Ike
entered the White House in 1953, the Democrats were in the
unusual position of being out of power both in Congress and
in the White House, and were consequently reeling from the
new normal, which they feared would send them hat in hand
begging for crumbs from their Republican masters. On the Republican side, Robert Taft, Ike's primary opponent, would be
majority leader of the Senate, and Joseph Martin, a conservative Taft supporter, Speaker of the House. Again to Ike's shock,
the worst resistance from Congress too often came from his
own party.

And yet in large part, the Eisenhower years were devoid
of the angry partisanship that would characterize most future
administrations—even though in six of his presidency's years
the government was divided. Seeking to explain his success
with the legislative branch, Ike zeroed in on two words in his
farewell speech to describe the relationship between Congress
and the White House: *intimacy* and *interdependence*.

By intimacy he meant a rapport born out of a shared common ideology. First experiencing it in wartime, he later came to
see this common bond as essential to the business of governing.
Eisenhower was magnanimous in his view that most people in
government were at heart public servants, and while their immediate goals and philosophies might differ, their dedication to
the cause of America was usually honorable. Even in debate he
sought shared ground where he could find it, and was quick to
offer praise when it was earned, in spite of the dustups on the
road to agreement. In eight years as president, he resisted the
temptation to blame Congress for his failures or use it as a con-
venient political whipping post, as his predecessor Harry Tru-

man had done. It wasn't Ike's style to demonize those who were potentially his partners.

The best example of Ike's talent for intimacy came early in his presidency in relationship to Robert Taft. In spite of their strong differences regarding America's role in the world, Ike had always admired Taft as a smart and experienced public servant, and he thought he was a decent man. He knew they would need to get along if they were to accomplish anything. So he reached out to Taft and they made an uneasy peace, even playing golf on occasion. In his diary Ike wrote that although they had not achieved a "Damon and Pythias" sort of relationship (referring to the ancient Greek ideal of friendship), "we have reached a very amicable and definite understanding as to the methods of handling common problems and, to date, he has never failed to attack vigorously any particular chore that I ask him to undertake within the Senate."

Then, three months into Ike's first term, the two clashed over the new president's first budget. In his diary Ike called the day of the encounter, April 31, 1953, the "worst day" since he took office. His administration had spent three months making proposed reductions to the budget Truman submitted to Congress at the end of 1952. They'd managed to make substantial cuts while preserving the important programs and a strong defense budget. When Ike presented the result during a meeting of Republican leadership, he expected the experienced legislators to appreciate "the agony of work and scheming that had gone into the business of making this kind of cut." Instead he was blindsided when Taft blew his stack. Taft called the cuts "puny" and suggested—in what Ike termed a demagogic tirade—such a program would ensure Republican defeat in the midterm election.

As Taft spoke, Ike could feel his temper rising, and only

the intervention of Secretary of the Treasury George Humphrey gave him room to cool down. The more positive opinions of others around the table likewise cooled Taft down, and by the end of the meeting, calm was restored.

What the president didn't know was that during that late April meeting, Taft was troubled by a pain in his hip that had sent him to Walter Reed Hospital for tests. The doctors said it could be arthritis. Further tests in May, however, revealed the worst: pancreatic cancer, which had metastasized. In June Taft transferred his duties as majority leader to William Knowland of California, though he was confident he'd beat the cancer, even telling Ike at a June 29 meeting that he was well on his way to recovery. But sadly, on July 31, in the hospital for exploratory surgery, Taft died of a brain hemorrhage. Ike grieved his passing, and he never developed the same relationship with Knowland, who served as majority leader until the Republicans lost the Senate in January 1955.

In his farewell address Ike spoke of the way he and Congress had achieved a "mutually interdependent" relationship during his presidency. It was hard-won. The Republican Congress Ike inherited in his first two years and the Democratic Congress he earned in the remainder of his term would prove to be a demanding test of his commitment to bipartisanship. This was not a sentimental endeavor, but a hard-nosed negotiating process, where each party's agenda was given a place at the table— not equally, of course, but in a subtle dance of give-and-take.

We have little experience in recent memory of relationships built across party lines. The most famous example is from the 1980s. Now elevated to mythic status, the relationship between President Reagan and Speaker of the House Tip O'Neill (who was, coincidentally, elected to the House the same year as Ike was elected president) is often cited as a perfect example of cross-party collaboration. Reagan and O'Neill might have been miles apart on ideology, but they formed a relationship based on what they shared—both were Irish Americans from humble beginnings; both wanted to achieve what was best for the nation, not just their respective parties. As a result, they were able to transcend their ideological disputes in recognition of the human being on the other side, and thus begin to talk. This was Ike's way as well.

One of Eisenhower's key principles was collaboration. Every Tuesday at 8:30 A.M., he officiated a bipartisan meeting of congressional leadership. Before the meeting, he would select two—one from the House and one from the Senate, on a rotating basis—to have breakfast with him at seven thirty. In particular, he made clear, he believed the nation's foreign policy needed to be approached as a bipartisan matter. He often had Secretary of State John Foster Dulles at leadership meetings, and the discussion would be freewheeling.

Ike came to the presidency unsure of exactly how to achieve a broad coalition—his rancorous end-stage conflict with Truman evidence of that—but he was determined to find a way. It's surprising today to note that his was the first administration to establish an organized liaison office with Congress. Jerry Persons was tapped to head up the effort, followed by Bryce Harlow. Persons and Harlow had what in Ike's view were perfect credentials for the task, having been the congressional liaisons to General Marshall during World War II.

Harlow described the job as not just about selling Congress on the president's program, but also a wide range of "cat herding" activities: "the care and feeding of members, plus also the blunting, thwarting, discouraging congressional activities—spiteful investigations, spiteful speeches, spiteful actions, excessive partisanship, that kind of thing . . ."

To accomplish this, weekly meetings of the executive branch's departments and agencies were held on Saturday mornings to present realistic proposals. Harlow said, "I used to say to the department fellows, 'you can't come running in here and give us a lead weight and ask us to float it across a pond. It's no way. Now, we can put some sails on it, and we can put some Styrofoam around it, and we might be able to float that baby across the pond.'"

Unlike the layered bureaucracy of today, Ike's cabinet members had a more informal and direct access to the process. It was commonplace for, say, the secretary of labor to come over, sit down with Persons, Harlow, and others, and talk through the details of what they wanted to advance in Congress. Everyone had access. (According to Harlow, this informality changed in Nixon's administration with the gatekeeper approach of H. R. Haldeman and John Ehrlichman, followed by the creation of a more system-wide role for the Office of Management and Budget.)

Eisenhower was fortunate to take office with Republican control of the House and Senate, but it only lasted for two years. After 1954, the Democrats controlled Congress. Still, as we've seen, some of Ike's fiercest battles were not with Democrats but with members of his own party. In the end he felt that a certain blindness to party ideology was the key to leadership.

It is in the interests of the nation for the president and Congress to get along. First and foremost, there is the need to keep the government running, to further American interests abroad, and to do the practical business of governing—all this is quite apart from pet programs and initiatives the president might want to make. At all costs, Harlow noted, both sides want to avoid "hardening of the political arteries," leading to a collapse of relations. Ike had the advantage of being not only immensely popular with the public, but also a heroic figure. As the historian Doris Kearns Goodwin observed, Lyndon Johnson, who was majority leader for six of Ike's eight years, felt that to attack Eisenhower would be "like telling children that their father was a bad man."

As minority leader during Ike's first two years, Johnson made a calculation: noting the dissent Ike was receiving from conservative members of his own party, LBJ eyed a way to wedge the Democratic agenda into the process. He didn't expect to get everything he wanted, but he thought he could make incremental progress. After 1954, when he became majority leader, he was poised to make a difference.

After the 1954 midterms, Eisenhower set out to woo Johnson, as well as Rayburn, who had been restored to Speaker of the House. Although Ike had warned before the election that a Democratic Congress would lead to "a Cold War of partisan politics," that didn't happen. Personally, Rayburn and Johnson liked Ike, and even teased that the president was, like them, a Texan, having been born in Denison. ("Us three Texans got to stand together.") At least once a month they'd have drinks and canapés together upstairs in the White House; once they got a bit lubricated, they'd have a great time together. In these meetings, after a few cocktails, they found a remarkable degree of candor. It was an unusual bonding. Sherman Adams, who was in Congress during the Roosevelt administration, remarked he could not recall an instance when FDR called the Republican leadership to the White House for a drink. Eisenhower did it often with the Democrats. "You had," said Adams, "the rather anomalous situation of having a bi-party convention in the upstairs Oval Room in the White House."

Unfortunately, this intimacy burned Vice President Nixon, who never received such invitations from Ike. On one occasion, when it was suggested the Eisenhowers invite the Nixons to their home in Gettysburg, Mamie declined, saying, "What on earth would Mrs. Nixon and I talk about?" There's no kind way to spin Ike's cool and often awkward relationship with his vice president, but a more pragmatic reading might be that he simply didn't need Nixon the way he did Rayburn and Johnson.

Ike was under no illusions that he, Rayburn, and Johnson were on the same page, or that these powerful politicians could be entirely trusted. Privately, he said of Johnson, "That fellow's such a phony," and of Rayburn, "That fellow would double cross you." But in his political relations with both men he managed to rise above these judgments. He understood "the leader of a minority party has a different set of references." That was a view Rayburn appreciated. In 1953, facing a Republican Congress, he had warned his members, "Any jackass can kick down a barn. It takes a good carpenter to build one." He had a core philosophy: go along to get along. Ike concurred: "You can't be a leader and ask other people to follow you unless you know how to follow, too."

The president and Speaker's relationship was so successful that before he left office Ike wrote to Rayburn: "Over these eight difficult but inspiring years your personal friendship and selflessness in cooperating in those things involving the vital welfare of our country have meant a great deal to me."

For his part, Johnson was perhaps one of the most purely ambitious political animals Ike had ever met, but he was also crafty about establishing close relationships with his opponents that he could later use to his advantage. Right up front Johnson told him, "Mr. President, when I agree with you, I'll come tell you. I'll disagree with you with dignity and decency, and I won't talk about your dog or your boy."

Later on, Ike and LBJ would bond over being members of

the same club—heart attack survivors. On July 2, 1955, the forty-six-year-old Johnson experienced cardiac arrest so severe it nearly killed him. Less than three months later, Ike, sixty-four, had the heart attack that briefly threatened to limit his presidency to one term. Both men resisted calls from friends and family to end their political careers, and even gained strength in the aftermath of their brushes with death. While Ike was in the hospital, Johnson sent him a note wishing him well and saying he'd recovered so completely from his own heart attack he'd even gone dove hunting. In other words, *we're not done yet.*

The ability to get things accomplished in the absence of a synchronized choir of approval is one of the great tests of leadership. Harry Truman had a reputation as a forceful leader, yet he mostly had a Congress of his own party. During the sole two-year period when Republicans held Congress, as Truman was running for reelection and angrily calling them a "do-nothing Congress" on the campaign trail, the legislative branch had passed more than nine hundred bills, making Truman's accusation a very partisan—and untrue—statement.

In the context of his farewell address, Ike's call for interdependence—another way of saying bipartisanship—was an outlier in a speech otherwise devoted to the drama and dangers on the world stage. And yet the refrains of leadership and collaboration were among the chief themes of Ike's life and presidency. Historian Michael Beschloss put it this way: "He saw himself . . . as a balance wheel poised to let postwar prosperity roar ahead under a balanced budget." And, wrote Beschloss, he wanted to stamp out isolationism from the Republican Party and the nation at large. Pause and consider how different the American mouthpiece would have been had Ike chosen to pass on a presidential run and the isolationist Robert Taft been elected instead. According to Beschloss, Ike and Taft were at such loggerheads on this matter that right before he announced his candidacy in 1952, Ike went to Taft and said, "I feel so strongly about defending the free world against the Soviets that I will make you a deal. If you renounce isolationism, I won't run against you for president." Needless to say, there was no deal.

Though committed to checking government expansion, Ike recognized the value of domestic programs and public works. Notably, he was not interested in obliterating all aspects of FDR's New Deal. He told his brother Edgar, probably accurately, "Should any political party attempt to abolish Social Security, unemployment insurance, and eliminate labor laws and farm programs, you would not hear of that party again in our political history." Instead, he sought a middle way, cutting where he could, proposing where he needed to, and always trying to be sensitive to what the American people wanted and expected. Although his most prominent actions were in the arena of foreign affairs, he secured one achievement on the domestic field that was huge, visionary, and literally reshaped the American landscape.

The Federal-Aid Highway Act of 1956 created the country's modern transportation infrastructure and opened the nation to a new way of being, defined by the open road. It took Eisenhower two years of unceasing effort to get it passed (it was the biggest public works project in U.S. history at the time), but in the end a strong bipartisan coalition shepherded his dream to fulfillment. Today, the Interstate Highway System that Ike created is the backbone of America's infrastructure. Our economy and our way of life are unimaginable without the Eisenhower-era arteries that connect our lives from coast to coast. (Were he alive today, Eisenhower would surely be pained by the crumbling roads and bridges in many parts of the country, and he might have something to say about the debate in both parties about how to fix it.)

THE PRESIDENCY AND CONGRESS are coequal branches of government; as such, power struggles are inevitable. A big one with international implications came early in Ike's presidency. Conservatives in Congress were concerned that the unbridled power of the executive branch to make treaties through the United Nations could stymie America's independence and even undermine American liberties. On this front, Ohio senator John Bricker, who had been a strong supporter of Taft, carried the banner against the administration, proposing an amendment to the Constitution that would restrict the presidential power to make treaties. In stipulating that "a treaty shall become effective as internal law in the United States only through the enactment of appropriate legislation by the Congress," the amendment would effectively give power over international treaties to the states through their legislative representatives—at least, that's what its critics claimed. The amendment's underlying goal seemed to be to limit internationalist efforts in favor of a more isolationist framework. In effect, the Bricker Amendment would be a repudiation of the postwar agreements made at Yalta and Potsdam, a reality that struck quite close to Ike's heart. "Adoption of the Bricker Amendment," he wrote to Knowland, "would be notice to our friends as well as our enemies abroad that our country intends to withdraw from its leadership in world affairs."

Writing in his diary, Ike expressed his frustration, calling Senator Bricker "almost psychopathic" and lamenting that so many senators had taken up his cause. He was particularly annoyed that a cadre of constitutional lawyers was on Bricker's side. "This fact does not impress me very much," he wrote.

"Lawyers have been trained to take either side of any case and make the most intelligent and impassioned defense of their adopted viewpoint."

In the Senate, Johnson shared much of Ike's philosophy concerning a strong foreign policy, but ever opportunistic, he also figured the conflict over the Bricker Amendment, which was dividing Republicans, could work to his advantage. The Texas senator's strategy was to seek a middle ground. Johnson managed to engineer a compromise amendment put forth by Senator Walter George of Georgia, the ranking member of the Senate Foreign Relations Committee. After the Bricker Amendment was defeated, George's amendment came up and lost by one vote. The *New York Times* reported the administration's position was saved by "a coalition of all-out Eisenhower Republicans and liberal Democrats."

In *Master of the Senate,* LBJ's biographer Robert Caro wrote that the Bricker Amendment was "the high-water mark of the non-interventionist surge in the 1950s" and "the embodiment of the Old Guard's rage at what it viewed as twenty years of presidential usurpation of Congress's constitutional powers." That theme intermittently gains favor in our current public debate, particularly when the president and Congress are from different parties. The Founding Fathers hotly debated the question of executive powers, always mindful of the dangers of creating a de facto monarch. On the other hand, a legislating body without an executive branch to enforce the law would be weak and unwieldy. Ultimately, the understandable fear of executive overreach in the years following the former colonies' revolt against the British crown were eased by the assumption that General Washington, the most admired man in the land, would serve as the nation's first president. Parallels between Washington and Eisenhower are unavoidable.

Unlike most presidents, who tend to view Congress as an oppositional force, Ike's outlook was straight out of a civics text. Congress was coequal, and as such, he thought his job included restoring the confidence of the American public in that institution. In the military he had been taught to respect the civilian institutions; now that he was in the White House, he could do no less.

EISENHOWER EVEN TRIED TO mend fences with Harry Truman, who as the former president was the titular head of his party. Although Truman publicly complained about never being invited to the White House during Ike's administration, the record shows otherwise. The instigator of rapprochement was Bryce Harlow, who in 1958 mentioned to Sherman Adams that the president had yet to invite Truman to the White House. It would be a shame, Harlow suggested, if Ike left office before doing so.

Adams replied, "Have you lost your mind? Are you going to go in and tell him? I'm not."

Next Harlow tried Jerry Persons, who said, "I'll be goddamned if I'm going to tell him that."

Harlow finally bit the bullet and spoke to the president himself. Although Ike thought the idea was "crazy as hell" and opined that Truman would never accept an invitation, he told Harlow to go ahead. The first invite was for the Trumans to join the Eisenhowers at Arlington National Cemetery for the dedication ceremony in honor of an unknown soldier from the Korean War. Truman declined, citing plans to be in Europe. A second invitation was made—which Truman claimed to have never received. A third time, Ike invited him to a stag dinner for Winston Churchill. Truman declined because of prior plans to be in New York, grumbling, "The invitation came too late—as intended."

A story regularly repeated over the years involved a snub by Ike that was said to have occurred back in October 1953. Learning that Ike was traveling in Kansas City, Truman said he phoned him because he wanted to visit and pay his respects. But he claimed that whoever answered the phone told Truman the president was too busy to see him on this trip. Ike said he never received the call—and it seems highly unlikely that an unnamed assistant would have delivered such a message. Whatever the truth is, the perceived slight inflamed their relationship further, and Truman did not even invite Ike to the dedication of his presidential library in 1957.

Unlike "give 'em hell" Harry, Ike refused to make personal attacks. It wasn't in his nature, and he didn't believe it was the way to get things done. He had a heightened sensitivity to the way his words were disseminated. Harlow remembered an occasion when he was working with Ike on a statement to be issued to the press. He presented Ike with a draft, and he began to read, striking out a word. Then he sat back and said, "Bryce, let me explain something to you. I have just stricken the word 'deliberate' out of this document. I want you to understand why." Harlow listened while Ike gave a brief discourse, based on his belief that in context the word had a negative connotation. He said, "A man will respect you and perhaps even like you if you differ with him on issues and on principle. But if you ever challenge his motives, he will never forgive you. Nor should he. So don't ever again, in any document submitted to me, include a word which questions a man's motives." By today's standards, that seems downright quaint, but it was effective. He also issued a standing order that any member of Congress who wanted to speak to him should be put on the phone as soon as possible.

Mamie did her part, too. She took pride in the fact that White House entertaining was entirely apolitical, and said half the time she didn't even know the political parties of those around the table or at receptions. After a luncheon for Senate wives, Jackie Kennedy sent Mamie a note: "I think it is so wonderful the way you make everyone feel so much at home. Thank you so much for having made such a memorable occasion possible. I will never forget it."

REPUBLICANS WEREN'T ALWAYS SO happy with Ike's bipartisan approach. They thought he wasn't interested enough in party building, but that wasn't true, either. Ike cared very much about the future of the party, and he stumped vigorously for Republican candidates. The best way to put it is that he was devoted to the party but not at the expense of the nation. Robert Anderson, the Treasury secretary during Ike's second term, described his principles this way: "I've always thought that this was a man who felt that his mission in life was to do whatever he thought was in the national interest, regardless of how it affected him or anybody else. I don't have a single recollection of the president ever talking to me and saying, 'Bob, let's just sit down and figure out what's good for the Republican Party.' I have many recollections of his saying, 'Tell me what you think is the best thing for the country.'"

Anderson recalled a dinner they attended where a man from Pennsylvania came up to the president and started berating him over a court vacancy that was slowing down the hearing of cases. Ike said to him in a very stern voice, "Look, if you want some judges in Pennsylvania, don't send me any political hacks. You select them on the basis of the recommendation of the American Bar Association, and recommendations of people in the professional field, and you send them down on that basis, and I'll nominate them. But I'm not going to put a political hack in anywhere, for life."

For expedience's sake, Ike, of course, might have preferred to have a Republican Congress throughout his presidency, but he cobbled together a coalition of moderate Republicans and mostly southern Democrats who functionally carried out his Republican agenda. He achieved this in direct ways that nonetheless seem hard to picture today—particularly his Tuesday morning legislative meetings at the White House, where everyone was encouraged to get their two cents in, regardless of party. One can't underestimate the power of being heard as a minority.

He instinctively understood the desire of people in Congress to promote their own stature with constituents by being able to tell them they'd talked to the president or had done this or that to further their state's interests. It was his way of inspiring cooperation. At the same time, he respected and even appreciated it when legislators stuck to their guns on critical issues. He did not expect Republicans to march in lockstep with his policies. And he took special pains to woo the more prickly members.

One of these was Republican senator Margaret Chase Smith from Maine, though an incident shortly after Ike was inaugurated made things doubly difficult. The Senate Republicans had decided to honor the new president with a dinner at the Burning Tree Golf Club, outside Washington. The problem was, Burning Tree had a strict no-women policy, so someone had to tell Senator Smith she would not be able to attend. When Connecticut senator Prescott Bush (father of George H. W. Bush and grandfather of George W. Bush) was asked to break the news to Smith, he balked. Maybe Burning Tree would make an exception. They would not. Unhappily, Bush told Smith, and in his recollection, "She absolutely hit the ceiling. . . . She was simply furious—*furious*."

Bush didn't feel he could let the insult stand, so he went back to Burning Tree and finally got them to make an exception, but it was too late. Justifiably, Smith told him, "I wouldn't come for anything! Nobody could make me go!" But Bush begged, lying and saying he'd already told Ike she'd be sitting on his right at the dinner. To his relief she finally agreed to attend—and presumably Ike was ignorant of the drama. But he might have wondered at Smith's chilly reception.

One could hardly call their relationship warm, but on one occasion Smith invited the president to her home in Skowhegan for a lobster and clambake. Ike sampled the Maine fare and then seasoned and cooked his own steak, and was happier than a proverbial clam.

But perhaps the most dramatic gesture Smith made on Ike's behalf was to be his surrogate in a 1956 campaign debate—which, as it happens, was the first presidential debate ever held, albeit without the candidates. It's a remarkable story. Ike's opponent, Adlai Stevenson, challenged him to a debate that would take place between two party surrogates. Ike agreed, and Stevenson chose Eleanor Roosevelt, seventy-two, to represent him. Ike chose a reluctant Margaret Chase Smith. The two women debated on *Face the Nation* on November 4, two days before the election.

Smith wrote in her memoir, *Declaration of Conscience*, of her reluctance to debate Mrs. Roosevelt. Smith thought Mrs. Roosevelt would be confident and authoritative—which she was—and decided to draw a contrast by making her presentation brief and to the point, and to avoid getting into any arguments. But in her closing statement she let Mrs. Roosevelt have it, aggressively defending Ike's leadership. She pointed out that her late husband, Congressman Clyde Smith, and Winston Churchill had selected Ike to lead the Allies to victory in Europe. (She didn't mention Eleanor's husband, FDR.) "They chose him on a nonpolitical basis of principle," she concluded. "They now attack him just because he is not a partisan Democrat." It was such a strong closing Mrs. Roosevelt refused to shake her hand after the debate.

The idea of using surrogates in a presidential debate is unthinkable today, though Ike had little problem letting others take the stage—and even outshine him. As a result, the press didn't always understand how vigorously engaged Ike was in every aspect of his administration, because he so often let other people grab the credit. Jerry Persons recalled numerous occasions when cabinet members and lawmakers would be in meetings with the president and reach an agreement. Invariably they'd say, "Mr. President, when I go outside, I'm going to be hit by reporters. How do you want the publicity on this to be handled? Would you like to call them now or would you like me to handle it?" And usually the president would say, "You handle it." The press would conclude the president was merely a bystander.

The collaborative process in Ike's White House was reflected even in the language Ike used to present his policies. For example, rather than saying, "I directed the secretary" to do such-and-such, he'd say, "I approved the secretary's proposal" to do such-and-such. Although some people privately called him "the Boss," harking back to his military days, he was not authoritarian. Senator Knowland, who was both majority leader and minority leader during Ike's presidency—and who wasn't always in agreement with him—acknowledged he had seen Ike change his position on issues in leadership meetings once the other side was fully aired. This was simple common sense to Ike, who once said, "It is better to have one person working with you than three people working for you."

Cooperation was his natural way, said Milton. "It just happens that this was the kind of leadership and talent that could bring the diverse elements of an Allied Army and leadership together. And as I think back—incidentally, I was close to this too; I spent time at his war headquarters and worked with him—I don't think any other kind of leadership could have done what he did, as Supreme Commander. So it was natural for him there, and my God, if it's natural in a military setting, where you have utter obedience to what you say, why wouldn't it be natural for him to use it in a more political situation?"

These working relationships earned Ike friends in places where resistance had once been a seemingly settled matter. Everett Dirksen, from the Taft wing, who was a supporter of McCarthy and one of only nineteen senators who refused to censure him, gradually became more centrist. In time he was one of the administration's most reliable supporters.

"Eisenhower relied more on the art of personal persuasion," Adams observed, "whereas Roosevelt relied on the use of political power and strength through his own congressional establishment." Remarkably, in evaluating legislation, the question of veto power was rarely discussed. "He judged the legislation on its merits," Persons said, "and that's the way he proceeded from there." The question of whether it would pass a veto was not considered. Was this approach effective? Ike thought so, but Adams was not so sure. The Democratic leaders, he said, liked to come down to the White House. They enjoyed the drama of the president trying to persuade them on one issue or another. Still, it often seemed to work.

IN HIS FAREWELL ADDRESS, Ike sought to send a message to Kennedy that seeking unity was not tantamount to weakness. In fact, Kennedy's own relationship with Congress would be more tumultuous, largely due to the opposition of southern Democrats to his signature legislation. (LBJ once said sarcastically, "Kennedy wouldn't get the Ten Commandments past Congress.") But at the end of his administration, Ike was determined to do what he could to send up a flare about what was possible in the best of times. He also had a more solemn message that transcended parties and the nonsense of politicians. There was a deep pain and loneliness when you were the man in charge, he'd learned, writing poignantly: "The problems a president faces, are soul-racking. The nakedness of the battlefield, when the soldier is all alone in the smoke and the clamor and the terror of war, is comparable to the loneliness—at times— of the presidency, when one man must conscientiously, deliberately, prayerfully scrutinize every argument, every proposal, every prediction, every alternative, every probable outcome of his action, and then—all alone—make his decision. All alone— because just when a new president needs allies, his circle of trust shrinks. No one with the possible exception of his family, treats him the same, and no one, with the exception of his predecessors, knows what it is like."

CHAPTER 7

THE HOSTILE LANDSCAPE

We face a hostile ideology global in scope, atheistic in character, ruthless in purpose, and insidious in method. Unhappily the danger it poses promises to be of indefinite duration. To meet it successfully, there is called for, not so much the emotional and transitory sacrifices of crisis, but rather those which enable us to carry forward steadily, surely, and without complaint the burdens of a prolonged and complex struggle—with liberty the stake. Only thus shall we remain, despite every provocation, on our charted course toward permanent peace and human betterment.

—From Eisenhower's farewell address

Looking serious but at ease, in his characteristic manner, Ike faced the White House press corps for the last time on January 18, 1961, the day after delivering his farewell address and two days before leaving office. He had one thing on his mind. When asked about the greatest disappointment of his presidency, he replied without hesitation it was the failure to achieve "a permanent peace with justice." If he felt any sadness in the remaining days of his presidency, it was in having wanted to change the world in this way—to light a torch for peace that would "flame brightly until at last the darkness is no more"— and having been unable to make it happen.

This painful reality had lent special urgency to the farewell speech he'd delivered the previous evening. If it accomplished nothing else, he hoped it would cement key ideas into the consciousness of the nation, while imparting hard truths to Kennedy. As he'd told him at their December 6 meeting, speaking of the presidency, "That fellow in the White House doesn't get many easy problems. If they're easy, they're solved down the government line. It's only the virtually impossible problems that come to the president's desk."

This was a grave and humbling fact. A president, Ike knew, could not afford to be cocky. The hostile landscape of our world was an ever-present reality. Although he had found Kennedy to be respectful and sober-minded during their first meeting in December, the myth growing around the vigorous young president-elect had so invaded the press that the problems of the world seemed to fade away in his wake. He spoke of the New Frontier, which listeners took to mean a time of optimism and progress, but which even Kennedy admitted held both "unfilled hopes and unfilled threats." The old realities could not so easily be dismissed. The following day, January 19, Ike would have his last chance to lay it out to Kennedy when he visited the White House for a final meeting.

Ike had inherited the whirlwind when he took office in 1953, and, like it or not, his presidency had been defined by the Cold War, the centerpiece of which was our changing relationship with Russia. Though we were Allies during World War II, the end of the war revealed just how far apart we were in fundamental principles. Stalin's rhetoric grew increasingly harsh— against NATO, and against any efforts of the free world to unite around common principles of peace and freedom. He was a ruthless dictator whose antidemocratic stance was impossible to align with American interests.

Stalin believed victory against Nazism was proof of communist supremacy and that the world wars could be laid in the lap of capitalism. In a famous speech on the subject in 1946, Stalin stated: "The uneven development of capitalist countries usually leads, in the course of time, to a sharp disturbance of the equilibrium within the world system of capitalism, and that group of capitalist countries regarding itself as being less secure . . . usually attempts to change the situation and to redistribute 'spheres of influence' in its own favor—by employing armed force. As a result of this, the capitalist world is split into two hostile camps, and war breaks out between them." In other words, he implied, the fight was not between *us* and *them;* it was between *us* and *us.*

In Stalin's view, Soviet communism was noble and transformative—a system not of private greed but of collective duty. During Ike's visit to Russia after World War II, he stood next to Stalin on a viewing stand atop Lenin's tomb as they watched Russian gymnasts perform in a seamless ballet of synchrony. "This develops the war spirit," Stalin told Ike. "Your country should do more of this." One supposes he meant the discipline, which, of course, Ike had seen in our own armies but was too polite to mention. He wasn't about to argue with Stalin while standing on Lenin's tomb.

Relations between the United States and the Soviet Union were on Ike's mind from the first day of his presidency. Indeed, during the campaign, his strongest rhetoric was reserved for the communists. He called them "barbarians" and said, "Hope for peace among men disappeared under the monstrous advance of communist tyranny." Even so, once in the Oval Office, Ike knew he could not govern by bluster; it was in his hands to reach for a solution. A lifelong strategist and problem solver, Ike wondered what he could do to begin mending the relationship. He still believed the two nations, so recently united in the takedown of Hitler, could find common ground. Shortly before the election, while flying from Boston to New York City with his brother Milton to make a televised speech, Ike said, "I want to write in a paragraph emphasizing that we should start at once negotiating with the Soviet Union for mutually beneficial trade between us, because many good things can flow from all the contacts that will develop in trading between our two nations."

Milton discouraged the idea. "This is a vast subject of which there is enormous misunderstanding in the United States," he told his brother. "If you put in a paragraph, it will probably hurt you because it won't be understood."

"Now you're trying to make a politician out of me," the candidate complained. But the idea of reaching a warm hand across the chasm of ideology appealed to him and he couldn't stop thinking about it. One evening after he was president, Ike and Milton sat upstairs in his White House study and he mused, "Wouldn't it be wonderful if we could send fifteen thousand of our university students to study in universities in the Soviet Union, and they would send fifteen thousand here?" He sat up straighter at the idea.

"Get Secretary Dulles on the phone," he instructed. Dulles came on and the president repeated his thought. Dulles told him the State Department was in the midst of negotiating a cultural agreement that would include an exchange of students, among other things. But he warned Ike off talking about it publicly until such an agreement was signed.

Unlike most politicians, including Truman, Ike had a firsthand experience of working with the Soviets for a common goal. He tried to see them not as the great red enemy, but essentially as people who wanted the same things for themselves and their families that everyone wanted. Human beings, he believed, craved peace and security and a way to make a living, and he sought ways of conveying that core commonality.

AMONG EISENHOWER'S TOUCHSTONES WITH respect to his understanding of the Soviets were his fond memories of the "soldierly camaraderie" that developed between him and Georgy Zhukov in the year after the war. In spite of their differences the two men genuinely liked each other, and they bonded over their shared experience. At a time when candor was in short supply, as their nations jockeyed for position in the postwar landscape, they always spoke honestly, trusting their conversations would go no further. Ike came to admire Zhukov so much he once referred to him as "the man whom the United Nations owes a greater debt than to any other military figure, for his triumphs against Hitler's armies."

With Zhukov, it felt possible to spar without destroying the relationship. For example, Zhukov was easily offended by what he felt were inaccurate portrayals in the American media—which he consumed voraciously. On one occasion he complained to Ike that an American newsmagazine had written he was shorter than his wife, a grave insult in his mind. He wanted to know what Ike was going to do to punish the offending press, and Ike tried unsuccessfully to explain to Zhukov why he was not able to do that—the press was free, even in its inaccuracies. The incident continued to bother Zhukov, however. Months later, Ike walked into a reception for Red Army Day to find Zhukov and his wife greeting people in the receiving line. Zhukov motioned to his wife. "Now—do you think my wife is taller than I am?" She wasn't, and Ike said so.

After the 1952 election, Ike took note of an interview Stalin gave in which the Soviet leader suggested he would like to meet with America's new president. Ike was cautious about the idea. He wasn't sure such a meeting could be productive, and when a reporter asked him about the possibility once he was in the White House, he chose his words carefully: "I would meet anybody, anywhere, where I thought there was the slightest chance of doing any good, as long as it was in keeping with what the American people expect of their chief executive."

Ten days later, Stalin suffered a stroke and lay on his deathbed. It was a tricky moment for the United States. Dulles warned Ike that any comment, no matter how it was phrased, could easily be misconstrued. But in his official statement, Ike tried to see beyond the chess game—to reach down and find the common human ground that the United States shared with Russia and with all peoples of the world:

> [T]he thoughts of America go out to all the peoples of the U.S.S.R.—the men and women, the boys and girls— in the villages, cities, farms and factories of their homeland. They are the children of the same God who is the father of all peoples everywhere. And like all peoples, Russia's millions share our longing for a friendly and peaceful world.

The following day Stalin died, and Ike felt the burden of deciding what to do next. At a cabinet meeting he raged at how everyone inside government had been talking for years about what the United States should do in the event of Stalin's death. "Well, he did [die], and we went to see what bright ideas were in the files of this government, what plans were laid. What we found was the result of seven years of yapping was exactly zero.

We have no plan. We don't even have any agreement of what difference his death makes." He glared at them. "It's criminal, that's all I can say."

Ike was well aware this might be a moment of opportunity. He watched with interest as Georgy Malenkov took the leadership position. But within a week a second name appeared on top of the Soviet leadership roster—Nikita Khrushchev. Perhaps, Ike thought, this was a chance to break the iron grip of the Lenin-Stalin eras, to open people's minds even a crack to the potential of a cooperative relationship.

Contemplating the future, Ike confessed to speechwriter Emmet Hughes that he was tired of the bombast that characterized speeches about the Soviets. He felt emotional about it—but what to say? Searching for a premise, he wondered how there could be a chance for peace as long as the sides were dedicated to an unending armaments race. And so he set out with Hughes, over many drafts, to write the speech that would stun the nation and give the world pause. Delivered April 16, 1953, before the American Society of Newspaper Editors in Washington, D.C., and broadcast over television and radio, "The Chance for Peace" was among the most radical speeches of the Cold War era. In plainspoken terms, Ike laid out his concern about the need for caution in establishing military spending priorities, and put forth concerns that have been virtually buried in the ensuing years:

> Every gun that is made, every warship launched, every rocket fired signifies, in the final sense, a theft from those who hunger and are not fed, those who are cold and are not clothed. This world in arms is not spending money alone. It is spending the sweat of its laborers, the genius of its scientists, the hopes of its children. The cost of one

modern heavy bomber is this: a modern brick school in more than thirty cities. It is two electric power plants, each serving a town of 60,000 population. . . . We pay for a single fighter with a half-million bushels of wheat. We pay for a single destroyer with new homes that could have housed more than 8,000 people. . . . This is not a way of life at all, in any true sense. Under the cloud of threatening war, it is humanity hanging from a cross of iron.

Ike also called on the Soviet Union to join a global coalition based on freedom, peace, and nonaggression. "The Soviet system shaped by Stalin and his predecessors was born of one world war. It survived with stubborn and often amazing courage a second world war. It has lived to threaten a third." Now, he urged, it was time to take hold of this "critical moment" to come together.

It was a provocative speech, presenting ideas that had never been considered before, and most people were unaware Ike was in the throes of a severe ileitis attack when he gave it. He was in extreme pain, flushed and beset by chills, but he carried on. There were moments during the speech when he felt dizzy and was afraid of fainting, and he gripped the lectern to steady himself. But his words commanded all the attention and his pale, sweating demeanor was little noted.

It was perhaps the most impassioned speech of Ike's life. He saw an opportunity after Stalin's death to place the arms race in this riveting context. But it wasn't, as some would believe, a conciliatory speech. The *Houston Chronicle* called it "an olive branch held in a mailed glove that covered the hand of friendship." That is, Ike was issuing an opportunity but also a challenge, making it clear the Soviets were the instigators of

the standoff, and they must change. He was also offering a
vision—a chance for people to see what was possible.

Our current reading of Cold War history always empha-
sizes the frozen terrain, hardening over decades, pitting a defiant "evil empire" against a freedom-loving West. But during
Ike's administration there were constant and serious efforts to
bring humanity into alignment. It was a battle. Breaking his
promise not to pursue a strategy of "sovietization" across Eastern Europe, Stalin had set the Cold War tensions in motion by
doing the opposite. The "Iron Curtain" came down, effectively
separating the East and West, but even then Ike attempted to
strategize out of the standoff.

In truth, since the end of World War II he had been intent
on resolving the seemingly intractable conflict—to soften Truman's hard line. Truman's relationship with Stalin was somewhat amicable at the end of the war, but within a year he was
raging, "I'm tired of babying the Soviets." On March 12, 1947,
he laid down his marker with the Truman Doctrine, stating, "It
must be the policy of the United States to support free peoples
who are resisting attempted subjugation by armed minorities or
outside pressures." This was a line in the sand, placing America
and its interests directly in opposition to the Soviets.

Eisenhower took a different tack—one might say he was
more focused on peace than on conflict. Up to a point. At the
very least, he wanted to reduce the inflammatory rhetoric,
knowing how easily posturing could get out of hand. Ike had
been at war, and more to the point, he had been intimately
involved in the making of a fragile peace. He knew what was
possible, and feared what was not.

And so, right away, during the summer of his first year,
he convened a high-level study group to strategize an effective
foreign policy. Named Project Solarium, after the location of

meetings in the White House's upstairs solarium (built by President Taft as a sleeping porch for hot summer nights), the group debated how to address Soviet expansionism. They considered three approaches—rollback, containment, and drawing the line.

After a few weeks of study and discussion the groups gave their presentation to more than one hundred White House cabinet members, the Joint Chiefs of Staff, department heads, and others. After the presentations, Ike got up and said, "Now I'd like to summarize this as I've seen it." In the end he favored containment, and he explained his reasons. Above all, he wanted to avoid war. He wasn't interested in a showdown—and although a strategy of brinksmanship was generally favored by Dulles, Ike hated that word and the assumptions behind it. He urged those in the room to be mindful always of nonmilitary as well as military strategies in fulfilling American goals.

Ike's definition of containment was to treat the conflict as a management issue, not a crusade against a wicked and dangerous enemy. This was very different than the public mood at the time, which was a roiling stew of fear and demagoguery. Schoolchildren learned of a godless communism where people weren't allowed to pray, under penalty of exile. Caricatures of humorless communists, their hearts cut out, their faces robotic, filled the tabloids. Joseph McCarthy promoted these fears in the Senate. Yet, while calling upon the public to be resolute, Ike was constantly tempering his words, speaking of common values built from within rather than based on abhorrence of the "other."

AT THE FRONT OF his mind during those early months in office was armistice in Korea, for it was impossible to move forward on détente without a resolution to the war that had evolved into a conflict between communism and the West—albeit fought on Asian soil. As he approached that hoped-for resolution, Ike knew America was suffering from a feeling of despair over a war no one wanted and which felt unwinnable. Polls that spring told the tale: a majority of Americans believed the Korean War was "not worth fighting." More important in Ike's view was that two-thirds of Americans approved of armistice.

Looking at the stalemate, Ike had examined all the options. It was intolerable, in his view, to let the war drag on as it was going. Nor did an aggressive attack on the North seem viable. He judged the timing was right to make a truce. But why would negotiations work now when they had failed in the past? The answer was timing and circumstances. He believed his election created new unease in North Korea and its allies, with the presumption the famous general might be more decisive about exerting extraordinary force—even nuclear—than his predecessor. (He'd as good as implied the threat in his pre-inauguration visit.) In addition, Stalin's death had softened the Soviet resolve in Korea. Everyone just wanted the conflict to end—even if the truce felt much like an extension of the postwar status quo.

Eisenhower's decision to seek an armistice did not sit well with Secretary of State Dulles, who believed that if the United States didn't act forcibly, we would look weak. Ike didn't listen. Later he told an aide, "If Mr. Dulles and all his sophisticated advisers really mean that they cannot talk peace seriously, then I'm in the wrong pew." He believed we had to "cut all this fooling around and make a serious bid for peace."

The biggest potential stumbling block was South Korean president Syngman Rhee, who did not support armistice. But with the threat of having all American aid and military support cut out from under him, he ultimately gave in. The truce, which would leave a divided Korea, the sides separated by a demilitarized zone, was scheduled for Sunday, July 27. On Saturday, Ike worked with Hagerty on the remarks he planned to give, and he found his thoughts turning to the words of Abraham Lincoln. That Saturday night he broke with his usual custom, staying up late into the night with close friends. He asked them to join him at church Sunday morning, and afterward he called Hagerty with more changes in his remarks. He had decided to end his speech with Lincoln's words of reconciliation, delivered at the end of his second inaugural address:

> With malice toward none, with charity for all, with firmness in the right as God gives us to see the right, let us strive on to finish the work we are in, to bind up the nation's wounds, to care for him who shall have borne the battle and for his widow and his orphan, to do all which may achieve and cherish a just and lasting peace among ourselves and with all nations.

At the last minute Ike scribbled his own ending: "This is our resolve and our dedication."

Bringing an end to the Korean War was the sterling accomplishment of Ike's first year. As 1953 wrapped up, he thought he could feel good about how it had gone. The nation was at peace, he believed in his team, he was making headway on the economy—even lowering taxes.

But his initial optimism was tempered by world events. The hostile landscape expanded even as it contracted. There was a mess in Indochina that seemed to place Southeast Asia on the brink of communist domination, and Ike knew it. With the French trying to take back the colonial control they'd lost in World War II, the area was becoming a nagging hotspot, with communist North Vietnam, under the leadership of Ho

Chi Minh, fighting for purchase. The possibility that Indochina could fall to communist control was deeply disturbing. "You have a row of dominoes set up, you knock over the first one, and what will happen to the last one is a certainty that it will go over very quickly," Ike said, fearing the loss of the region. But was it enough to warrant American intervention? Having just concluded one war in Asia, the president wasn't willing to jump back into another conflict. "I am not going to land any American troops in those jungles," he said.

According to the recollections of Dean Abel, a *New York Times* correspondent, the most "resonant voice" against military involvement was General Matthew Ridgway, who had succeeded Eisenhower as Army chief of staff. In a report to Ike on the topic of military involvement in Southeast Asia, he advised, "The French are fighting a colonial war, no matter what kinds of noises they make. That is how it's regarded in Asia, and if we go in there to pull their chestnuts out of the fire, it becomes the White Man's War against Asians, and it's going to be a very hard war to win." Ike essentially shared this view. As he would write in his memoirs, it was almost impossible to make the case to average Vietnamese people that the French colonialists were fighting for the cause of freedom, while those of their own ethnic origins were threatening to subject them to a form of slavery.

In notable opposition was John F. Kennedy, the young senator from Massachusetts, who favored a robust intervention. "Vietnam represents the cornerstone of the free world in Southeast Asia—the keystone to the arch, the finger in the dike," he said—an eerie foreshadowing of the debacle to come.

Although Ike rejected military intervention, he supported the French with other resources, and helped bring about an unhappy compromise in a divided Vietnam ("an old communist trick," Thomas Dewey called it, referencing Germany and Korea). Later he sent military advisors to shore up the South Vietnamese government. Many have speculated how Ike would have acted had he been in Kennedy's shoes, or Johnson's, during the 1960s, but placing hypotheticals aside, the salient point is that when he had to decide whether or not to send troops, he said no.

IN HIS RHETORIC, IKE was always "very restrained," said General Andrew Goodpaster, who served as an invaluable staff secretary and defense liaison officer (and was so highly regarded that Kennedy asked him to stay on). Goodpaster emphasized that Ike was particularly careful in any public comments about military action or weapons. "He was always trying to cast things in quite a different way—he was not given to bluster or to framing issues in military terms," Goodpaster said. "Now, he was a great poker player and he did think of things in poker terms, but it was more in terms of the psychology operating on the other man. One of the things he always talked about was getting inside the other man's head."

After Stalin died, the question became, which man's head? The power struggle between Malenkov and Khrushchev went on for two years after Stalin's death, and others came to the forefront, including Nikolai Bulganin, who became the titular head of the Soviet Union in 1955—though he was rumored to be Khrushchev's puppet. Ike, who despised political posturing, might have smiled to consider that the Soviets were the most political animals of all. The power struggle after the death of Stalin was epic. For two years the United States wasn't quite sure who the leader was. Appearances didn't always reflect reality. But at the Geneva Summit in July 1955, Ike began to understand the power dynamic. It was a meeting of the "Big Four"—Eisenhower, Prime Minister Anthony Eden of Great Britain, Prime Minister Edgar Faure of France, and Premier Nikolai Bulganin. The Americans proceeded cautiously. Was Bulganin the man in charge? Khrushchev was also there, a prominent presence. Did they share power? That seemed unlikely. In subtle but convincing ways, Khrushchev steered the Soviet contingent at the summit, although he would not officially become premier until 1958. Ike took note.

When the president flew to Geneva, he had reason to feel in charge of his agenda. Two weeks earlier, the July 4 issue of *Time* magazine had published a glowing review of Ike's presidency: "From Franconia Notch, N.H. to San Francisco, Calif, this week, there was clear and convincing evidence of patience, determination, optimism and faith among the people of the U.S. In the 29 months since Dwight Eisenhower moved into the White House, a remarkable change had come over the nation. The national blood pressure and temperature had gone down; nerve endings had healed over. The new tone could be described in a word: confidence."

Encountering their Soviet counterparts in Geneva, Americans thought Bulganin and Khrushchev were an odd pair. More than one person noted that Bulganin, with his burly frame and prominent goatee, resembled Colonel Sanders, while Khrushchev was fat and seemed uncultured—by terms jovial and petulant. Still, appearances do not always speak truth, and those who looked carefully saw signs that, titles aside, Khrushchev held power and needed to be reckoned with. Hagerty recalled that when the sessions were held, the American, British, and French delegates would drift in as they arrived, but the Russians always entered in a group, all ten of them with Khrushchev in the lead, almost like a march.

It was in Geneva that Ike and Khrushchev met and planted the seed of a working relationship. Khrushchev seemed to be an anomaly. "How can this fat, vulgar man with his pig eyes and ceaseless flow of talk really be the head—the aspirant Tsar?" British foreign secretary Harold Macmillan wrote, reflecting the question many in the West had. Ike was more circumspect, keeping his opinions about Khrushchev private.

Ike was pleased to have his son John along for the conference. John, now thirty-three, fresh out of the Command and General Staff School, was poised for a post-Army career. The president was also happy to see his old friend Georgy Zhukov and spent as much time with him as possible. He'd been hopeful Zhukov would become a key voice in Soviet policies, but now he feared that was far from the case. One evening there was a stag dinner at the villa, and during the cocktail period, Ike and John sat alone talking to Zhukov. Zhukov mentioned his daughter was getting married that very day, but he had passed on the wedding for the chance to see his old friend. Immediately, Ike summoned an aide and ordered gifts, including a transistor radio and a pen set, be sent to the couple. During their conversation, Zhukov said quietly, "There are things in Russia which are not as they seem," and asked Ike if they could find time for a private chat during the conference. They agreed on a meeting time.

Near the end of the conference Ike and Zhukov met in Ike's villa. As they talked, Ike was pained to see that "Zhukov was no longer the same man he had been in 1945." As Eisenhower later wrote, "In our wartime association he had been an independent, self-confident man who, while obviously embracing Communist doctrine, was always ready to meet cheerfully with me on any operational problem and to cooperate in finding a reasonable solution." Now Ike found Zhukov to be "a subdued and worried man." John's take: "Zhukov looked like a man who'd really had the rubber hose taken to him. There was no spirit left in him at all." As Zhukov repeated the party line, Ike became convinced he was acting on the instructions of his superiors. "I obtained nothing from this private chat other than a feeling of sadness."

Ike was concerned for his old friend. He knew life had been difficult for him, first with Stalin and then with the rocky transitional leadership. Why Zhukov had fallen out of favor is subject to debate, but one reason might have been his tremendous popularity after the war, something Stalin and his successors could not tolerate. Ike worried; the journalist Joseph Alsop once noted that Zhukov's poor treatment was one of the reasons Ike developed the perception of the Soviets as "dangerous and peculiar."

Years later, when Khrushchev visited America, he assured Ike, "Don't worry about your old friend. He is living happily in retirement, doubtless writing his memoirs." He told Ike Zhukov loved fishing, and Ike sent him a box of fishing tackle, which he was said to use for the rest of his life. But Ike never saw him again.

It was during the Geneva conference that Ike made his bold recommendation that the United States and the Soviet Union should allow planes to do reconnaissance over each other's countries. The proposal came to be known as Open Skies. He'd been thinking about it for months, and hadn't necessarily planned to bring it up in Geneva, but at the last moment he decided to spring it. Here, he argued, was a foolproof way to hold each other accountable to any arms accords they might make. He, the president of the United States, was willing to put his cards on the table. Was the Soviet Union prepared to do the same?

As soon as he stopped speaking there was a loud crack of thunder and the lights went off. Laughing, Ike said, "Well, I expected to make a hit, but not that much of one." Shortly after, the lights came back on, but the incident broke the tension.

Bulganin seemed mildly favorable, but after the meeting, as they were walking out of the room, Khrushchev pursued Ike with a more dismissive tone. "No, no, no," he called, "that is a very bad idea." He charged Ike with wanting to look into their bedrooms and assured him the idea would never fly. Ike later said that at that moment he knew Khrushchev was really the man in charge. Unsurprisingly, the Open Skies initiative never came to fruition.

Immediately after the summit there was optimistic talk of the "spirit of Geneva," and it was Bulganin, not Khrushchev, who graced the cover of *Time*. For a time there did seem to be an easing of tensions after the summit, as Bulganin spoke of the "spirit of cooperation and the desire for mutual understanding." The success of the conference, from the standpoint of U.S.-Soviet relations, might have come down to a simple matter of respect—something Ike excelled at. "During the summit the Soviet leaders, in their own estimate, achieved their most important goal," wrote Vladislav Zubok, a Soviet-born historian of the Cold War, based at the London School of Economics. "They forced the Americans to talk to them as equal partners, without intimidation or condescension." If this was truly the case, it was Ike's doing—without being forced. He sought a meeting of the minds. Unfortunately, the Soviets would prove more difficult to bring to the table once the bloom was off the conference.

In the coming months Bulganin proceeded to send Ike voluminous correspondence, detailing potential agreements, baiting him about nonaggression pacts, and suggesting treaties. Unrav-

eling the spools, Ike found little was different in Bulganin's recommendations. And while he would normally say that as long
as the two sides were talking, that was progress, there was a
bottomless quality to Bulganin's prose that did not help further
negotiations. This continued after Bulganin stepped down and
was replaced by Khrushchev.

A crucial backdrop to U.S.-Soviet relations was the fate of
East Germany. In the waning days of World War II, Ike, as
commander, made a decision that had a seismic impact on the
way Cold War politics would unfold in the coming decades.
Berlin was arguably the jewel in the crown of victory at the end
of the war, and as the Allies moved into Germany it was left to
Ike to decide how to take it. His philosophy was that it was the
job of a commander to achieve a military victory in the most efficient way. Churchill originally wanted to take Berlin to secure
that prestigious victory, but Ike and Bradley estimated the effort
would mean up to fifty thousand additional casualties. So ultimately Ike determined (and Churchill reluctantly agreed) that
the Russians were better poised to take Berlin. Ike held Western
Allied forces short of the city. Many people considered this the
start of the Cold War, and wanted to blame Ike, the general, for
allowing a Russian foothold in Germany in the first place. After
the war, Germany was divided into sectors, which ultimately
led to Russia dominating the east and the Americans and Euro-
peans controlling the west, an arrangement that was doomed to
conflict from the start. The west pursued reunification, the east
sought domination—and the simmering tensions threatened to
reach an explosive end. (Interestingly, even as tensions escalated
through the 1950s, Ike remained tremendously popular in East
Germany, where they idolized him as the man who had overthrown the Nazis.)

With all these matters, Ike had one firm rule: he would not

The Eisenhower boys, the early years. Ike is front right, with Edgar behind him; Arthur is holding baby Roy. *Courtesy of the Eisenhower Library*

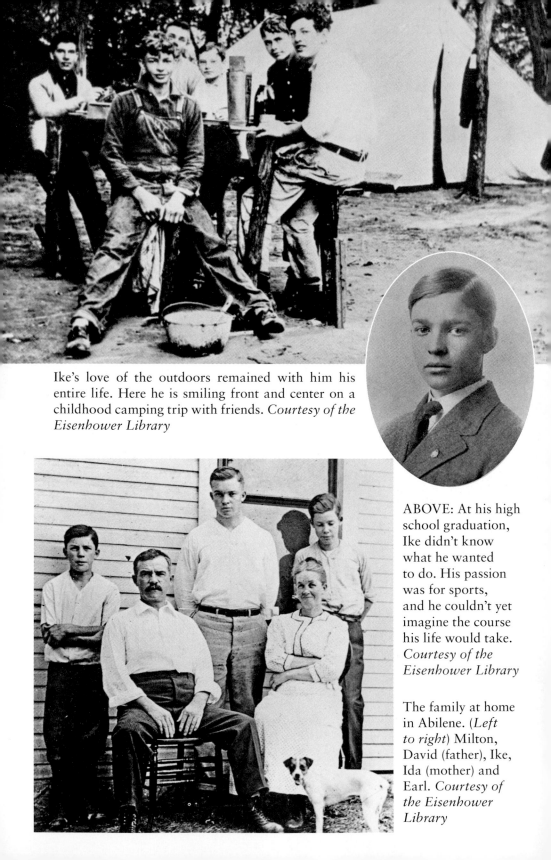

Ike's love of the outdoors remained with him his entire life. Here he is smiling front and center on a childhood camping trip with friends. *Courtesy of the Eisenhower Library*

ABOVE: At his high school graduation, Ike didn't know what he wanted to do. His passion was for sports, and he couldn't yet imagine the course his life would take. *Courtesy of the Eisenhower Library*

The family at home in Abilene. (*Left to right*) Milton, David (father), Ike, Ida (mother) and Earl. *Courtesy of the Eisenhower Library*

Ike's first impression of Mamie was that she was attractive and saucy. She also had a steely will and an endless supply of devotion and support, which she provided during their fifty-three-year marriage. *Courtesy of the Eisenhower Library*

Ike the soldier and commander, as America knew him. He was buried in this uniform. *Courtesy of the Eisenhower Library*

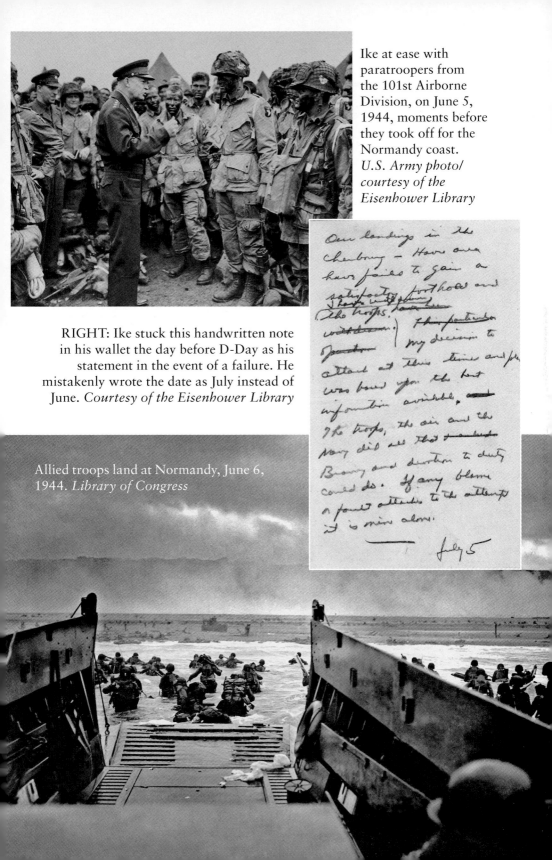

Ike at ease with paratroopers from the 101st Airborne Division, on June 5, 1944, moments before they took off for the Normandy coast. *U.S. Army photo/ courtesy of the Eisenhower Library*

RIGHT: Ike stuck this handwritten note in his wallet the day before D-Day as his statement in the event of a failure. He mistakenly wrote the date as July instead of June. *Courtesy of the Eisenhower Library*

Allied troops land at Normandy, June 6, 1944. *Library of Congress*

"ALL HONOR TO OUR HERO": General Eisenhower returns home. New York City, 1945. *Library of Congress*

"We Like Ike": a once-reluctant candidate on the campaign trail, 1952. *Courtesy of the Eisenhower Library*

Inauguration Day, 1953. Ike took the oath of office on two Bibles—one, a gift from his mother when he graduated from West Point, and the other, the Bible George Washington used to take his oath as the first president. *National Park Service photo/courtesy of the Eisenhower Library*

Cowboy Montie Montana lassos the new president during the inaugural parade, January 20, 1953. *National Park Service photo/courtesy of the Eisenhower Library*

The Castle Bravo nuclear test, March 1954, the
largest nuclear detonation at the time. The specter of
atomic warfare hung over the Eisenhower years, but Ike
navigated the world safely through.
National Nuclear Security Administration

RIGHT: "President-elect Eisenhower [*left*] during inspection tour at Kimpo [Air Base], Korea," December 1952.
Ike made ending the Korean War a priority from the
outset, diffusing a dangerous flashpoint in the deepening
Cold War. *Seymour Johnson AFB Library*

September 25, 1959.
When Ike and Khrush-
chev (*center*) were alone
at Camp David, their
conversations were
warmer than on the pub-
lic stage. They bonded
over a shared love of
westerns, but the Cold
War tensions remained
after the visit. *National
Park Service photo/
courtesy of the
Eisenhower Library*

President Eisenhower with Senate Majority Leader Lyndon Johnson (*center*) and Secretary of State John Foster Dulles (*right*), posing outside the White House during a bipartisan luncheon in March 1955. Ike's record of reaching across the aisle should be a model for today's politicians. *Library of Congress*

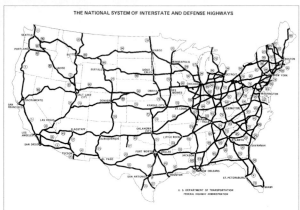

ABOVE: The 1956 National Interstate and Defense Highways Act was the largest public-works project in U.S. history and revolutionized the nation's infrastructure. Today it is known as the Eisenhower Interstate System. *Library of Congress*

BELOW: The "Little Rock Nine" desegregate their high school under escort of the 101st Airborne. Ike had ordered the elite army unit to Arkansas to uphold the Supreme Court's *Brown v. Board of Education* decision. *US Army*

PEACE ★ PROSPERITY ★ PROGRESS

"Peace, Prosperity, Progress"—the Eisenhower-Nixon campaign theme in 1956. During the Eisenhower years, the nation's economy grew at a record rate. *National Park Service photo/courtesy of the Eisenhower Library*

Ike's second inaugural parade, January 1957. *Library of Congress*

Thanksgiving Day, 1953, at the farm in Gettysburg—Ike always carved the turkey. It was a particularly happy occasion that year because Dwight and Mamie's son John was home from the Korean War, which Ike brought to an end in July. *Bettman/Getty Images*

Taking a break at the White House, Ike sometimes stepped outside the Oval Office and hit golf balls on his putting green. *HWG/ Associated Press*

JFK bounded up the steps to greet President Eisenhower at the White House on December 6, 1960, as the press corps looked on. *National Park Service photo/ courtesy of the Eisenhower Library*

Ike and JFK posed in the Oval Office after a serious discussion of the nation's business during the December 6 transition meeting. *National Park Service photo/courtesy of the Eisenhower Library*

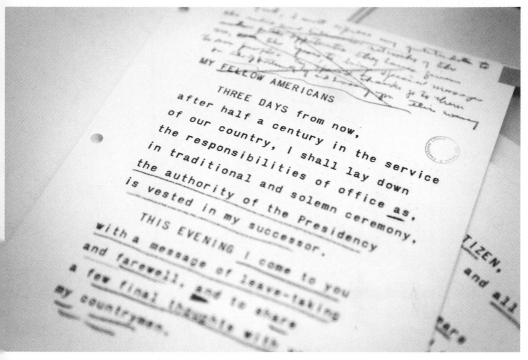

Ike was a relentless editor, revising his farewell address some thirty times since 1959. *Photo by Cory Keller*

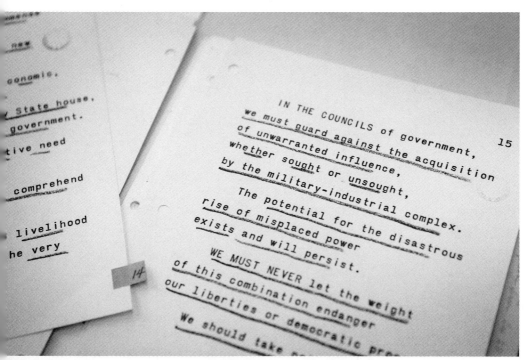

By the final transcript, the scribbling was gone, but Ike underlined key lines in the speech for easier reading. *Photo by Cory Keller*

Eisenhower delivering his farewell address, January 17, 1961. *Bill Allen/Associated Press*

Ike hated using a teleprompter, and although it was rolling during his farewell address, he mostly read from his notes. *Eisenhower Library and Museum/ photo by Cory Keller*

John F. Kennedy's inaugural address, January 20, 1961. *JFK Library*

Stunned by the Bay of Pigs fiasco, President Kennedy flew Ike to Camp David for a sober conference on April 22, 1961. "No one knows how tough this job is until he's been in it a few months," Kennedy confessed—a reality Ike had warned him about months earlier. *Paul Vathis/ Associated Press*

Ike by the fireplace in a reflective moment late in life. The prophetic words of his farewell address would continue to resonate for decades to come. *Courtesy of the Eisenhower Library*

The author visits Ike's chapel, where a quiet spiritual energy and peace pervades. Ike's grave at the Eisenhower Presidential Library in Abilene, Kansas, is surrounded by engravings of his most important quotes. *Photo by Cory Keller*

negotiate under a threat—and on many occasions, particularly with Germany, the Soviet stance was very much a hostile one.

IN SPITE OF THESE seemingly insurmountable conflicts, the United States and the Soviet Union moved ahead on cultural exchanges. The Soviet exhibition opened in New York City in June 1959, while the United States exhibition opened in Moscow in July, with Vice President Nixon on hand for the occasion. Nixon hosted Khrushchev for a private showing. On display were the wonders of the free enterprise system, designed to inspire envy in the communist state. The term "American exceptionalism" had not yet made it into the vernacular, but it captures the intention. Nixon was particularly enthusiastic about taking the Soviet leader on a tour of an American kitchen. What followed was a heated exchange, dubbed in the media as the "Kitchen Debate."

> **Nixon:** I want to show you this kitchen. It is like those of our houses in California.
> [Nixon points to dishwasher.]
> **Khrushchev:** We have such things.
> **Nixon:** This is our newest model. This is the kind which is built in thousands of units for direct installations in the houses. In America, we like to make life easier for women. . . .
> **Khrushchev:** Your capitalistic attitude toward women does not occur under communism.
> **Nixon:** I think that this attitude towards women is universal. What we want to do, is make life more easy for our housewives. . . . This house can be bought for $14,000, and most American [veterans from World

War II] can buy a home in the bracket of $10,000 to $15,000. Let me give you an example that you can appreciate. Our steelworkers, as you know, are now on strike. But any steelworker could buy this house. They earn $3 an hour. This house costs about $100 a month to buy on a contract running 25 to 30 years.

Khrushchev: We have steelworkers and peasants who can afford to spend $14,000 for a house. Your American houses are built to last only 20 years so builders could sell new houses at the end. We build firmly. We build for our children and grandchildren.... The Americans have created their own image of the Soviet man. But he is not as you think. You think the Russian people will be dumbfounded to see these things, but the fact is that newly built Russian houses have all this equipment right now....

Nixon: I appreciate that you are very articulate and energetic....

Khrushchev: Energetic is not the same thing as wise....

And so it went. In the end, Khrushchev acknowledged it had been a debate. "You're a lawyer of capitalism, I'm a lawyer for communism," he said genially. "Let's kiss."

The Kitchen Debate feels strange and even cringe-worthy by today's standards—"our appliances are better than yours" hardly seems like a productive argument when describing the differences between capitalism and communism. Back home, however, Nixon's performance was praised, and the media was quick to declare Nixon the "winner." Americans were perhaps relieved to see that an American official could hold his own against the Soviet leader—who most people thought of as mysterious and threatening. Khrushchev likewise received kudos in

Moscow, where the "debate" was televised. Looking at it now we see how the back-and-forth shines a light on the most widely held stereotypes of both nations. In the 1960 presidential campaign, Kennedy made a pointed reference to the Kitchen Debate when he said to great applause, "Talk is cheap, words are not enough, waving our finger under Khrushchev's face does not increase the strength of the United States, especially when you say to him—especially when you say, as you wave your finger, 'You may be ahead of us in rockets, but we are ahead of you in color television.' I will take my television black and white."

Less than two months after Nixon's visit to Moscow, Khrushchev was in the United States for a visit that would take him not only to Washington but on a tour of the country before finishing with private meetings with the president at Camp David.

Before coming, Khrushchev was nervous. Upon receiving an invitation from the president to join him at Camp David, he didn't know what to think. "What in the world is Camp David?" Khrushchev asked his advisors suspiciously. Nobody knew. Khrushchev wondered if it was a place Americans invited people they didn't trust—like a quarantine area. Such was the fear of being humiliated during his visit that Khrushchev actually contemplated this possibility.

When Khrushchev first arrived in Washington, Ike wanted to show him the sights from a helicopter, but Khrushchev at first refused to fly in one. But Ike convinced him. Seated side by side, with Khrushchev's interpreter in front, they rose up off the South Lawn and flew over Washington and its suburbs. Khrushchev noted the rows of single-family houses—"we have apartments in Russia; this is very inefficient"—and the heavy automobile traffic—"we have buses in Russia." All of this was said with a determined poker face, as if he was loath to express anything approaching amazement at the sites—even though the landscape around the nation's capital is quite beautiful, and the highways were streamlined and impressive.

Pointing out a golf course, Ike said, "There, Mr. Khrushchev, is where I play golf. I love that game. What do you think of it?"

"I haven't the slightest idea about that game," Khrushchev said. "We don't have it in our country."

Before Khrushchev left Washington for a trip across America, he asked James Hagerty, "How are you going to tell the American press to report my visit across your country?"

"Mr. Khrushchev," Hagerty replied respectfully, "I don't understand what you mean. In our country we don't do that. All I can assure you is that you will get fair treatment in the American press as you visit our country."

"Yes," he pressed, "but what are you going to tell them to say?"

"Mr. Khrushchev, I'm not going to tell them to say anything."

Hagerty didn't feel as if he'd made his point—he assumed Khrushchev thought he was lying. He just didn't believe the press representative of the president of the United States had no power over the press—much less the local press in the states Khrushchev would visit.

During his travels across America, which he enjoyed enormously, Khrushchev was aware of being a source of curiosity: "The Americans seemed to take a tolerant attitude toward us, as though to say, 'We'll see how things turn out. Let's see what kind of sly fox [literal translation 'goose with paws'] it is who heads their government,' " he wrote in his memoir.

Ike looked forward to meeting with Khrushchev when he returned to the East, and their time together at Camp David was surprisingly intimate. Ike could smile recalling the way

Khrushchev revealed his humanity when the two men were in close quarters. For example, Khrushchev confided to Ike he shared his love of western movies. "When Stalin was still alive, we used to watch westerns all the time," he told the president. "I too have a weakness for this sort of film." Delighted, Ike pulled out a list of movies on hand—*The Big Country, Shane, High Noon,* and the like. And that night the two men watched movies together.

Ike observed that when he and Khrushchev were alone, they spoke much more openly and in a friendly manner. Khrushchev wanted to talk about consumer goods, how the economy worked, how much clothing cost, the automobile industry, and even the idea of American know-how. Ike found Khrushchev had a charming side, with a good sense of humor.

In fact, on a visit to Ike's farm in Gettysburg, Khrushchev spent time with Ike's grandchildren. Barbara Eisenhower was struck by Khrushchev's seemingly genuine enjoyment of the children. He talked to them and translated their names into Russian (or tried to—unfortunately there was no equivalent for Susan). In addition to beautiful blown-glass Christmas tree ornaments, he gave the children little red stars to put in their buttonholes. Barbara was not so charmed by that. Recalling Khrushchev's threat years earlier—"We will bury you"—she made the children give her their stars when they got in the car to drive home, and she threw them out the window onto the road.

David, who was eleven, recalled the impact Khrushchev's visit made on him: "the imminence or the possibility of war with the Russians was something, as a child, that I can remember worrying about all the time. And suddenly the leader of it all, Nikita Khrushchev, in your wildest fantasy, is suddenly standing there in front of you, and he's not that much taller than you are."

In a press conference at the National Press Club the following day, Khrushchev had a teasing, grandfatherly manner. "I would like to reveal a secret," he said, noting he hadn't asked Ike's permission. "Yesterday the president was kind enough to invite me to his farm, where I met his wonderful grandchildren. I established direct contact with those wonderful grandchildren of his, and we held a conference with them as to whether they should accompany their grandfather to our country, and if so, when. At that conference with the president's grandchildren, they and I reached a unanimous decision that they certainly should come with the president."

Ike had a gift for human relations, and he loved meeting with his foreign counterparts, because in those private settings the curtain was drawn back and they were just human beings together. He took Khrushchev's warmth and good humor at face value—for the time, at least. It was not enough, Ike thought, to fight; one had to understand. And in that spirit, he asked himself, what was the appeal of communism? True, it was atheistic, a worldview he could not comprehend. True, in its Soviet manifestation, it was a totalitarian philosophy that did not respect human freedom. True, it was the antithesis of the open markets of capitalism. True, it was oriented toward domination, not collaboration. But what was its appeal? He looked at the scene and saw an illusion where people were promised liberation at the expense of personal freedom; community at the expense of individuality. There was the myth of superiority grounded in a rickety economic system. Ike was clear about the choice: communism, which sliced an ever-smaller pie into ever-smaller pieces, or capitalism, which kept expanding the pie. But his feelings went deeper. As a child in Abilene he had been blessed by a parental attitude treasuring self-determination, and this was the critical element missing in the communist philosophy. It was a sad picture, but he knew the people had to believe, had to hope in these principles in which they had invested so much.

But he favored understanding to demagoguery. General Goodpaster later said of Ike, "he never tried to whip up hatred toward the Soviets. He felt they had a mistaken system and a system that didn't respond to the needs or the possibilities for the people of the world, but he did not try to fan any kind of hatred or emotion." Goodpaster also observed that Ike often went out of his way to recognize the role Soviet armed forces had played during World War II, and said they had paid a tremendous price.

Ike appreciated the way everyday moments could have profound meaning—how differences could evaporate in a shared pleasure. He had an uncanny knack for being able to meet foes on human terms. After Khrushchev returned home, Eisenhower was determined to work through the fog of fear that had developed around the arms race.

Khrushchev's visit seemed to have been a success. The Soviet leader enjoyed this type of personal diplomacy, and he even trotted out the favorite "spirit of" characterization, now speaking of "the spirit of Camp David." There was talk of future summits, and the trip to Moscow by Ike and his family was in the planning stages. For a brief time, the winter cold gave way to a spring blossoming.

And then, on May Day 1960, a Soviet surface-to-air missile shot down an American spy plane over Sverdlovsk, Russia, and the pilot, Gary Powers, was captured. According to the Soviets, Powers had confessed the plane was under the direction of the Central Intelligence Agency. And all hell broke loose.

In fact, the United States had been flying U-2 spy planes over Russia to keep track of its military and missile development since 1956—and Khrushchev knew this quite well. But prior to the

Powers incident, the planes had been too high to shoot down, and rather than embarrass themselves by admitting their vulnerability, the Soviets had kept quiet about it. The subject never came up during the Camp David discussions. Thus, the U-2 incident, if not a real disaster, was a PR nightmare for Ike and gave the Soviets a ready excuse to freeze relations once again. "Khrushchev had his hawks and doves," noted presidential advisor Admiral Evan P. Aurand, analyzing the incident. "Every president does. Every head of government does. [The U-2 incident] gave the [Russian] hawks a lever on Khrushchev. He had to respond to it. He couldn't keep talking about the Spirit of Camp David." The invitation Khrushchev had extended for Ike and his family to visit Moscow was abruptly withdrawn. Powers was paraded before the public and put on trial in Moscow, where he was sentenced to ten years in prison, including seven years of hard labor. Later, during Kennedy's second year in office, a prisoner exchange was made between Powers and a Soviet spy in an American prison. (The story was dramatized in Steven Spielberg's 2015 movie, *Bridge of Spies,* starring Tom Hanks.)

In the immediate aftermath of the U-2 incident, Ike had to figure out what he was going to tell the American people. Malcolm Moos began to work on a speech, but he was frustrated by the rigid dictate of the State Department that the president could never admit spying was going on. Moos put together a draft with that in mind, and then raced to meet Ike at National Airport so he could review the speech in the limo.

Reading the draft, Ike scowled. "Malcolm, it'll never do." He tossed it on the floor of the limousine.

"You know why that's wrong?" he asked.

"I think I do, Mr. President," Moos said.

"This is exactly what they want to hear, the communists, Khrushchev, that I'm a lackey, I'm a tired old man, I'm in the collar of these capitalist imperialists, I don't know what the hell's going on in my country—and that is the *last* thing we want to say."

Following Ike's revisions, the result was a forceful speech, declaring that the program of aerial reconnaissance was under his direction and approval, and arguing strongly about the need for constant vigilance—citing Pearl Harbor. The Soviets also conduct espionage, he added. The speech was honest and strong—no apologies—and was well received by the American people. Privately, Ike was angry about the incident, and he later told Merriman Smith he regretted it, saying if he'd had it to do all over again, with the Russians ready to talk, he would have pulled the spy planes, at least during that period.

Like the automatic pinsetter at the Camp David bowling alley that impressed Khrushchev when he visited, the Cold War pins were reset in their conventional order after the U-2 incident. Khrushchev closed down all talks, deciding to do no more until the United States had elected a new president. Ike was deeply disappointed.

WHEN HE SET OUT to finalize his farewell address, what might have been warmer sentiments were replaced by a harsh view of the "hostile" and "atheistic" landscape—the communist threat that remained strong after eight years of steady effort on his part. It would not have been boastful for him to believe that if he, with his knowledge, experience, resources, and convictions, could not make progress with the Soviets, JFK would be hard-pressed to do better. For Ike, the Camp David meetings seemed liked a mirage—the tantalizing specter of peace disappearing to reveal an arid plain. Now the United States must invoke its true power with the best card it had to play—leadership.

One of Ike's central precepts was that America must be willing to use all of its military might where warranted—no empty threats. "My boy," he said to Hagerty, "there isn't any such thing as a little force. If you have to use force, you have to use it in overwhelming superiority. If you resort to it, you have to do it that way. Now, I don't want to resort to it, but if I have to, I will use it in the strong numerical superiority of men and weapons and everything else that I have."

At the same time, he understood true success would be measured by finding nonmilitary solutions. Ike strongly believed America's wealth and might were not the sole measures of its dominance on the world stage. He often cited America's moral center and spirit as the keys to its success. For what would be the point of being dominant in the world if we had nothing to transmit?

It was, he believed, a long game, and his point in the speech was to urge Americans to resist falling into a crisis mentality, bouncing from one failed military action to the next. Liberty was at stake, not only in the face of America's enemies, but in the false bravado of military power.

This was a particularly strong warning from an old soldier who resisted sending troops onto new battlefields—and although he was speaking to the nation, in a sense he was focused on an audience of one, the president-elect. He knew that Kennedy was less inclined to follow his strategic long game, proclaiming a more aggressive approach to communism. Ike abided by his policy not to discuss personalities, but privately he deemed JFK callow, itching for a fight. Once in office, would Kennedy heed Ike's advice and take a more strategic view?

CHAPTER 8

DUST TO DUST

Disarmament, with mutual honor and confidence, is a continuing imperative. Together we must learn how to compose differences, not with arms, but with intellect and decent purpose. Because this need is so sharp and apparent I confess that I lay down my official responsibilities in this field with a definite sense of disappointment. As one who has witnessed the horror and the lingering sadness of war—as one who knows that another war could utterly destroy this civilization which has been so slowly and painfully built over thousands of years—I wish I could say tonight that a lasting peace is in sight.

—From Eisenhower's Farewell Address

In the 1960 campaign, JFK had pounded away at the so-called missile gap between the United States and Soviet Union—a misrepresentation that Ike knew to be nonexistent. Presumably, Kennedy understood this as well, since he was briefed on the matter by the CIA during the campaign. Nevertheless, he pushed the theme, crying, "I don't want to be the president of a nation perishing under the mushroom cloud of a nuclear warhead, and I intend, if president, or if I continue in the Senate, to build the defenses which this country needs, and which freedom needs."

It was a clever, yet devious, tactic. It was impossible for the average citizen to know whether or not the Russians were actually building more missiles than America, or what it all meant if they were. Did it matter whether you could blow up the world twice over, or a hundred times? But the rhetoric was compelling—and it well might have won Kennedy the election. Of course, within two weeks of assuming the presidency, Kennedy's administration would acknowledge there was no missile gap. In this instance, such shading of the truth—or outright lying—though common to campaigning, angered Ike for two reasons: first, America had a sufficient weapon supply for its defense needs; second, Ike recognized the need to emphasize restraint in ever having to use it—to be less muscular and more thoughtful when the future of the planet was at stake.

The campaign attacks stung, both for their lack of accuracy and their spirit of negativity. Bristling at the tone of JFK's speeches, Ike said he was "terribly tired of hearing America run down."

Whereas America's isolation in a "new world" afforded it unique protection for much of its history, Ike's presidency faced a looming threat of attack on the continental United States. How does one defend a nation against nuclear attack? What bunker could be sufficient? The day he took office, Ike had noticed a locked drawer in his desk in the Oval Office. Asking for a key he found a report, which had been commissioned by Truman, predicting a frightening arms race between the United States and the Soviet Union, involving thousands of nuclear weapons and the strategic missiles that could carry them across the hemisphere. On the question of survivability in the event of a nuclear attack, the report was blunt: most of the country would be a moonscape of radioactive ash.

Ike wanted to get the matter out in the open. It was too important for locked drawers. He encouraged the report's author, physicist Robert Oppenheimer, "the father of the atomic bomb," to write an article on the topic, which was published in the July 1953 issue of *Foreign Affairs*. Oppenheimer's calculation was a shock to those who took any consolation in America's lead in the arms race. "The very least we can say," he wrote, "is that, looking ten years ahead, it is likely to be small comfort that the Soviet Union is four years behind us, and small comfort that they are only about half as big as we are. The very least we can conclude is that our twenty-thousandth bomb, useful as it may be in filling the vast munitions pipelines of a great war, will not in any deep strategic sense offset their two-thousandth. . . . We need to be clear that there will not be many great atomic wars for us, nor for our institutions. It is important that there not be one."

So when Kennedy talked about the missile gap, Ike understood it was not only inaccurate, but also probably irrelevant. Although our nuclear stockpile had grown from about 1,000 warheads to about 23,000 during Ike's presidency, it was his firm belief that we could not be saved by building many more missiles than the other guy.

Khrushchev knew it, too. At the 1955 Geneva Summit, sitting together after dinner one night, Ike and Khrushchev had an informal discussion about nuclear arms. Ike said flat out, "Of course, this is something we can never resort to."

"I agree," replied Khrushchev. And then he went on. "I understand completely, Mr. President. We get your dust, you get our dust, the winds blow around the world and nobody's safe."

"Yes," said Ike, "that's what it's all about."

Later, at Camp David, Khrushchev admitted he had always been haunted by Chairman Mao's 1957 speech at the World Communist Representative Meeting in Moscow, in which the

Chinese communist leader stated that if there were a nuclear war, there would be 50 million Americans and 50 million Russians left, but there would be 450 million Chinese survivors.

Knowing the stakes was a heavy burden. Observed Hagerty, "The President of the United States has, sitting right on his shoulder all the time, that atom bomb or nuclear bomb, or whatever you want to call it. And so has the man on the other side. They're about the only two that have it, and they're about the only two that realize (. . . in my own opinion) the complete and utter futility of nuclear war. There won't be anything left. It's as simple as that."

The threat of massive retaliation as a deterrent—which Ike always kept in his hip pocket—wasn't such a slam dunk. As Ike well knew, the very idea gave rise to endless speculation. For example, in a press conference on the fate of Berlin, when the crisis with Russia was mounting, a reporter asked, "If the Russians press us on Berlin, are you prepared to use nuclear weapons?"

The president snapped, "No, you can't *defend* anything with nuclear weapons."

The overwhelming picture could get discouraging. "Sometimes you feel, almost, that we can be excused for getting a little bit hysterical, because these dangers come from so many angles, and they are of such different kinds, and no matter what we do they still seem to exist," Ike told the American people in mid-1954. That's not to say he was unwilling to use nuclear weapons if the worst happened—the option was on the table with respect to Korea. Unquestionably, the nuclear threat acted as a barrier to conflict. Referring to the Soviets, Andrew Goodpaster said, "The thought of their troops being hit by an atomic round would be very sobering, and I think Eisenhower was well aware of the way that the Soviet Union would think about the possibility of this being used against them." Of Eisenhower, "It was a deterrent in his mind, and not just a deterrent to war of their initiation, but a deterrent also to their attempting to use pressure tactics or threats to force concessions. They faced the problem that if they tried to back that up with military action, they could very well have a nuclear attack against them, against their forces in the field or against their airfields, and so on."

In his heart, Ike was determined to find another way. In the early years of his presidency he became obsessed with the idea of how to slow the arms race. Notwithstanding the terrible destructive power of nuclear weapons, he wondered if the nuclear technology could also be used for positive ends. It was a new idea. On December 8, 1953, as his first year in office drew to a close, he stood before a packed meeting of the United Nations General Assembly and gave a speech that would later be dubbed "Atoms for Peace."

He began by reminding all present that the United States certainly had the nuclear capability to lay waste to any enemy who would provoke retaliation by attacking the United States or its interests. There was no doubt about our capability or our resolve, he stressed.

Then he pivoted. "To pause there would be to confirm the hopeless finality of a belief that two atomic colossi are doomed malevolently to eye each other indefinitely across a trembling world," he said. "To stop there would be to accept helplessly the probability of civilization destroyed, the annihilation of the irreplaceable heritage of mankind handed down to us from generation to generation, and the condemnation of mankind to begin all over again the age-old struggle upward from savagery towards decency, and right, and justice. Surely no sane member of the human race could discover victory in such desolation. . . ."

Instead, he presented another path—a peacetime harnessing

of nuclear energy that might do good. To that end, he proposed the United States and Soviet Union agree to deposit certain amounts of uranium into an international uranium bank. Not only would this reduce their supplies of material for bombs, but it would also open up the potential for other nations to draw from the bank for peaceful purposes—once the technology became available. He told the gathering he was prepared to present to the United States Congress any such plan in support of four goals: 1) encouraging a worldwide investigation into the most effective peacetime use of fissionable material; 2) diminishing the destructive power of the world's atomic stockpile; 3) showing the people of all nations that the world powers—of both the East and West—were more interested in human aspirations than war; and 4) opening up channels for peaceful discussions and problem solving.

As soon as Ike finished delivering his speech, it received huge publicity around the world, and was extremely popular with the American people. Suddenly nuclear power was being described in a different context—as a breakthrough in medicine, in electricity, in agriculture, in space, in myriad applications that might build civilization rather than destroy it—in effect, to turn weapons into plowshares. The proposal led to the creation of the International Atomic Energy Agency, which promulgated cooperation in science and technology across all borders.

Ike was a believer in incremental progress, and he thought that even if we could make "the tiniest of starts" in getting the Soviet Union to collaborate on a peaceful direction in the atomic field, it would be worth the effort. His trump card was the knowledge of just how much weaponry the United States possessed. He wrote in his diary, "[E]ven in the event that the USSR would cooperate in such a plan for 'propaganda purposes' the United States could unquestionably afford to reduce its atomic stockpile by two or three times the amounts that the Russians might contribute to the United Nations agency, and still improve our relative position in the cold war, and even in the event of the outbreak of war."

However, the true policy could feel a bit schizophrenic, because everyone was still determinedly producing weapons and trying to figure out how to survive a nuclear attack. During the 1950s and into the early 1960s, the American people were in the grip of a civil defense fever—the misperception that surviving a nuclear attack was a simple matter of preparation. Americans were trained to "duck and cover" as the bombs fell. Schoolchildren performed drills where at the sound of an alarm they dropped and huddled beneath rickety wooden desks, hands over their heads—and even many of these naïve youngsters must have guessed it was a futile exercise.

A new economy in home fallout shelters bloomed. Americans were taught how to build them in basements and underground in backyards, and told how to stock them. Home shelters were the new middle- and upper-class accessory, and magazines and television specials featured advice, recipes, and ideas for entertaining the kids during the nuclear winter. Survival stores sold basic products like freeze-dried foods, flashlights, first-aid kits, and battery-operated radios. By 1961, the effort was in full flower. *Life* magazine even featured a newlywed couple spending their honeymoon underground in a homebuilt shelter. The accompanying article had the unfortunate assertion, "Fallout can be fun."

Communities built fallout shelters in the basements of public buildings, in subway tunnels, and in other underground spaces. Major corporations built fallout shelters for employees. The black and yellow signage can still occasionally be seen today. In 1962, President Kennedy would call for "a fallout shelter for everyone"—his administration's version of "a chicken in every pot." By the mid-1960s, there were more than 200,000 fallout shelters languishing in American communities, littered with rotting crackers and stale bottled water. A re-creation of a fallout shelter, at the Eisenhower Museum, shows just how morose and unlivable it would be, when one imagines an average family crammed into a room with canned foods and cereal lining a small shelf.

There was a madness to it, or perhaps it was just a distraction, creating the illusion of control. The idea that one could survive a nuclear blast by huddling in a steel box belowground (never mind what would greet you when or if you finally emerged) was something of an opiate that might have prevented mass fear and revolt. It didn't change the depressing calculations of men like Oppenheimer, nor did it calm Ike at all. In a letter to Winston Churchill in the spring of 1956, Ike wrote that nuclear buildup was not necessarily a strategy of deterrence. "I think it would be unsafe to predict that, if the West and the East should ever become locked up in a life and death struggle, both sides would still have sense enough not to use this horrible instrument. You will remember that in 1945 there was no possible excuse, once we had reached the Rhine in late '44, for Hitler to continue the war, yet his insane determination to rule or ruin brought additional and completely unnecessary destruction to his country; brought about its division between East and West and his own ignominious death."

Sometimes when his advisors were in the Oval Office advocating to increase the number of missiles, Ike would get up from his desk and stand looking out the window, collecting his thoughts. With his back turned to them he would calmly muse about his experiences as a general, expressing his hope they would trust his judgment in the field. Repeatedly he said he didn't believe there was a likely possibility of a conventional shooting war with the Soviet Union.

In 1956, Ike appointed retired Air Force General Harold George to work with a staff group to calculate the damage that might be inflicted in the initial stages of a nuclear war between Russia and the United States. George presented two scenarios:

In the first, the attack came without warning until the DEW line (early radar warning line) had been reached. The result: complete economic collapse for at least six months to a year; members of the federal government wiped out, with government improvised by the states; and enormous casualties, with 65 percent of the population requiring medical care, and little opportunity to receive it. In the second scenario, there was a month of strategic warning, but no specific information about when the attack would take place. The outcome was much the same, and the idea that the United States would launch its own secret first-strike attack during the warning month was deemed highly unlikely. There was no way, Ike thought, to put a hopeful spin on the matter.

Americans panicked when the Soviets launched the world's first artificial satellite in October 1957. There had always been a presumption America was a technological giant and the Soviets were light-years behind in technology and capability. Sputnik brought us up short, opening our eyes as a nation to the strength of the Soviets. Disturbingly, it came as a complete surprise to the White House and to Ike's science advisors. Now the "space race" became a euphemism for a nuclear threat as the realization dawned that satellites could serve as a delivery system for nuclear weapons.

Ike knew we were in a superior position in terms of nuclear strength, but the idea that the Soviets were ahead in space was a blow to American prestige—as well as a worrisome sign of unpreparedness. Was America falling behind? The criticisms began to fly. In the Senate, Lyndon Johnson said the Soviets could one day be "dropping bombs on us from space like kids dropping rocks onto cars from freeway overpasses." Edward Teller, the "father" of the hydrogen bomb, called it the worst defeat since Pearl Harbor.

Ike was annoyed by the criticism. Most of all he hated fear-mongering. After all, the Soviets had never hidden their ambitions about space. And it seemed wrong to conflate a satellite with nuclear capabilities. He faulted his critics in the military for amping up a panic across America in an opportunistic drive to get more money from Congress for their favorite weapons systems.

But with the midterm elections approaching, Sputnik also became a useful campaign topic for Democrats. Massachusetts senator John F. Kennedy, running for reelection in 1958, was already being talked about as presidential material. He spoke often about Sputnik and the need for better science education. (As president, Kennedy vastly expanded the space program and dramatically challenged America to put a man on the moon before the end of the 1960s. It happened in 1969—under Nixon's watch.)

Politics aside, the educational appeal carried a great deal of weight, both in the White House and in Congress. Many, including the president, believed that if America was to be prepared to meet the challenges of a new scientific and technological age, we had to invest more heavily in science and math education. The result was the National Defense Education Act, which Ike signed into law on September 2, 1958. The act allotted up to $1 billion in a four-year effort to improve American education, with a special emphasis on the sciences.

Shortly after the launch of Sputnik, Ike empaneled the President's Science Advisory Committee to study the nuclear threat and make recommendations. Its findings, called the Gaither Report after its chairman, Horace Rowan Gaither, head of the Ford Foundation, proposed a $30 billion investment in fallout shelters and more missiles—not the path Ike favored. His reluctance left him open to attacks from Democrats, and laid the groundwork for Kennedy's campaign appeals. But Ike continued to speak out against fear-mongering. At his final State of the Union address, delivered just eight days before Kennedy's inauguration, Ike wrote, "We must not return to the 'crash-program' psychology of the past when each new feint by the communists was responded to in panic. The 'bomber gap' of several years ago was always a fiction, and the 'missile gap' shows every sign of being the same."

It has often been said U.S. presidents make up a tight and very exclusive club, in the sense that only they know the total weight of responsibility and the full truth of what our nation faces at home and abroad. Once in the Oval Office, Ike had seen, even presidents with thin resumes were capable of rising to the occasion, and he prayed this was true of Kennedy.

He had to put faith in the future and hope for the best for the new young president-to-be. At his final press conference, one of the reporters asked if it was true that he and Kennedy had hit it off pretty well.

"Well," said Ike with his typical candor, "I don't know if you could put it that way. But I could see that he was willing to learn."

And Ike was more than willing to teach—with a lesson not just in might, but in balance, delivered in his farewell address.

Our arms must be mighty, ready for instant action, so that no potential aggressor may be tempted to risk his own destruction. But each proposal must be weighed in light of a broader consideration; the need to maintain balance in and among national programs. . . . Good judgment seeks balance and progress; lack of it eventually finds imbalance and frustration.

And, he might have added, the potential for destruction.

CHAPTER 9

THE MILITARY-INDUSTRIAL COMPLEX

In the councils of government, we must guard against the acquisition of unwarranted influence, whether sought or unsought, by the military-industrial complex. The potential for the disastrous rise of misplaced power exists and will persist.
> —From Eisenhower's farewell address

JFK's false campaign rhetoric, ratcheting up fears that America wasn't keeping pace with the arms race, had been bad enough. But it was against an insidious backdrop. The war economy was in full flower by the early 1960s, and Ike was disturbed by the ubiquitous display of missiles—missiles!—in advertisements in some of America's most popular consumer magazines. Full-page ads and double-page spreads were purchased by companies like Goodyear, McDonnell Douglas, General Electric, General Motors, and Boeing. They weren't only featured in trade publications like *Aviation Week,* or even *Scientific American* and the *Smithsonian,* but also in *Life, Newsweek, Time,* and *U.S. News & World Report.* What could possibly be the point of advertising to ordinary Americans in this way? Working folks didn't buy missiles. Housewives didn't stock up on bombs. But they could be swept up in the drumbeat of a war economy—persuaded by muscular images wrapped in the flag. Thus more, better, and increasingly expensive missiles could be equated with military might and greater patriotism. It was at best a simplistic notion, and at worst a form of profiteering by companies whose incentive was profit, not necessarily patriotism.

In Ike's view, these advertising campaigns were nothing more than an attempt to make the case for more weaponry directly to the American people so they in turn would place additional pressure on Congress. Science advisor James Killian witnessed Ike's fury: "Repeatedly I saw Ike angered by the excesses, both in text and advertising, of the aerospace-electronics press, which advocated ever bigger and better weapons to meet an even bigger and better Soviet threat they had conjured up."

Ike had been agitating on this topic for years. And although one might think it was a distinctly modern concern, brought on by the advances in science and technology, Ike was intrigued to find a similar concern expressed in George Washington's farewell address. Washington urged the young nation to "avoid the necessity of those overgrown military establishments which, under any form of government, are inauspicious to liberty, and which are to be regarded as particularly hostile to republican liberty."

Balance was the theme, both for Washington and Eisenhower. Although Ike's administration undeniably orchestrated the buildup of a massive nuclear arsenal, he was very interested in having a conversation with the American people about how to achieve balance between military strength and domestic needs. He didn't want America to be a nation only concerned with its firepower. He thought this new direction should be managed wisely, and he was particularly concerned about the undue influence the military and contractors could have on Congress.

"We don't want to become a garrison state," he emphasized at a press conference during his first year in office. "We want to remain free. Our plans and programs have to conform to a free people, which means essentially a free economy." Ike had never been in lockstep with the military when it came to questions of whether certain weapons systems were worth the money. He challenged the nation to balance all of its priorities.

That was evidenced in his "Chance for Peace" speech, also delivered in the first year of his presidency—Ike's granddaughter Susan would later call the farewell address "a bookend" for that speech. But the warning now did not just concern the cost of military buildup—it was about its nature, and it went right back to the Founding Fathers and their intention. His worry was not about the strength of our military but the source of its power. It wasn't that this military-industrial complex was an organized effort by people with diabolical intentions, as much as it was the natural outcome of a free market economy combined with a surging industry in technologically based weapons. It was the job of the president to place restraints on these massive enterprises. Democracy, Ike believed, could be defined as public opinion in action, but leadership played a role in helping to form and direct that opinion. And the promotion of military hysteria was not helpful to the security of the country.

And so, with the final days ticking down until the transfer of power, Ike made his case to the American people—and, he hoped, to his young successor—planting a seed with one provocative phrase: *the military-industrial complex*.

Looking back in time, the American tradition was a civilian military—a relatively small permanent force, plus reserves, which could be expanded in times of emergency. The Founding Fathers were committed to the idea the military not be a power base in its own right—thus leading to military dictatorship—but rather the servant of a free society governed by the people.

The Continental Army was disbanded after the Revolutionary War, and a national military wasn't funded until 1879.

Likewise, the commander in chief of the military would be a civilian, but he alone could not choose to go to war. At the Constitutional Convention, the Fathers clearly determined that Congress, not the president, had the power to declare war. But in the twentieth century, especially after World War II, the executive branch took on more power. Congress never declared war on North Korea, but Truman sent forces under the principle that if we were attacked first, we could respond. Ike felt the nature of Cold War conflicts opened the door for abuses of executive power. The White House, he knew, had vast resources available to constantly shape the popular will—it was the most efficient propaganda machine in the nation. The White House could in effect become the controlling lever of the military-industrial complex.

The size and structure of the military had changed in dramatic ways since the vision of a civilian military was first imagined by the Founding Fathers. As Ike took office, he was aware the nation could not rely on the typical peacetime concessions that would weaken the military and leave us vulnerable. But military expansion came with consequences to the entire principle of the civilian military. During his administration, as he would later write, "In the making of every military budget, my associates and I . . . did our best to achieve real security without surrendering to special interest." Ike viewed himself as the guardian of a permanent peace, and yet this other force—this military-industrial complex—was selling a different vision to America. When consumers opened their favorite magazines to see pictures of a Titan missile, they saw the nation's emphasis on the weapons of war—enabled by rhetoric on the campaign trail warning of a missile gap. It sent the wrong message, Ike thought. "Down the long lane of the history yet to be written," he would state in his farewell address, "America knows that this world of ours, ever growing smaller, must avoid becoming a community of dreadful fear and hate, and be, instead, a proud confederation of mutual trust and respect."

Ike was particularly concerned about the ways industries might inappropriately affect congressional decisions. In a June 1959 meeting with legislative leaders on the subject of defense appropriations, he restated in the strongest terms his concern that the munitions industry might be exercising undue influence on Congress. He once again mentioned his pet peeve—those full-page ads.

The origins of a military economy could be traced to the years before Ike even took office. One might say the military-industrial complex was an invention of FDR, who established the War Production Board in 1942, to conscript companies, such as those in the auto industry, into service to produce war machinery. (During World War II, for example, General Motors converted all of its factories from making cars to building trucks, tanks, airplanes, and weapons for the military.) FDR also created the top-secret Office of Scientific Research and Development during the war. This would be the genesis of the Manhattan Project. Not only were the nation's leading scientists recruited for this project; the DuPont and Kellogg companies were also among the leadership. Prior to his death, FDR took action to make the war industry permanent, and indeed, companies like Boeing and GM kept their defense divisions operational. Truman continued the charge. Before 1950, President Truman's advisors had been pushing to amp up expenditures for both nuclear and conventional weaponry to protect the nation against a potential Soviet threat. The National Security Council report, "NSC-68," which outlined a plan for American rearmament, stated that increasing Pentagon spending would also boost the gross national product "by more than the amount being absorbed for additional military and foreign assistance purposes." To sell the public on such an expensive buildup during peacetime was a real challenge, as it would mean raising taxes. But, as one State Department official noted frankly, "Thank God Korea came along."

When peacetime came again, in 1953, it was tough to convince Americans to sink national treasure into the development of weapons whose benefits were basically invisible. So an unrelenting PR campaign was launched, with the constant goal of demonstrating that the more we spent on military, the greater the economic stimulus on the domestic front. In effect, we needed war as an avenue to prosperity. And the appeal largely worked.

Ike's own military buildup further increased the role of private industry in military affairs. But it troubled him deeply as he saw how easily members of Congress—and perhaps future presidents—could be persuaded by military and private-industry "experts" who might be more interested in their bottom lines or careers than in a reasonable approach to military policy. The foxes of industry had made their way into the government henhouse. This was Ike's final warning.

Undue influence—even corruption—was inevitable, as demonstrated most tangibly when a Martin Aircraft executive revealed the company had flown the chairman of the Joint Chiefs of Staff and the secretaries of the Air Force and Navy to the Bahamas for weekend parties. It was not unusual—nor is it today—for industry to court government officials. But more meaningful than a pleasure trip was the promise of jobs and infrastructure that military industries could bring to local communities. Furthermore, the American people were easily persuaded that heightened military expenditures equaled improved national security. As Charlie Wilson once remarked in understated fashion, "If we ever go to the American people and tell them that we are putting a balanced budget ahead of national defense it would be a terrible day."

The warning about the rise of a military-industrial complex would become the centerpiece of Ike's speech, and in the decades to follow his words remained the most referenced and widely misinterpreted statement in modern history—readily co-opted by the antiwar movements of the 1960s and beyond. The subtlety, the seriousness, and the measured tone were lost in the usual fight to paint things in black and white, swept up in the "sides"—something Ike never intended but which was probably inevitable. While it's true Ike was a measured commander in chief, his warning about the military-industrial complex was geared toward a more pervasive threat. He wasn't saying, as some believed, that there was too much military. His concern was how deeply the military economy had burrowed into communities across America. Every community that housed a military installation or a related manufacturing plant reaped jobs and welfare, and the citizens let their congressional representatives know they wanted to keep it that way. But how much influence was too much? How could wise minds in government and the military structure an effective yet not excessive defense apparatus when presented with a virtual blank check? How could the nation achieve real security without overspending? How could we thoughtfully respond to the pressures from the military to give more and more without abdicating the responsibility to be as strong as we could be? How could we face down communism, with moral as well as military might, without becoming a garrison state? And how could we balance the expenditures with the pressing priorities domestically?

What was the honorable course? What was the intelligent course? Where were the best minds to achieve this goal? When Ike appointed James Killian in 1956 to be his science advisor, many people in the Defense Department felt blindsided and there was a scuffle of controversy. "It was clear that the President's announcement of my appointment was viewed with some alarm by Secretary [Neil] McElroy [who had replaced Wilson as secretary of defense] because the press interpreted the appointment to mean that I was to serve as the President's lieutenant, to have responsibility for the missile program, and there were many statements in the press that I was to be the missile czar," Killian recalled. Killian had been involved in Ike's Technological Capabilities Panel, which was, in effect, a bulwark against military advisors—a balancing view. "My scientists," Ike called them fondly. Eisenhower received plenty of advice from his military advisors, but he sought a heavier weight on the opposite end of the seesaw to give him a full range of input. He wanted an objective view of the weapons development program. In the end, the Technological Capabilities Panel earned the support of the Department of Defense and, according to Killian, "reestablished a new confidence . . . between the scientific community and the government which had been badly impaired by the Oppenheimer case."

Ike was also intent on improving the scientific groundings of the nation's defense system, and to advance American prospects through a vital space program. At the same time he knew science and technology were not solely the domain of the military, but also the bedrock of domestic progress in areas like consumer technology and health care. Yet after World War II, the elevation of the physicist as a servant of military technology had become the norm. When people talked about the need for science and technology, too often they were speaking about missile capabilities. Throughout his presidency, Ike pressed for a sensible balance, but by the end he felt stymied by the sheer size and complexity of what had been created.

THE IDEA OF EXPRESSING his concerns about the military-industrial complex in a farewell speech did not just come to Ike in his final days. According to Hagerty, he had been talking about it since he became president. "We had many, many hours over the years alone—in a plane, in a car, in a hotel suite, for breakfast, for late dinner—where he would, to some extent, just let his hair down and I'd listen. The military-industrial complex was a rising concern to him from the day he became president."

Halfway through his second term, Ike told Hagerty, "Jim, I'm going to make this speech. I'm going to make it as the last major speech before I leave office." In 1959 and 1960, Ike and his speechwriters set to work on this final address, with the urgency of speaking in a sober way about this new reality high on everyone's minds. Crafting the original military-industrial complex premise, Malcolm Moos found what he saw as a tripod of concerns.

The first leg of the tripod involved the forceful presence—almost a takeover—of the military by industry. Some of the input for the idea came from Ike's own military advisors. Ike's naval aide, Captain Aurand, took to leaving piles of aerospace journals on Moos's desk. Paging through them, he counted some twenty-five thousand different companies involved in the military's aerospace efforts—a figure that alarmed Moos.

The second leg of the tripod involved the revolving door from the military to industry. Moos was working on a study tracing the number of people retiring from the military at young ages (in their forties) and immediately becoming directors of aerospace and other related industries. This idea never made it directly into the speech, but it was on Moos's mind—whether such a transfer of influence could be damaging. The implication, of course, was that a massive underhanded quid pro quo had become virtually institutionalized. As a side note, this concern continues today. In 2008 the Government Accountability Office found 2,435 former generals and senior officers employed by 52 large defense contractors—some working on the same contracts they oversaw while in service. This revelation led Congress to pass a law requiring the Pentagon to maintain a database of high-ranking military officials who pursued jobs with defense contractors. But according to a 2014 *Washington Post* investigation, the Pentagon failed to do so, calling the law "an unfunded mandate."

The third leg was the domination of military pursuits in the awarding of federal and private grants for scientific research—massive funding outlays that made the federal government and its military interests the de facto shaper of the knowledge industry. Again, not all of these ideas would make it into the speech, explicitly, but they unpinned Ike's broader argument.

Ralph E. Williams, a staff assistant to Aurand, summarized the concerns Moos expressed in an October 31 meeting on the subject—a week before the 1960 election:

> The problem of militarism—for the first time in its history, the United States as a permanent war-based industry . . . Not only that but flag and general officers retiring at an early age take positions in war based industrial complex shaping its decisions and guiding the direction of its tremendous thrust. This creates a danger that what the Communists have always said about us may become true. We must be very careful to insure that

the "merchants of death do not come to dictate national policy."

IKE'S FAREWELL ADDRESS WAS crafted against the backdrop of his own presidency. Certainly he'd had many opportunities to engage in land wars while he was president—not just Indochina. There was Germany, Formosa, Suez, and, of course, Cuba. As his presidency drew to a close, Ike still had something going for him that seemed lost on his political foes: eight years of peace. He came into office to end a war—Korea—just as he had ended the previous war, but as the civilian commander in chief, his primary intent was to prevent another one. Those who suggest he might have pursued a similar policy in Vietnam were he in office instead of Kennedy and Johnson, can only speculate. What *is* knowable is that Ike strongly felt the hill-by-hill, field-by-field process of ground wars was folly. Observing it in Korea sealed his conviction to end that war short of full victory. He used the threat of massive retaliation to force a negotiation.

In increasingly strident tones during the campaign, Kennedy had charged the Eisenhower administration—and by extension Nixon—with a flimsy if not coddling foreign policy. "In the last seven days," he cried, "Mr. Nixon has suggested that if he is elected president of the United States, he will go to Eastern Europe. He has also indicated if he is elected president of the United States, President Eisenhower will go to Russia. He has also indicated that if he is elected President of the United States, President Hoover and President Truman will also go behind the Iron Curtain. I want to make it clear that if I am elected president of the United States, I am going to Washington, D.C. If there is any lesson which this country should have learned in the last eight years, it is that the communist system and the communist leaders are not impressed by good will missions. They are impressed by the power, strength, and determination of the United States, and that is what must be built."

But what was he really saying? Ike found Kennedy's words empty, meant to stir the pot rather than strengthen America's hand. He feared the unschooled bluster of Kennedy, and worried the new president would rush carelessly into conflicts, would administer an untenable buildup of the war machine, and would not be a cautious steward of America's phenomenal power. He knew Kennedy planned to increase defense spending, which was already 50 percent of the federal budget.

Eisenhower recognized the nation was entering a new era; increasingly warfare was a matter of sophisticated weaponry and technologies capable of taking us places we might not want to go. The stakeholders in these developments were not necessarily wed to the people's principles of patriotism and the national interest. Increasingly they were from the ranks of scientists and the private sector—an influence Ike feared could unduly affect the decisions of elected officials.

The military that Ike now bequeathed to Kennedy bore little resemblance to the one Eisenhower had known when he first joined the Army. Instead of rifles, artillery cannons, and cavalry mounts, a dominant Cold War military needed a supply of high-altitude bombers, long-range submarines, intercontinental missiles, jet fighters, spy planes, radar networks, and more. The "permanent armaments industry" was now a requirement of a new era of weaponry, and he understood that necessity. From the speech:

Until the latest of our world conflicts, the United States had no armaments industry. American makers of plowshares could, with time and as required, make swords as well. But now we can no longer risk emergency improvisation of national defense; we have been compelled to create a permanent armaments industry of vast proportions. Added to this, three and a half million men and women are directly engaged in the defense establishment. We annually spend on military security more than the net income of all United States corporations.

But necessity or not, Ike fought the idea of being beholden to this new industrial reality. We needn't give over our precious heritage and "American way" to an overbearing mammoth. In the speech Ike acknowledged that research had become essential, but also more complex and costly—and too often at the expense of the federal government:

Today, the solitary inventor, tinkering in his shop, has been overshadowed by task forces of scientists in laboratories and testing fields. In the same fashion, the free university, historically the fountainhead of free ideas and scientific discovery, has experienced a revolution in the conduct of research. Partly because of the huge costs involved, a government contract becomes virtually a substitute for intellectual curiosity. For every old blackboard there are now hundreds of new electronic computers.

The prospect of domination of the nation's scholars by Federal employment, project allocations, and the power of money is ever present—and is gravely to be regarded.

Yet, in holding scientific research and discovery in respect, as we should, we must also be alert to the equal and opposite danger that public policy could itself become the captive of a scientific-technological elite.

Surely the man who had presided over the largest military expansion in American history was not having second thoughts about the buildup. How could a nation be both militarily strong and not beholden to a military-industrial complex? His views seemed to contradict each other. But as Ike prepared to leave office he had reached the conclusion that nuclear weapons were useless in procuring peace, and thus their expansion, at the expense of other interests, was indefensible and potentially dangerous.

Journalist Dean Abel reflected, "Ike, I think, was a very complicated man, and his relationship with the Pentagon was highlighted, I think, by a fairly sincere feeling that precisely because he was a professional soldier, he had to be a peace president."

The conflicts over our military buildup and the criticisms from Congress were so intense that at one point in early 1958, only three months after suffering his stroke, Ike put his head down on his desk one day and murmured, "I don't know whether my poor brain is going to be able to take it." But Ike was a natural optimist, in that he always believed that with time and consideration, no problem was unsolvable—even this one. Still, though he was strong and confident throughout the speech, Ike allowed a note of sadness at the end. Longing for peace, he could only glimpse its elusive glory.

Yet his ace in the hole in making the final appeal about the dangers of the military-industrial complex was, he knew, that in the eyes of the nation he was still *General* Eisenhower— they trusted his judgment. Bryce Harlow once observed that Ike *looked* like the American eagle—embodying the symbol of the nation. "And he had this astoundingly mobile face, which can look craggy one minute, and the next minute that warm, friendly grin of Ike of Kansas."

As the television cameras lit up Ike's face in his final address, Americans did not see the heady charisma of the New Frontier, but a sober veteran confronting a reality the nation was reluctant to face. "Surely, it is impressive that the old soldier should make this warning the main theme of his farewell address," wrote the prominent columnist Walter Lippmann the next day, adding that if it "were not a real and serious problem, General Eisenhower would not have devoted to it so much of the emphasis of his last official message to the Nation."

The media politely took note of Ike's farewell address, but few column inches were spent on its review. Ike "was striving to reach tomorrow's conscience, not today's headlines," Moos said. But he was also hoping Kennedy was listening.

PART THREE

THE FINAL MISSION

CHAPTER 10

AN UNKNOWABLE SUCCESSOR

January 18, 1961

Dressed in black tie for a family dinner-dance organized by his sister Jean Smith and her husband, Stephen, at their Georgetown home, on the evening of January 17, JFK stayed to watch the president on television before leaving for the party. Jackie had not yet arrived in Washington from Palm Beach, Florida, and he was alone. One can imagine Kennedy either watching the speech intently, or perhaps idly glancing at the screen while he fiddled with his tie, his thoughts miles away on his own inauguration.

However, there is reason to think Kennedy was paying attention, particularly as he prepared to give the speech of his life, three days from then. Historian Thurston Clarke, who wrote about Kennedy's inaugural speech, deemed Ike's farewell "both a stinging reply to Kennedy's campaign rhetoric and an advance rebuttal of his inaugural address." Clarke believed Eisenhower figured Kennedy would warn against American weakness in his speech—since that had been a key theme of his campaign— and Ike was preempting the attack by highlighting the size and strength of the military, to the point of suggesting that it was too influential.

On the morning of January 18, there was a sprinkling of media commentary on Ike's address. However, Kennedy made no public remarks about the speech or his reaction to it, and if he commented privately to his people, they never spoke of it. We do know that his private view of Eisenhower was never particularly admiring, in spite of their cordial first meeting on December 6, and at least one member of his transition team referred to meetings with the president as basically the necessity of protocol more than a source of vital information. If Kennedy *did* pay close attention to the speech, he might have taken exception to Ike's warning about the military-industrial complex— his worldview already established as more interventionist than Ike's, and also more on edge, as his claims about the missile gap evidenced.

In most respects, Kennedy, a son of privilege following a dynastic pathway, was unknowable to Ike. He was as different from Eisenhower as he could be, as well as from Truman, who didn't much care for him. JFK was named for his maternal grandfather, the notorious Boston politician John F. "Honey Fitz" Fitzgerald. In 1946, when Kennedy launched his political career by winning his grandfather's seat in Congress, Ike was busy receiving accolades as a war hero and planning the organization of a peacetime world. He was not then interested in politics, but certainly knew of JFK's father, Joe Kennedy, who was FDR's ambassador to Great Britain in 1937. The elder Kennedy's stance as a Chamberlain ally (and thus an alleged Hitler appeaser) led to a bitter rift with Roosevelt. Truman also despised Joe Kennedy, and during the campaign dustup about JFK's Catholicism quipped, "It's not the pope I'm afraid of, it's the pop."

The common narrative about the Kennedys—intact to this day—was that the patriarchal Joe Kennedy intended for his sons to be political giants, and they stood in line to follow his wishes. As a World War II hero, JFK was perfectly poised to accept the familial mandate to run for political office. The story of his bravery was well documented (indeed it would be highlighted in all of JFK's political campaigns); when a Japanese destroyer sank the PT 109, the boat Kennedy was commanding in the South Pacific, he saved ten of his men. Kennedy received the Navy and Marine Corp Medal and a Purple Heart for the wounds he suffered. In June 1944 the *New Yorker* dramatized the PT 109 incident in a five-thousand-word nonfiction article titled "Survival," which was reprinted in the mass-circulation monthly *Reader's Digest*. By the end of the war Kennedy was viewed as an up-and-comer. In fact, his first meeting with Eisenhower came in 1945 when he was asked to accompany Secretary of the Navy James Forrestal to the Potsdam meeting. Ike was at the airport to meet Forrestal, and the two future presidents shook hands for the first time. Later, as a senator, JFK rarely crossed paths with Ike.

Ike could find the Kennedy power train baffling, right down to the immaculately coutured family and the relentless displays of youthful vigor, all stamped with the patriarchal—and matriarchal—signature. Rose Kennedy was as overbearing as her husband, albeit in the domestic arena. Memos to Jackie were full of instructions: "Will you please remind Jack about his Easter duty; I'm sure that he could go to confession some morning in Washington as the church is quite near," or "Will you see about some old socks for Jack—for him to wear playing golf or walking in the rain. . . ." The Kennedy lifestyle seemed shallow but provocative, infused with tremendous cash. (In 1956, Ike had expressed dismay on hearing that Senator Kennedy was going to spend more than a million dollars on his reelection campaign, a sum Ike deemed "immoral.") During the election

Ike had been well aware of the contrast with Nixon, a tabloid illusion that unfairly cast the vice president in an unfavorable light. He was conscious of the visceral public longing for something fresh and new, even though the problems on the world stage were severe. They didn't go away because the population was in thrall to youth and glamour. This was a turning of the page, but the Democratic Party had to be dragged kicking and screaming into alignment.

According to Malcolm Moos, prior to the Democratic National Convention, after Congress had adjourned for the session, Speaker Rayburn and LBJ had dropped in to see Ike. Hammering his fist on the desk, Rayburn said they had to "go out there and lick that little bastard John Kennedy, and make Lyndon the President of the United States as the Democratic nominee." Ike roared. Then, a day before Johnson, now a candidate himself, flew to the convention, he visited Ike one more time. "Ike, for the good of the country, you cannot let that man become elected President . . . he's a dangerous man," he railed. But when Kennedy could not be thwarted, Johnson folded and agreed to become his vice presidential nominee. Typical Johnson, Ike thought. The truth was, Ike's relationship with Johnson had already begun to cool after a contentious year. Once Johnson was chosen as Kennedy's running mate, and entered the election season, there was no longer a forum for bipartisanship. Now they were clear adversaries, and Ike, who had never really trusted Johnson, despite courting him for pragmatic purposes, gave him little attention. He sent only the briefest one-sentence message of congratulations after the election. And since Johnson was well in the background during the transition, there was no collaboration between them.

Bryce Harlow perhaps captured the mood of the times best when he recalled a striking moment on the last day of the 1960 campaign when the two candidates were leaving a hotel in New York. "I paused just for an instant to glance at the television," Harlow said. "And there was Jackie and Jack, right there in the middle of that tube, smiling and talking to the American people. And I glanced and stopped there for a moment and watched them. And I walked out of there and I thought to myself, how in the world can anyone vote against a pair that is so incredibly lovely. . . . I think the country had there briefly the most spectacularly attractive personalities. And it just was a kind of flower that opened up and then the stem was plucked and away it went." In the minds of many voters, who didn't really know Kennedy very well, the optics overwhelmed everything else that season.

It's comforting to imagine that American history unravels in forward motion, the accomplishments of one administration building upon those of the last. But of course it has never been that way, so each retiring president, especially when the party changes, can be left with a sense of depression. Ike felt this deeply, and feared everything he'd worked so hard to achieve would be relegated to history's dustbin. He was sickened by concern that the New Frontier would be a wasteland. But if he allowed himself some brooding in the early days after the election, he quickly snapped back into action as the timeline advanced. In his leave-taking he felt compelled, in the manner of a general on a training mission, to guide and educate the young president-elect. Those around Ike saw no signs of a retiring mind. Rather, he was busier than ever. He saw the transition period as a final opportunity to put his stamp on the next president's term. And he would do that through what was later applauded as the most detailed and orderly transition in history—though it wasn't always easy to get Kennedy's people to sit still for the lessons.

The heady confidence—a sense of *we've got this*—pervading the Kennedy operation could be hard to stomach, even among some Kennedy loyalists. After Kennedy took office, Clark Clifford acknowledged, "the men around President Kennedy were inordinately cocky. It bothered me some."

Also, Ike found the media's slavish regard for his successor irritating. In particular, he cited the liberal syndicated columnist Ralph McGill, who he complained had sold himself on a "naïve belief that we have a new genius in our midst who is incapable of making any mistakes and therefore deserving of no criticism whatsoever."

Ike wanted to ensure that Kennedy and his advisors felt the full weight of the deeply complex and troubling issues on the table. Kennedy's view of Ike was that he was a passive president, who merely presided over the vast bureaucracy, not a fully responsive president, up to his elbows in the muck. No one who had ever been in Ike's orbit saw it that way. He was a card player to Kennedy's tag football team, shading his motivations and thoughts—his hidden hand—while Kennedy tackled issues on a public stage. The proof of Ike's engagement was in his accomplishments—the end of the Korean War, the creation of the Interstate Highway System, civil rights legislation, Cold War diplomacy that prevented a "hot war" in a charged environment. But his age and lack of pretension provided an opportunity for his critics to cast him as a benchwarmer.

Although during the campaign Kennedy had liked to portray Ike as a doddering chief executive whose best days were spent on the golf course, this was, in modern vernacular, nothing more than "throwing shade." Kennedy, too, was an avid golfer, but he played in secret. It was said that during the campaign he was playing golf one day in California, away from the cameras, when a tee shot on a par-three hole began rolling toward the hole. Kennedy shouted, "No! No!" and was relieved when it didn't go in. He explained if it had it was inevitable the news of the hole in one would get into the papers and he would be stained with the reputation of being another golfer seeking the White House. After the election he dropped his guard and played golf in Florida every day for a month. Kennedy had other things in common with Ike, including a love of bridge and westerns. The two men also shared an advertising agency—BBDO—to manage their very different images.

Kennedy's people underestimated Ike, and Clark Clifford, his transition front man, an esteemed Democratic Party member and advisor to Truman during his presidency (he was credited with masterminding Truman's 1948 election), tended to gaze longingly back to Truman, and many of his thoughts were culled from the archives of that administration—never mind how much the world had changed. This was in part a nod to party loyalty, but more directly it was a condemnation of Eisenhower's tenure. For his part, Kennedy viewed himself as the second coming of FDR, a forceful leader with a tight cadre of advisors.

Among Ike's chief concerns was the makeup of Kennedy's administration, how important it was to bring in the best minds and most experienced advisors. Arthur Larson once told a revealing story about Ike. During a campaign one of his team was complaining about all the things going wrong. Ike grumbled to a friend, "I wish these amateurs wouldn't bother me," to which his friend replied, "There are two professions in which the amateurs always think they are better than the professionals—military strategy and prostitution." He knew how important experience could be in the gut-check, war-room moments, and he hoped Kennedy was choosing a strong team.

To this end, JFK did make an effort toward continuity. He

retained Allen Dulles, brother of the late secretary of state, as director of the CIA. J. Edgar Hoover would also remain FBI director.

In their December 6 meeting, Kennedy had asked to keep Andy Goodpaster for at least two months. General Goodpaster, Eisenhower's staff secretary and invaluable military advisor (and some said "alter ego"), was a soldier through and through, who was looking forward to his new commission as deputy commander of the Third Division in Germany. Ike told Kennedy that Goodpaster deserved and desired this assignment, but Kennedy wanted him to stay on for a time, and urged Ike to make it happen and see to it that he could then take his command. Well, Ike reminded him, you'll be the commander in chief, so you can do whatever you like. Ike didn't necessarily approve of the deal, but he did see it as a sign Kennedy appreciated the solemnity of the task ahead and the need to have the very best people by his side.

Kennedy's most surprising and controversial appointment was the choice of his brother and campaign manager, Robert, only thirty-five, as attorney general. In the decision one could see the hand of Joe Kennedy, who pressured Kennedy to appoint his brother, even knowing how such nepotism would be criticized. Once the selection was made, the pressure was on for Democrats to get behind the choice. Although there was no love lost between LBJ and Bobby Kennedy, Johnson went to bat for the appointment. LBJ told Bobby Baker, his protégé and now the secretary to Mike Mansfield, the vice president–elect's replacement as Senate majority leader, "I want you to lead all our Southern friends in here by their ying-yangs" to support RFK, claiming it was a matter of personal survival for him. Those who argued that JFK's relationship with his brother was no different than the one between Ike and Milton missed the point that Milton never had a government office—much less one as significant as attorney general, a position notable for its required independence from the White House.

There had been times during his presidency when Ike was asked why he didn't give Milton a cabinet position. He certainly had the qualifications. But Ike felt strongly the cabinet should be a team of equals. If one of them was the brother of the president, he knew others would instinctively defer to him. It was just human nature, and he wanted to avoid it.

RFK's youth might have bothered Ike as well, as he said, "One of my biggest concerns is that government be run by wisdom instead of by callow youth." But JFK disarmed the protests with a funny quip: "You know there are a number of people who have complained bitterly about my appointing Bobby, my brother, as Attorney General," he said. "But I just tell them. I say, 'Friend, he's got to get experience someplace.'"

There was another potential appointment that stuck in Ike's craw. His undersecretary of state, Douglas Dillon, had been approached by Kennedy to serve as secretary of the Treasury, and in a blisteringly frank letter, Ike advised him to reject the offer. He warned Dillon he risked becoming "a scapegoat of the radicals," arguing, "You and I are both dedicated to the prevention of debasement of our currency through any cause, domestic or foreign. I can think of no one who could do this better than you, provided you were working with a President who agreed with you in this philosophy"—which, he warned Dillon, Kennedy did not. A lifelong Republican, Dillon was a surprising choice for Kennedy, and also a controversial one among liberals, but he personally did not think there was a substantive philosophical difference between Eisenhower and Kennedy. Although Dillon's first reaction on being approached by Kennedy's people had been "You're crazy," he came around to the idea and did not take Ike's advice. He would serve as secretary of the Treasury under both Kennedy and Johnson, leaving the post in 1965. However, Ike's forceful, uncharacteristically harsh letter was a sign of how deeply troubled he was about the future. The trend lines of the election bothered him, as he would later write in his memoir, reflecting that the campaign illustrated several things. "It showed the influence of television: for some reasons one man projects well, another does not. It showed again how much elections can be controlled by sentiment and emotion rather than by facts and experience. And it showed the successful appeals to large interest groups." None of these were comfortable truths. Uneasily, Ike vowed to do what he could in his remaining days.

Since their meeting on December 6, the vast mechanism of the federal government was shifting gears, preparing for the incoming administration. Few people appreciate how enormous the task of transition actually is. Even before the election, Kennedy had asked Clifford and Richard Neustadt to prepare a detailed memo for the transition, saying, "I don't want to wake up on the morning of November 9 and have to ask myself, 'What in the world do I do now?'" In his initial report, Clifford definitively set the stage for a new era. "The turning over of government to a Democratic President elected today differs substantially from the transition to President-elect Eisenhower in 1952. Much of the 1952–53 experience is irrelevant." In spite of this tone, the transition proceeded well. There had been talk early on that Ike was a bit "peevish" about having Kennedy people wandering around the White House willy-nilly. But if so, his main concern was that the transition be kept orderly, with Jerry Persons and Clifford being the main points of contact. It helped that Persons and Clifford were social friends. There was no animus. They were the adults in the room, older and presumably wiser than the young people flooding JFK's administration. They knew how to put their cards on the table and avoid power struggles and demoralizing spats. The two men spoke several times a day, and saw each other two or three times a week. Persons arranged for Clifford's staffers to have desks in the various cabinet offices and even put them on the payroll beginning New Year's Day so they wouldn't be working for free. Serving as backup for Clifford were the stalwarts of the Kennedy inner circle—Ted Sorensen, Arthur Schlesinger Jr., and Pierre Salinger—who would remain his closest aides.

IKE BELIEVED THE PEACEFUL handover of power was a signature achievement of democracy—no matter the size of the victory, which in Kennedy's case was fewer than 120,000 votes. At the same time, the process was fraught with an opportunity for mischief. You had a sitting president, a lame duck with all the authority of the office, and a president-elect with an outstanding pulpit but no authority.

There hadn't been a presidential transition of any kind for twenty years when Ike took office, so the process was rusty. And in Ike's mind, never before had the stakes been so high. True, previous presidents had faced the Great Depression and the daunting burdens of world war, but Ike's peacetime handover carried the pressing dangers of the nuclear age and the kinds of threats requiring strategic minds and well-honed bureaucratic skills to manage America's might.

Ike was intimately familiar with how difficult the transition process could be, dependent as it was on the goodwill of two men, often from different parties. Until 1936–37, the presidential transition period was longer, with the inauguration on March 4, leaving plenty of room for the collision of opposing visions. This was most vividly illustrated by the changeover from

Hoover to FDR. With the economy collapsing around them, Hoover and Roosevelt took to their respective corners and essentially did nothing. Hoover wanted Roosevelt more engaged; Roosevelt didn't want to dirty his hands with Hoover's crisis. When Hoover asked him to participate in naming delegates to an urgent global economic summit, Roosevelt was curt, writing to Hoover, "I think you will recognize that it would be unwise for me to accept an apparent joint responsibility with you when, as a matter of constitutional fact, I would be wholly lacking in any attendant authority."

Hoover kept asking, and Roosevelt deflected. As a result, the Great Depression grew worse during the long months between the election and the inauguration. Although Hoover tried to place some of the blame on Roosevelt's inaction, historical scorekeepers put the Depression on Hoover's tally sheet, while crediting Roosevelt with the recovery. In fairness to Roosevelt, his reluctance to sign on to Hoover's plan was his prerogative and completely understandable. His New Deal was a vastly different strategy than Hoover's.

On the other end of the spectrum, Harry Truman had no transition at all, and had been vice president less than three months when Roosevelt died. There was no chance for a learning curve, and notably, he approved dropping the atom bomb on Hiroshima and Nagasaki within *four months* of taking office. In effect, the nuclear age was launched by a man with slim to no experience in the Oval Office.

Of his own transition after the 1952 election, Ike said very little, and never explained precisely why he gave Truman the cold shoulder, though the feeling was obviously mutual. The simplest—and most disheartening—explanation is the two men had become engaged in an unbreakable grudge match made up of perceived betrayals and slights, which neither was interested in resolving. Truman, who had once so passionately urged Ike to run for president when he thought he could be a Democratic Party standard-bearer, haughtily said of him once he was elected, "Poor Ike. It won't be a bit like the Army. He'll sit here and he'll say, 'Do this, do that,' and nothing will happen." Thus, Truman's intransigent partisanship, coupled with Ike's dislike of political gamesmanship, fueled a mutual mistrust so great that when Truman seemed to offer an olive branch during the transition, Ike stiffly rejected it.

Surprisingly, the two men's first and only transition meeting, on November 18, 1952, was surrounded with fanfare, orchestrated by Truman. Eisenhower landed in Washington to crowds lining the roads, including government workers given the day off by Truman for the occasion. But when Truman greeted Ike at the White House, both men were solemn and unbending.

Truman spoke of the need for continuity, and pressed Ike to collude on key foreign policy statements. Ike, according to Truman, had a "chip on his shoulder," and the meeting was testy. Ike assumed the whole show was a trap designed to humiliate him. In fact, according to Emmet John Hughes, Ike's speechwriter at the time, the "mere mention of Harry Truman's name brought fast flashes of antipathy."

More substantively, coming into office Ike had very strong feelings about the ways in which Truman's stewardship had strayed away from America's best interests. He felt the nation's prestige had been damaged by "numerous instances of malfeasance in office, disrespect for fiscal responsibility, apparent governmental ignorance or apathy about the penetration of Communists in government, and a willingness to divide industrial America against itself." Truman took the criticism personally and couldn't rise above it.

As a result, Ike did not have the advantage of much wise

counsel during his transition, and while he never admitted missing out, he eventually realized that a more orderly and in-depth consult was needed.

Ike's reflections on the transition period even led him to conclude the inauguration should happen earlier than January and the date of the election pushed back. "I think that we ought to get a constitutional amendment to change the time of the inauguration and to give dates for election and assumption of office in such fashion that a new President ought to have at least eighty days or something of that kind before he meets his first Congress," he told the press. A possible change was for the election to be held in September, with the inauguration before the end of the year. Ike thought it was silly that the sitting president had to go before Congress to give a State of the Union address mere days before the new president took office. His own final State of the Union address on January 12 was not delivered personally but was read into the record by the House clerk, and was barely a blip on the public screen, as the nation and Washington were consumed with inaugural plans. In fact, only forty Democrats and fifty Republicans bothered to attend the reading. It lacked all the fanfare and gravitas of previous speeches before joint sessions of the House and Senate, with crowded galleries and television lights. But it delivered a final jab at the party preparing to take office—as one Republican put it, the speech "throws away much of the smog and murk which all too frequently occurred in the last political campaign." Still, it was more a summary of the past than a challenge for the future.

Furthermore, there was the obligation, on January 16, to send his final budget, for fiscal 1962, to Congress—the largest to date at $80.9 billion—to which Senate Majority Leader Mike Mansfield responded, "Very interesting. Now we'll wait and see what the real budget looks like." Fair enough, as the new president would be taking office four days later.

In manner, Ike determined to be solemn and circumspect during the transition, offering support and counsel but staying somewhat removed from the fanfare. He was determinedly not thin-skinned, as Truman had been, even though he must have known how the incoming team felt about him.

And make no mistake about it, there *was* sniping beneath the surface—typical generational putdowns that didn't account for much but were prevalent nevertheless. Ike, much sharper than the Kennedy gang gave him credit for, sensed these attitudes, and responded by rising above them to show full respect. Believing in the office above the man, he never uttered a public word of personal criticism about Kennedy, and did not allow his people to do so, either.

IKE COULD STILL REMEMBER the overwhelming sense of responsibility that settled on a new president, an atmosphere of chaos thwarting the best-laid plans. His own first days in office were such a mad swirl of activity he loudly complained at one point, "When does a man get a chance to think around here?" For him the leadership and organization of the office of the presidency had some parallels to the military. Once stripped of the romanticism attached to either field, these were systems demanding careful calibration and a clear eye. Too often people were in thrall to the individuals who led them. Hero worship was the realm of boys playing soldiers, not men leading battalions. It warped perceptions. Eisenhower had a near reverence for the structure of leadership—the coordination and interaction of agencies, the many spokes of the giant wheels of power. He took great pains to impress these things on his successor, mindful that many of Kennedy's young team thought him a fogey. And while it was true that Kennedy had been a heroic leader in his small corner of the war, he wasn't an *organiza-*

tional leader, and he spoke often about his distaste for a layered bureaucracy.

People might joke about overreliance on administrative details or structural diagrams, but in Ike's long experience, these could have tremendous consequences. A disorganized mind, a shoot-from-the-hip style of leadership wasn't appropriate to the modern complexities of the presidency. General Goodpaster recalled a conversation he had with Nixon after it became apparent he would be the Republican nominee in early 1960. Goodpaster was appalled by the chaotic manner in which the vice president ran his office. He sat him down and said, "Now look, you're going to be running for the presidency. You'll be dealing with all kinds of people. Many of them are sensitive, and many of them are even important or they think they are, and the kinds of letters you write me I take it are a fair sample of the kinds of letters that go out of your office. Sometimes they come a month late or two months late, and sometimes I don't know for whom they're intended. Now the president has a system under which letters get answered within two or three days, and no matter where he is, whether he's in Washington or Paris." In other words, Goodpaster stressed, Ike's White House was a well-run, disciplined shop, and these things mattered.

Goodpaster hastened to explain that Ike wasn't a slave to bureaucracy—just that he expected an orderly discipline. To that end, before he left office, Ike told Goodpaster—and likely others—"I want you to leave things in your area in apple pie order for my successor. I want everything cleaned up so that when I go out of office and the new administration comes in, it's ready to roll."

In sum, Ike was a field commander—a leader by training and by nature, and in Goodpaster's view that meant he had a gift for discarding the trivial and getting to the heart of the matter, and he expected his team to cultivate similar qualities. Ike might not have been an experienced politician when he became president, but he was an experienced military commander, and as such his meetings with military leaders had far more depth and breadth than was typical. He knew what they were talking about; he spoke their language.

Kennedy, aware he'd barely squeaked out a victory in the election, while Ike's two elections had been landslides and his popularity was intact, was overtly gracious. The gossipy tidbits would not emerge until much, much later. One of these involved Mamie Eisenhower's reception of Jackie Kennedy, which was awkward, at least in the timing. Jackie visited the White House a mere two hours after leaving Georgetown University Hospital, where she had prematurely delivered a son, John F. Kennedy Jr., by Caesarian, fourteen days earlier. Concerned about Jackie's well-being during the long tour, Mamie had asked that a wheelchair be available in case she should want it, but Jackie chose to walk alone with Mamie through what must have been a grueling tour. Accounts of the day paint Mamie in a harsh light. Usher J. B. West implied Mamie had not offered the wheelchair, yet Jackie herself told the press that day she knew of the wheelchair and thought it was "very gracious" of Mamie, but it was her decision to walk. West said Jackie had told him she was afraid to ask the first lady for the wheelchair. In a breathy description, taped much later, Jackie was very critical of Mamie, and said following the visit she had "a weeping fit that lasted two days." Frankly, the whole story seems puzzling, as Jackie was hardly a shrinking violet, and Mamie had earned a reputation for being a gracious hostess, who surely would have accommodated Jackie if she or her aides had expressed the need.

Jackie also spoke about how shabby the White House was, describing the family quarters as having all the style of a low-class hotel. She compared the upstairs Oval Sitting Room to the Lubyanka—the Moscow prison—and complained about

Mamie's color schemes, especially the "ghastly pink." If nothing else, the remarks underscored an attention to style, if not an elitism, that the more homespun Eisenhowers, veterans of Army housing, would not have appreciated. It's unfortunate this anecdote is the sole takeaway of Mamie and Jackie's meeting— especially since their husbands went to such great lengths to put forth a picture of cooperation and respect.

"Eisenhower didn't like the man, but he revered the office," said presidential historian Timothy J. Naftali, whose lecture "The Peacock and the Bald Eagle: The Remarkable Relationship Between JFK and Eisenhower," explored the ways the two men worked out their differences, even into JFK's term. He credited Eisenhower with having a "superhuman ability" to not undermine Kennedy—and that was ultimately good for the country.

On January 18, the day after his farewell address, Ike held his last press conference—his one hundred and ninety-third. The press never seemed to "get" Ike. He wasn't politically driven, wasn't interested in seducing them. Pressured to finally attend a cocktail party for the White House press corps, he grumbled, "I am to drop in for the purpose, I suppose, of showing that I am not too high-hat to do so." He didn't care for the press's obsession with personalities and gossip, feeling it played to the lowest nature of mankind. If some in the press faulted Ike for being distant and removed, the facts tell another story. In the first year of his presidency Ike gave thirty-three press conferences—and he continued a similar number throughout two terms. JFK would give eighteen press conferences in his first year, and by the time Reagan was elected, the average annual number was down to six. (Obama averaged between seven and eight a year.)

Jerry Persons believed any difficulty Ike had with the press was the result of his being an atypical political animal. "I don't think the Washington press really understood Eisenhower, or perhaps some of them didn't want to understand him," he mused. "They were so accustomed to dealing with politicians to whom publicity is life-blood that they couldn't bring themselves to believe that a man in public life didn't strive to get all the publicity possible." It's very likely this lack of understanding resulted in Ike constantly being underestimated and rarely getting the credit he deserved for his boldest moves.

"He was not very good in his press conferences," said *Newsweek*'s Kenneth Crawford—noting that these were the only occasions the press met with Ike, as he didn't give private interviews. "He was called 'Bubblehead' by some of the people, because he seemed to bumble in news conferences." However, with hindsight Crawford was more generous in evaluating Ike's administration. "The Eisenhower administration was not an innovator," he said. "It was rather a consolidator. And although I was not in sympathy with that at the time, as a matter of hindsight, it seems to me it was perhaps a fairly wise course at the time."

Additionally, Ike was consumed with the same frustrations every president, regardless of party, comes to feel—the press is too subjective, and too opinionated (at the expense of reporting facts). And the press, as always, compiled its own list of slights. It was the way the world turned, and although the makeup of the media would change substantively in the coming decades, this aspect was baked into the cake.

AT 3:55 P.M. ON January 18, Ike swept into the press room for the last time, smiling and confident. "I came this morning not with any particularly brilliant ideas about the future," he told the packed room of reporters, "but I did want the opportunity to say goodbye to people that I have been associated with now for eight years, mostly, I think on a friendly basis. . . ." He flashed his big smile, and the reporters laughed.

He began with a personal acknowledgment to Jack Romagna, the White House stenographer, whose nimble pen had raced across the page to record every press conference he had given—and that of Truman and FDR before Ike. Reporters cheered the quiet, self-effacing Romagna. None of them—least of all Romagna—could predict that months later he would be summarily fired by Press Secretary Pierre Salinger. The ostensible reason was that new technology was making his job obsolete. But insiders whispered the real reason for his dismissal was that he "slugged" (titled) a transcript of a telephone conversation JFK had with a mayors' conference in Miami as coming from the White House swimming pool. It was the kind of thin-skinned reaction not seen in Ike's White House.

Of course the press wanted to know Ike's impression of Kennedy, an obvious nonstarter for a man who never talked about personalities. "Well, now you know, that's the last thing I would do," he chided, but added he thought the transition was going "splendidly."

Basking a bit in the positive media about his speech the night before, Ike did not hesitate to further elaborate on the military-industrial complex, although there were relatively few questions about it. One from William McGaffin of the *Chicago Daily News:* "Mr. President, you sounded a warning last night of the dangers to our democratic process implicit in unparalleled peacetime military establishment. But some of your critics contend that one liberty, the people's right to know, has suffered under your administration because you have tolerated the abuse of executive privilege in the Defense Department and other departments and agencies and because you did not hold frequent enough press conferences."

Ike shrugged off the question, saying, "Well, they are critics and they have the right to criticize." But when Lillian Levy of the Science Service asked him to elaborate on his warning to the nation about a military-industrial complex, he was happy to do so. "When you see almost every one of your magazines, no matter what they are advertising, has a picture of the Titan missile or the Atlas or solid fuel or other things, there is becoming a great influence, almost an insidious penetration of our own minds that the only thing this country is engaged in is weaponry and missiles," he said. "And I'll tell you, we just can't afford to do that. The reason we have them is to protect the great values in which we believe, and they [our values] are far deeper even than our own lives and our own property, as I see it." He added that only an informed citizenry could stop the abuse.

When asked about his accomplishments, Ike pointed proudly to the patience and skill that kept the nation at peace during a combustible eight years. Pointing out that during this time our enemies developed strong missile programs and there were ongoing threats from the Chinese and the Soviet Union, he noted it was our consistent show of resolve and strength that prevented the worst from happening. Had we displayed moral or physical weakness it would have given the enemy the opening it needed. This was Ike's long-held position against the potential for aggression, and it had worked for him.

As for the greatest problem confronting his successor, Ike told the press, "Well, I think that is answered almost by the fact that the thing that causes all our problems is the intransigent, unreasonable attitude of the Communist bloc and therefore his basic problem and as a matter of fact not just the president, everyone else's, is what to do to keep ourselves strong and firm and yet conciliatory in trying to meet this—this terrible problem that is none of our making."

As for his predictions for the economy, Ike joked, "While I'm one of seven sons, I'm not the seventh son of a seventh son, so I'm not a prophet."

A poignant moment came when Ike was asked what kind of a United States he would like his grandchildren to live in. "I'd say in a peaceful world and enjoying all of the privileges and carrying forward all of the responsibilities envisioned for the good citizens of the United States, and this means among other things the effort always to raise the standards of our people in their spiritual, their intellectual, their economic strength. . . ."

When he was done, the reporters, whose difficult relationship with Ike was a matter of record, gave him a standing ovation as he left the room. He responded with the wide grin that had seldom been seen in press conferences before that day.

ALTHOUGH TWO DAYS FROM now he would be accompanying his successor to the Capitol, his work was not finished. The following day he would have his most important meeting with Kennedy, and that was his focus.

Ike was increasingly sober and thoughtful in his leave-taking. Walking through the White House with Admiral Aurand during those last days, he said, "You know, I've seen men who faced death and took it calmly, and who've been through all kinds of things without a tremor of emotion, come into this place with tears in their eyes."

CHAPTER 11

THE DAY BEFORE

January 19, 1961

The morning of his last full day in office, Ike sat at his desk and wrote a letter to Richard Nixon. His reason was twofold. First, he wanted to soothe his vice president, who was receiving mocking treatment in defeat, including a brutal joke from JFK making the rounds: "If I've done nothing else for this country, I've saved them from Dick Nixon." More important, though, Ike wanted to point a way to the future. Nixon, who had turned forty-eight ten days earlier, was still a young man with a political career ahead of him, if he wanted it. Ike might have also sought to offer an unspoken apology for an embarrassing moment during the campaign. Ike had been asked at a press conference if he could name a major idea of Nixon's he had adopted as president. Caught off guard Ike stumbled and replied, "If you give me a week, I might think of one. I don't remember." Ike said he'd meant it in a joking manner, the result of a barrage of questions about Nixon's influence, and hadn't intended it to be read as a slam at Nixon's contribution and abilities. Not that anyone believed him.

In the end, Nixon was perhaps done in by his personality as much as anything. As Eisenhower's personal secretary, Ann

Whitman, who had been by his side for eight years, wrote in her diary, remarking on the difference between her boss and Nixon, "The President is a man of integrity and sincere in his every action. . . . He radiates this, everybody knows it, everybody trusts and loves him. But the Vice President sometimes seems like a man who is acting like a nice man rather than being one."

Now Ike wrote to Nixon, encouraging him to press on: "The passage of years has taken me out, so far as active participation is concerned, but the future can still bring to you a real culmination in your service to the country. . . . As you know, I am not an individual that accepts defeat easily. When I have to recognize a major set-back, my sole reaction is to redouble the effort in order to recover lost ground."

Ike had to acknowledge Nixon had been gracious and pitch perfect in accepting defeat. In his role as president of the Senate, he even had to preside over the Electoral College roll call. Taking his place for what promised to be a humiliating moment, Nixon turned it around. "This is the first time in one hundred years that a candidate for the presidency announced the result of an election in which he was defeated," Nixon said. "I do not think we could have a more striking and eloquent example of the stability of our constitutional system." His attitude won him much praise.

Ike's final meeting with Kennedy was scheduled for nine that morning. The president viewed it as a brass-tacks summit, a chance to talk at length about the most pressing matters Kennedy would face in only one day's time. Unlike the December 6 meeting, which was introductory in nature, Ike planned a more strenuous—and even dramatic—meeting. Under threatening skies that would dump eight inches of snow on Washington in the coming hours, Ike completed the final acts of his presidency.

Shortly before the hour, Kennedy, accompanied only by the Secret Service, drove through the northwest gate and to the West Wing entrance. Jerry Persons met him there and ushered him into the Oval Office. To Kennedy's eye, Ike looked "very fit, pink cheeked and unharassed," although the president confessed he had been busier in the period of his leave-taking than he'd been when he first took office. For their private meeting, Ike decided to show JFK exactly how much power was at his fingertips at every moment. A president has to know the procedures that would get action in the worst-case scenario, he told Kennedy, and pointed out an officer sitting outside the door, carrying a satchel containing nuclear codes and a method for the president to instantly communicate with the Strategic Air Command. Would Kennedy like to see an example of the power a president had at hand if he had to rapidly leave the White House? Kennedy smiled and said yes. Ike reached over, pressed a button, and said, "Opal Drill Three." Only six minutes later, a helicopter landed on the lawn outside the Oval Office, ready to whisk the president away. Kennedy seemed to enjoy the display, although some of his aides would later joke about it. Ike's point was that only so much could be communicated with words; sometimes you had to see it with your own eyes.

On a more sober note, the two men had perhaps the most thoughtful and deep conversation of their relationship. "Neither of us apparently felt any impulse to minimize the significance of the transfer of immense responsibilities, now only hours away," Ike wrote. He enjoyed the intimacy of these one-on-one meetings far more than the more formal Cabinet Room gatherings that followed, and he lingered over the discussion. Eyeball to eyeball, he hoped to draw Kennedy into candid conversation. Once again Ike observed that despite his youth and relative inexperience, Kennedy was a quick learner, with a sharp mind and a willingness to study the reams of position papers he had to read and process. In their conversation, the president-elect was unfailingly polite and deferential, which Ike felt masked his true feelings. Ike never would know for sure what Kennedy thought, and the full content of their last private conversation was never detailed in a memo, as their first conversation had been. In *Waging Peace,* Ike only referenced it in a cursory way—with the exception of the helicopter demonstration. And, of course, Kennedy did not live to write a memoir. But Ike did say in an interview years after leaving office that they completely avoided one topic: politics.

After forty-five minutes, they rose and walked together into the Cabinet Room to join the larger meeting with key players, past and present: the outgoing and incoming secretaries of state, Christian Herter and Dean Rusk; secretaries of defense Thomas Gates and Robert McNamara; Secretary of the Treasury Bob Anderson and his presumptive heir, Douglas Dillon; as well as Persons and Clifford.

Though less enjoyable to Ike than the private discussions, this would turn into an extremely important meeting—in many respects a haunting prelude to Kennedy's most troubling conflicts in office: Laos and Cuba.

Ike began by asking Herter to speak about the existing crisis in Laos. The world did not pause to wait respectfully for a new president to take his seat. In particular, the danger Laos might fall to the communists was real and present. The Soviets, said Herter, were basically acting as troublemakers in the area, as if testing Western resolve. Kennedy came away from the meeting feeling Ike supported military intervention if it was necessary to stave off the communists. In later years both Kennedy and Johnson would cite Ike's tacit approval of this strategy. And while it was true Ike said, "We cannot let Laos fall to the Communists even if we have to fight—with our allies or without them," he asserted one giant caveat his successors largely ignored: "It's my conviction that if we ever have to resort to force, there's just one thing to do: clear up the problem completely. We should not allow a situation to develop, costly in both blood and treasure, without achieving our objective."

But the most immediate crisis they discussed that day was the one occurring only ninety miles off America's shores. On New Year's Day, 1959, the revolutionary guerrilla leader Fidel Castro had toppled the corrupt Cuban dictatorship of Fulgencio Batista, driving Batista out of the country. At first the United States was hopeful of a positive change, since Castro's early statements indicated he was willing to establish an elected presidency, and many Latin American nations were lining up in support. But then the wholesale murder of Batista's loyalists began, and by March the State Department was reporting that communists were insinuating themselves into the military and government. Accolades for the new regime came from both China and the Soviet Union.

Ike was appalled when the American Society of Newspaper Editors invited Castro to speak in Washington in April. Ike refused to meet him personally, deliberately planning a golf trip. He put Secretary of State Herter in charge. He also sent Nixon in his stead. Castro arrived in all his guerrilla glory, with army uniform and boots and a bushy beard, delighting the media as he chowed down on hot dogs, kissed babies, and charmed the country. His charisma created a headache for the administration, which was well aware of Castro's ruthlessness. Notwithstanding Castro's personal appeal, Herter was struck by how naïve Castro was: he "was very much like a child in many ways, quite immature regarding problems of government." Nixon's account of the meeting strengthened the fear Castro would be a more vicious dictator than Batista. At one point Nixon challenged him, asking, "Before you came to power you indicated that within a reasonable time there would be elections. When will elections be held?"

"The Cuban people have no faith in elections," Castro said in a boastful manner. "They want me. They want Fidel Castro, and I'm going to run the country."

Although he claimed not to be a communist, Castro embraced the support of communists in the region, and it quickly became apparent communism now had a significant beachhead off our shores. Throughout 1960, Castro expropriated American properties, nationalized refineries, and made it virtually impossible for the United States to continue doing business there. In October, Ike placed an embargo on exports to Cuba, even as Castro increasingly collaborated with the Soviet Union. By January, the United States had broken off diplomatic relations with Cuba, which was now a ticking time bomb off our southern coast.

This was, to say the least, a missed opportunity for Castro. Had he chosen differently, Cuba might have become a beacon of democracy and prosperity, whose influence would have lifted the foundering boats of his region. American trade would have enriched Cuba beyond all measure, and its cultural wealth would have been equally substantial. Instead, by choosing to align himself with the Soviet Union, he doomed his country to a miserable existence and took on the United States with revolutionary fervor.

The mass executions horrified Ike, but he understood Cuba was an incredibly tricky problem, because Castro was viewed as a hero throughout Latin America. Ike wrote, "They saw him as a champion of the downtrodden and the enemy of the privileged who, in most of their countries, controlled both wealth and governments. His crimes and wrongdoings that so repelled the more informed peoples of the continent had little effect on the young, the peons, the underprivileged, and all others who wanted to see the example of revolution followed in their own nations." Ike warned against underestimating Castro—he referred to him as "a little Hitler"; how to handle him was a more difficult matter.

Throughout 1960, Castro had ramped up the threat, making him a significant target of Kennedy during the campaign. Whatever the failures of the administration in preventing Castro's assault on democracy, Kennedy's words seemed hollow and bereft of practical strategies, with crowd-pleasing but empty lines directed at Nixon, such as, "If you can't stand up to Castro, how can you be expected to stand up to Khrushchev?" What Nixon could not say was that during that time the United States was covertly training Cuban exiles in Guatemala, preparing for the vague eventuality they might be used in an operation against Cuba. These were the most passionate anti-Castro forces on the planet, but what they had in the sheer desire to overthrow the regime, they lacked in organization and leadership.

Now in the meeting with Kennedy and his team, Ike laid out the situation. The Cuban exiles were being trained under the auspices of the CIA, and an assault was in the early planning stages. But lest anyone think the forces were ready to go, Ike emphasized to Kennedy that certain conditions would have to be in effect for it to be even remotely feasible. These included having a viable government in exile, as well as an individual who could serve as a replacement for both Batista and Castro. No such leader had emerged. He remarked that despite having created the paramilitary force, we were not obligated to use it. In Ike's eyes it was only one option, not the only or even the best option. Unfortunately, Kennedy and his advisors heard a different message in that meeting—with disastrous consequences. They would later say they had the impression Ike was urging them to go ahead, when actually he was urging them to be cautious. It should be noted that Eisenhower and his senior aides insisted Ike was always extremely careful and precise in his remarks; Kennedy's assertions to the contrary notwithstanding, he did not give a de facto go-ahead to an invasion.

But that morning Ike felt he'd done the best he could do to hand over wisdom and a template about how the new administration might begin. As he rose to leave, Kennedy shook Ike's hand quite sincerely. "Thank you for giving us everything we asked for, and even quite a few things we haven't, because we didn't know to ask for them," he said with a smile. It was, Ike mused, impossible to fully impart the extreme nature of White House life—an obligation that never lifted. One could work more than twenty-four hours a day, if such hours existed, and the desk was never cleared. But the most valuable currency a president had was the nation's trust and respect.

Here we can step back and reflect on what Eisenhower was trying to accomplish in those final days. He was handing over the presidency at a point of extreme complexity on the world stage to a man with little direct experience of global issues. While the United States had not marched onto battlefields since the end of the Korean War in 1953, Cold War tensions had only heightened. Potential hotspots in Laos, Cuba, and Berlin could erupt to put the United States, the Soviet Union, and China on a war footing, and that war could be nuclear. So in a sense the security of the nation was in greater jeopardy than it had been in a pre-atomic age. Hot-headed, unpredictable personalities like Castro, and often unreadable and inconsistent foes like Khrushchev, who wished America harm, could not merely be "handled" by rhetorical bravado; nor could the menace they posed be ignored. What pleased the crowds during election campaigns gave way to the grinding work of diplomacy and intelligence.

When he ran for president, Ike had had the benefit of understanding the seriousness of these negotiations; he had done them all before during and after the war. As president he built a layered fail-safe of advisors, much as he had in the war when each option debated literally had life-and-death consequences. Presidential decisions were often more nuanced than they were in wartime, but he trusted his system to steer him in the right direction. During his meetings with Kennedy he took pains to urge the president-elect to keep the structure in place. It had immeasurable value. Kennedy nodded and smiled, but it wasn't his way and he had no intention of doing it.

KENNEDY LEFT THE WHITE House as snow flurries began, for a busy afternoon of receptions, culminating with a private conference with Truman, who had arrived for the inauguration. Meanwhile, throughout the afternoon John Eisenhower went from office to office, accompanied by two janitors, collecting the last of the presidential papers that remained in circulation. The accumulated paper filled eight safes, and by the time he was done, the offices were completely free of all paperwork. As he finished he looked outside to see heavy snow still falling. At six thirty he took a call from the secretary of defense. "Tell your Dad that I'm turning out the whole Army to keep the streets clean," he said. In the course of the night, three thousand men and seven hundred plows would tackle the massive plowing effort.

Ike put in a call to Kennedy, telling him there would be hot coffee ready when the Kennedys arrived at the White House the following morning before the inauguration. The frigid weather did not carry over to an emotional chill as it had between Eisenhower and Truman.

As the outgoing administration fretted about snow removal, the incoming team was preparing for a spectacular gala, the last and grandest of the many parties that had set the social circuit in Washington alight. Excitement surrounded the glamorous new president-elect and his wife. Even Republicans got into the spirit. One Republican hostess served her guests a Kennedy cocktail, composed of "two-thirds Irish whiskey, one-third Southern Comfort, and a twist of Norman Vincent Peale."

The big event for inauguration eve was a gala at the National Guard Armory hosted by Frank Sinatra and actor Peter Lawford, JFK's brother-in-law. It was an extraordinary effort by the so-called Rat Pack, the heartthrob gang of Hollywood performers, which included Sinatra, Dean Martin, and Sammy Davis Jr., all of whom worked for Kennedy's election. However, Sammy Davis Jr. was asked not to attend the gala, on the instruction of Joe Kennedy, who was affronted by his interracial marriage to the actress May Britt. This sour note would not dampen the larger gala, which starred many of Hollywood's most famous performers—among them Harry Belafonte, Milton Berle, Nat King Cole, Tony Curtis, Janet Leigh, Ella Fitzgerald, Gene Kelly, and Ethel Merman. The sold-out seats went for $100 apiece, with seventy-two ringside boxes at $10,000 each, for the purpose of retiring the Democratic Party campaign debt, and while many people didn't make it through the snowy night to attend, those who did got the show of a lifetime.

Jackie was luminous in a white ivory silk gown, designed by Oleg Cassini. As she stepped out of the limousine, she looked like a princess against the snowy backdrop. Among the highlights of the evening was a performance by Sinatra of "That Old Black Magic," changing the words to:

That old Jack magic had them in his spell
That old Jack magic that he weaved so well
The women swooned, and seems a lot of men did, too
He worked a little like I used to do.

The festivities went on long into the night, and while Jackie bowed out early, the president-elect did not arrive home until three in the morning, giving him less than four hours of sleep before the most important day of his life.

BACK AT THE WHITE House, many of the staff were forced to usher out Eisenhower's presidency in an unexpected and somewhat ironic way. Snowed in and unable to go home that final night, they hunkered down in the bomb shelter in the basement of the East Wing. They took advantage of being stranded to hold a farewell party late into the night, while the president and his family were asleep in their beds upstairs.

Ike usually had no trouble going to sleep—a soldier's habit. But he'd once admitted to a friend that if there were weighty matters on his mind, he'd wake up after a few hours and ruminate. As the drifts of snow cocooned the White House, one imagines him taking a moment to consider the significance of his last hours as president. Often, when searching for meaning and historical comparisons, Ike let his thoughts travel back to the first president, who completed the nation's maiden transition from power on March 4, 1797. In an era when leadership of nations usually passed only after death or bloodshed, it was in Washington's hands to set a new precedent. After his successor, John Adams, took the oath of office in Philadelphia's Congress Hall, they prepared to walk out of the room. Adams stepped aside to allow Washington to precede him through the door. But Washington demurred, gesturing Adams to go first. After all, *he* was the president now, and Washington was a private citizen. From that moment forward, the peaceful passing of power was a settled matter in the United States.

On January 20, 1961, the ritual would be performed flawlessly once again. So the living presidency turned a new chapter. Ike had often heard people say the record of a presidency is left to history, and history would be the judge of its success or failure. That was a trite and limiting way of looking at it, he thought. For him the question always was, *am I doing my duty as a citizen to the best of my ability?* Citizenship had imparted for him special privileges and special obligations, and these would not go away once he was out of office.

CHAPTER 12

THE PASSAGE

January 20, 1961

As Ike rose at his regular hour of 6:15 A.M., the snow had stopped falling and the day was clear, with an icy wind. He could hear the distant roar of snowplows and the machinery of war turned to the task of removing more than a thousand stalled vehicles from around the capital.

He was at his desk early, to clear the final business of his presidency.

But there wasn't much to do. An informal attitude pervaded the West Wing. Ike chatted with Ann Whitman. His son, John, wearing his Army uniform for the day, went to his office and propped his feet up on the desk, reflecting. Most of the farewells had been said, and there were a lot of them. The people who worked in the White House—ushers, housekeepers, policemen, doormen, gardeners, cooks, waiters, Secret Service men, and others—had become like family, and it was hard to say goodbye. Many workers would stay on and, Ike hoped, make the Kennedys' life as happy as theirs had been.

He also said his final goodbyes to the White House staff who had served him so well. Most of them were tearful. Some had hoped to have a role in a Nixon White House, which was not to be. At least one group of White House staffers was planning to watch the inauguration on television at the Jefferson Hotel, drinking martinis and toasting the end of an era.

In the late morning, Ike and John left the offices for the last time. Shortly after eleven, John and Jackie Kennedy arrived at the North Portico, and Ike strode out to meet them, coatless and hatless, ushering them into the warm interior like the perfect host at the most envied party in town. Minutes later the Johnsons drove up, and once again Ike went outside to bring them inside. Coffee was served in the first floor state reception room, called the Red Room for its red upholstery, wallpaper, and draperies. The conversation was friendly and high-spirited. Sitting next to Jackie on a settee, John enthused about how much she would love the house and how wonderful the staff was. She smiled politely but he could tell her thoughts were elsewhere.

Ike did make one concession to tradition and to Kennedy's style. Although he had enraged Truman by not wearing a stove-top hat to his inauguration in 1953, he wore one now to match Kennedy's, causing Mamie to blurt unthinking to Jackie, who must have cringed—"Doesn't Ike look like Paddy the Irishman in his top hat?" Mamie seemed not to realize it was a slur.

At the Capitol, seated between Eisenhower and Johnson, Kennedy made small talk with Ike in a friendly manner before the ceremonies began. There were various delays. Washington was still battling back after the snowstorm. National Airport was closed; among the thousands impacted was former president Herbert Hoover, whose plane was turned back, causing him to miss the inauguration. Although a million people would be there to see the inaugural parade, it was no easy task. A further delay occurred almost as soon as the ceremonies began. As Cardinal Cushing of Boston began his invocation, smoke began pouring out of the lectern. Cushing's immediate thought was it might be a bomb, but it was only a short circuit. Ike leaned over and murmured to Kennedy, "You must have a hot speech."

Finally, the ceremony was under way. Cushing was followed by Marian Anderson singing the national anthem, and then the great Robert Frost, who had written a special poem for the occasion. The eighty-three-year-old Frost was frail and shaking, and after attempting to read his poem in the glare of a blazing winter sun, he gave up and recited another poem, "The Gift Outright," which he knew by heart. Johnson and Kennedy took their oaths of office, and at last it was time for the speech.

The pageantry of a presidential inauguration is always uplifting, regardless of which party is taking power, but Kennedy had a gift for embodying the ideas he wanted to express. Draping his coat over the chair and removing his stovetop hat, despite the frigid air that had all others bundled up, he appeared to Americans watching on TV as especially youthful and vigorous. (They didn't know he was wearing long underwear.)

JFK's inaugural address, brief and powerful, was a masterful blend of poetry and ideology—a stunning performance still regarded as one of the best speeches in our nation's history.

It's almost puzzling to see the rampant speculation, still ongoing, about the authorship of Kennedy's inaugural speech. That's like asking about the authorship of Ike's "Chance for Peace" speech or his farewell address. Ike never attempted to disguise the fact he had speechwriters—that the process was collaborative before he finally gave it his imprimatur. It's a reality most people understand and accept. In fact, the process of more than one head being put to the task of crafting words intended to move a nation is actually a positive. Good speechwriters come to inhabit the mindset of their subjects, to the extent they virtually hear the voice in their ears, and know what the person would say.

Malcolm Moos once had a confrontation with Merriman

Smith that put a lid on the matter. Smith thought a particular speech didn't sound like Eisenhower—it was too eloquent. "Where did this come from?" he asked Moos.

"It's the President's speech," Moos said.

"You know that's not true," Smith challenged him.

"Well," Moos said, "it is true that when the President of the United States delivers a talk, we've got to assume it's his speech, and we're carpenters but not architects."

Yet, although people around JFK knew of—and history would record—Theodore Sorensen's central involvement in Kennedy's address, there was some attempt to make it appear Kennedy had written the speech entirely on his own. Before his death in 2010 Sorensen acknowledged he had destroyed an early draft of the speech, which he had written by hand, at the request of Jacqueline Kennedy, who apparently wanted the authorship to be solely granted to her husband.

Over the years Sorensen was often pressed to say whether or not he had written the famous line, *Ask not what your country can do for you, ask what you can do for your country.* "Having no satisfactory answer, I long ago started answering the oft-repeated question as to its authorship with the smiling retort: 'Ask not,'" Sorensen wrote.

Sorensen would also offer a description of speechwriting that echoed Moos's: "As the years went on, and I came to know what he [Kennedy] thought on each subject as well as how he wished to say it, our style and standard became increasingly one."

At the time Kennedy himself was annoyed by the speculation of the speech's authorship, saying, "I don't want to hear any more about this at cocktail parties who wrote that and who wrote the other thing." He was sensitive about the subject, and was probably right to be.

It might be added that the very people relied upon to make great speeches are those who have the least time to contemplate their prose. Ike, who did try to do this during his presidency, also acknowledged that speechmaking was a big job. "The President of the United States, naturally, must be ready at an instant's notice to address himself fluently on any topic from the largest pumpkin ever grown—just that moment presented to him—to the State of the Union and of the world," he said in a speech on the subject after he left office. "And some day, to those may be added reports on the state of the Moon and Mars!"

Whatever the dispute, there is no doubt that, like Ike, Kennedy had a strong hand in his speeches; particularly in this one, his gift for eloquence was evident. Unlike his predecessor he chose soaring rhetoric over plainspokenness. Ike would never utter a line like "Now the trumpet summons us again." Kennedy was reaching for the heavens.

Edward R. Murrow would devote his final newscast, on January 22, 1961, to a comparison of Ike's farewell address with Kennedy's inaugural address. Eisenhower, he said, focused on the impact of the world situation on our society: "The Eisenhower concern, as I read it, was a fear that we may lose our liberties while preparing to defend them." Of the military-industrial complex, Murrow observed Ike was speaking back to Kennedy's claims in the campaign that our nation was growing weaker. Instead, Murrow said, Eisenhower "was, in fact, suggesting that the machine may get beyond human or political control, that we could reach a point where, in fact, 'things would be in the saddle and ride mankind.'"

By contrast, Kennedy's speech was muscular, even defiant, although Schlesinger later admitted that a key line—"we shall pay any price, bear any burden, meet any hardship, support any friend, oppose any foe"—was perhaps more bellicose than needed. "In retrospect," Schlesinger said, "I think it was an overreaction to Khrushchev's speech." The speech in question, delivered by the Soviet leader on January 6, was an incendiary offensive against the West: "Liberation wars will continue to exist for as long as imperialism exists, as long as colonialism exists," Khrushchev thundered. "These are revolutionary wars," which, he said, were fully supported by the Soviets. According to Schlesinger, Kennedy was deeply affected by this speech, and as a result his own was more hawkish than originally planned.

Sitting on the platform, Ike allowed himself one dark thought. The inauguration, he reflected, could be a moment of "practical dead center" for an attack on the entire mechanism of the government, as everyone gathered in one place and paused for the ceremony. Furthermore, the next twenty-four hours—Kennedy's first day in office—was equally precarious; if an emergency were to occur, a brand-new president might not be ready to respond effectively. He was glad he'd spared nothing in his effort to prepare Kennedy for what he might face.

AS THE INAUGURATION CONCLUDED Ike shook Kennedy's hand vigorously, feeling the weight of eight years fall away. Making his way to a side entrance, his arm around Mamie, Ike realized that for the first time in their married life, they were free—private citizens, beholden neither to the military or government, and though wistful to be leaving a life he had relished until the final moment, he was content with his standing and curious about what the next stage would bring.

Ike and Mamie avoided the escorting committees surrounding other dignitaries and walked alone to their car, which would take them to a private luncheon at the 1925 F Street Club, hosted by Admiral Lewis Strauss, the former chairman of the U.S. Atomic Energy Commission. It was a relaxed and thoroughly enjoyable affair, with heads of agencies, cabinet officials, and close friends sitting around reminiscing about the time they had spent together.

By midafternoon the Eisenhowers were on the road for home, traveling the eighty-five miles to Gettysburg in the family car, a 1955 Chrysler Imperial, with John Moaney behind the wheel. Moaney, an African American Army sergeant, had been by Ike's side as a valet and general aide since World War II. He along with his wife, Delores, became indispensable to the Eisenhowers. During Ike's retirement, Moaney would continue his service, and then stay on with Mamie after Ike died. In some respects, he was closer to Ike than any human being apart from Mamie.

As they crossed the snowy landscape, Ike and Mamie found themselves marveling at the life they had lived, noting that the White House had been their home for longer than any other residence in their forty-four years of marriage. They were touched to see crowds of adults and schoolchildren lining the roads, bundled against the cold, to cheer their return. The crowds grew larger as they neared the farm, and Ike recalled another occasion when their neighbors had turned out to wish them well—when they came home after his heart attack. The people were always there, he thought—those good, patriotic folks eager to unfurl a flag, wave a hand, and shout, "God bless you," and "We love you."

That evening the family gathered round for an intimate dinner at John and Barbara's house, prepared by the Moaneys. John gave the toast: "Leaving the White House will not be easy at first, but we are reunited as a family, and this is what we have wanted," he said. "I suppose that tonight we welcome back a member of this clan who has done us proud."

Everyone, including Ike, raised their glasses and shouted, "Hear! Hear!" For the first time that transitional week, Ike found himself fighting tears.

The next day Ike received a warm note from President Kennedy:

My dear Mr. President

On my first day in office I want to send you a note of special thanks for your many acts of cordiality and assistance during the weeks since the election.

I am certain that your generous assistance has made this one of the most effective transitions in the history of our Republic. I have very much enjoyed personally the associations which we have had in this common effort.

With all good wishes to you and Mrs. Eisenhower in the days ahead, I am

Sincerely,
John F. Kennedy

Ike was pleased to receive Kennedy's gracious note, and he could only hope the new president had taken the substance of the preparation to heart. He was still thinking about the final days, wondering if he'd done enough. Presidents operate in their own closed orbits, and the transition is that one precious moment in time when two administrations work together so intimately. Well beyond pro forma meetings and communications, the transition operations can make or break a new president's first days. In spite of what he considered meaningful personal conversations with Kennedy, Ike admitted to himself that he had no idea at all what effect they'd had.

PRIVATE LIFE WAS AN entirely new experience for Ike, who had spent much of his military career and then his presidency being staffed for his ordinary needs. Right away, he ran into trouble. On his first day home, he came barreling out of his office, calling for Dick Flohr, the Secret Service agent who had been assigned to him for thirty days. "There's something wrong with the telephone," he complained. "I keep trying to dial this number, and I keep getting wrong numbers or getting the operator. I wish you'd see what's wrong with it."

Flohr dialed the number and it worked fine. "That's how you do it," he said. "How have you been doing it?" Ike showed him; he'd been turning the dial as if it were a safe combination. He was also rusty when it came to driving a car. His grandson David recounted how terrifying it was to be with him when Ike was behind the wheel. And Henry Scharf, owner of the Gettysburg Hotel, where Ike and Mamie sometimes dined, admitted that when the president had a reservation, he made sure all the parked cars were removed from the front of the hotel to give Ike plenty of room to maneuver.

The reporter Merriman Smith and a few others made up a list of things Ike had not done for at least thirty years, and possibly ever. It was a long list: he'd never been in a drugstore or supermarket, never shopped for clothing, never been to a barbershop, didn't know what a drive-in movie was or a Laundromat—and so on. When a news story appeared detailing the list, Mamie was offended, but Ike said, "I don't see what's wrong with it. It's all true."

Having served eight years at the will of the people, what Ike wanted most was to return to the man he was—the soldier. To that end he'd asked a favor of Kennedy—that he propose to Congress it restore Ike's status as a five-star general. He was willing to forfeit the title "Mr. President" if this could be done. Kennedy didn't understand the request, couldn't fathom why Ike would rather be called General Eisenhower than Mr. President—a title earned by so few. But before he left office Ike drafted a bill for Congress, and when Kennedy presented it, it easily passed. On March 24, 1961, Kennedy signed into law the commission restoring the rank of five-star general of the Army to Ike. The following day the Army's five-star red pennant was raised on the flagpole at Gettysburg.

ON JANUARY 30, KENNEDY delivered his own State of the Union speech, only eighteen days after Eisenhower's. Ike was on a hunting vacation in Georgia with George Humphrey and didn't see or hear the address, which was probably good for his blood pressure. Although Ike's State of the Union was generally optimistic, Kennedy's was a harsh warning about the state of the economy, an "hour of peril," as he described it.

While Ike was reinventing himself at Gettysburg, Kennedy's team was busy imprinting its own signature on the White House. This meant effectively pulling up the guideposts and safety systems that had served Eisenhower so well. According to Schlesinger, National Security Advisor McGeorge Bundy quickly dismantled the natural security apparatus—"After the inauguration, Bundy promptly slaughtered committees right and left and collapsed what was left of the inherited apparatus into a compact and flexible National Security Council staff."

According to Carl M. Brauer, author of *Presidential Transitions: Eisenhower Through Reagan*, "new Presidents frequently overreact to a perceived flaw in their predecessor. In reaction to Truman, Eisenhower was too anti-political. In reaction to Eisenhower, Kennedy was too anti-organizational . . ." Kennedy's team let it be known the new president would chart his own course, and they would be unbound by the wary ca-

reerists who had so cautiously advised the previous administration. "The cabinet as such didn't make much sense to him
[Kennedy] because, you know, he felt that he was the president
and that a committee doesn't decide anything," one of his staff
assistants later explained, confirming Kennedy's preference for
a one-man show.

Admiral Arleigh Burke, chief of naval operations for the
Joint Chiefs of Staff, concerned about the dismantling, told
McNamara: "It only takes a few minutes to destroy an organization or to destroy a building or to destroy a structure, to
destroy things that a lot of other people have spent lifetimes, a
succession of lifetimes, in building up. It takes only ten seconds
to destroy your own reputation; it takes a lifetime to build it. It
only takes a little while to destroy any structure, but it takes a
long, long time and a lot of thought to build it. So before anything is destroyed, you should know what's going to be built to
replace it. You should have a pretty clear idea of what's going
to be built and be pretty sure in your own mind that it is really
good." Those were strong words, which mostly went unheeded.

Kennedy's time in the White House would be, as historian
Michael Beschloss described it, more a matter of crisis management than a grand vision. His first big crisis would come less
than three months into his term. It was, among other things, a
failure created by the lack of an organized system of advisors.
As Ike would write in *Mandate for Change,* "Organization
cannot make a genius out of an incompetent. . . . On the other
hand, disorganization can scarcely fail to result in inefficiency
and can easily lead to disaster."

CHAPTER 13

A SPRING DAY AT CAMP DAVID

April 22, 1961

As Ike's helicopter came into view over the treetops of Camp David, President Kennedy was standing near the helipad to greet him. The commander in chief was humble in meeting the man who had passed the torch to him three months earlier, was chastened by an early catastrophe he thought might ruin his presidency. He had sent the helicopter for Eisenhower, who made the twenty-six-mile trip from Gettysburg to offer his counsel.

Sober in a gray suit and homburg, Eisenhower alighted from the helicopter and greeted Kennedy warmly. The two men strolled along the tree-lined paths. This was Kennedy's first trip to Camp David, and Ike was in the position of showing him around the grounds, pointing out the sights and taking in the beauty of spring blooms. Camp David was originally named Shangri-La by President Roosevelt, but Ike had renamed it Camp David to honor his father and his grandson. "Shangri-La was just a little fancy for a Kansas farm boy," he wrote his friend Ed Hazlett. (On his last visit to the place, thirteen-year-old David hid a note reading, "I shall return.") Briefly, upon Kennedy's election, Democrats in Congress talked of restoring FDR's original moniker, but Kennedy vetoed the idea.

Kennedy aide David Powers, who months earlier might have thought Eisenhower was irrelevant, now viewed the matter differently. "When I saw them together that day . . . I was thinking of President Kennedy, the youngest man ever elected at the age of forty-three, and President Eisenhower, the oldest man up to that time ever elected President of the United States. And as I watched them I was thinking of the advice that President Kennedy was going to receive that day, not from President Eisenhower, from General Eisenhower, the old warrior."

As they strolled, members of the press were kept at a distance, but one photographer, Paul Vathis of the Associated Press, would snap a photo from behind that would win him a Pulitzer Prize. That photo (on the cover of this book) perfectly captures the solemn intimacy and heavy hearts of two men burdened by the weight only a president can feel.

They settled in at the president's house, Aspen Lodge, renamed for Mamie's childhood home in the state of Colorado. There, with majestic views of the surrounding countryside, including Ike's three-hole putting green, which was modeled after the course at Augusta, they talked about the Bay of Pigs invasion, five days earlier.

By almost every account, including Kennedy's own, the Bay of Pigs disaster was a fatal combination of mixed signals, poor planning, a naïve reliance on a ragged band of Cuban exiles, and a last-minute withdrawal of the vital air support that might have guaranteed success. Back in January, during their last meeting, Ike had forcefully declared that Castro needed to be dealt with, but so far he had not found the leader—much less the plan—that would make that happen. Judging by the comments of people in Kennedy's administration, Kennedy and his advisors took that as Ike's rubber stamp to go ahead.

At the CIA, Dulles strongly urged Kennedy to launch the invasion, and Kennedy's first instinct—the right one—was to consider alternatives. Others were telling him to wait. Senator William Fulbright, the powerful chairman of the Foreign Relations Committee—a Democrat—wrote Kennedy a memo stating, "The Castro regime is a thorn in the flesh, but it is not a dagger in the heart."

Called to a full court meeting at the White House to discuss the proposed invasion, Fulbright was more convinced than ever to oppose it. But he found Kennedy's national security advisors resistant to dissent. They had already decided on the course they wanted to take.

The voices of caution remained unheard. "[F]or God's sake be careful, be sure that the military and CIA are telling you the truth," NSC foreign policy officer Samuel E. Belk warned National Security Advisor McGeorge Bundy as the momentum for an invasion built. But his words had no effect.

Those who truly understood the dynamics of the invasion plan emphasized that American air support was crucial to victory. Kennedy waffled on that, telling the CIA he didn't want the invasion to be seen as an "American" program—which an air assault would most certainly be. It's unclear how Kennedy imagined the invasion succeeding without it. Perhaps Dulles thought the president would change his mind and allow the air assault to go forward. The invasion was scheduled.

Shortly after midnight on April 17, some 1,400 Cuban exiles landed on the coast of southern Cuba in an area known as the Bay of Pigs. When the unsupported invaders landed in Cuba and were faced with an enormous defense by Castro's forces (Castro having learned in advance of the "secret" mission), Kennedy personally canceled air cover for operation, still not wanting to put an American signature on the effort. His decision to withdraw support doomed the invasion force to defeat. One hundred and fourteen of the exiles were killed and more than twelve hundred more were captured.

It was the first test of his presidency, and it was an unqualified disaster. Just as the consequences were becoming clear, Kennedy gathered his team in the Oval Office—McGeorge Bundy, Dean Rusk, CIA planner Richard Bissell, and others. The president was morose. He told them in any other form of Democratic government he'd be out of office after a fiasco like the Bay of Pigs, and no English prime minister could have survived. He sighed, "Well, at least I've got three more years—nobody can take that away from me."

As a side note, perhaps one of Kennedy's flaws was the belief that he could essentially act as his own secretary of state, much as FDR had done. In selecting Rusk, he believed he'd found someone he could keep under his control. He would often bypass Rusk and seek advice from others. This was one of those cases. Rusk would later confess, "I myself did not serve President Kennedy very well. Personally I was skeptical about the Bay of Pigs plan from the beginning. Most simply, the operation violated international law. There was no way to make a good legal case for an American-supported landing in Cuba. Also, I felt that an operation of this scale could not be conducted covertly." Nor did he see evidence of a groundswell of support for an overthrow of Castro. But he never forcefully presented this view, instead sitting back in meetings and saying very little.

In a speech to the American Society of Newspaper Editors three days after the invasion, Kennedy promised, "We intend to profit from this lesson. We intend to re-examine and reorient our forces of all kinds, our tactics and our institutions here in this community. We intend to intensify our efforts for a struggle in many ways more difficult than war, where disappointment will often accompany us." But he didn't really understand why the mission had failed so completely, or what he could do about it, and that's when he called Ike, sending a helicopter to Gettysburg to whisk the former president to Camp David for an urgent meeting.

NOW FACE-TO-FACE WITH EISENHOWER, he confessed the whole operation was a complete failure. Everything about it had gone wrong—the intelligence, the timing, the tactics—*everything.* Kennedy was angry, disappointed, and, Ike thought, more than a little bewildered. Mere months after the heady moment of the inauguration, when he was full of such hope and confidence, he now worried that this failure, for which he took complete responsibility, could leave a permanent stain on his presidency.

"No one knows how tough this job is until he's been in it a few months," Kennedy said to Ike.

Eisenhower smiled wryly. "Mr. President," he replied softly, "if you will forgive me, I think I mentioned that to you three months ago."

Kennedy smiled back, rueful. "I certainly have learned a lot since then."

Ike would later reflect, "he seemed himself at that moment"—no longer the cocky king of the New Frontier, but a man steeped in truth.

Eisenhower had not been told of the invasion before it occurred. Now the man who had planned the greatest invasion in world history—D-Day—questioned JFK closely about the operation, walking him through the process he took to launch it.

Who recommended it? What were the nature of the meetings and debate? Were there changes in the plan while it was under way?

"Well," said Kennedy, "I just approved a plan that had been recommended by the CIA and by the Joint Chiefs of Staff. I took their advice."

Ike nodded. After a moment he asked, "Mr. President, before you approved this plan, did you have everybody in front of you debating the thing so you got the pros and cons yourself and then made the decision, or did you see these people one at a time?"

"Well, I did have a meeting. . . . I just took their advice."

His response troubled Ike. Clearly, Kennedy had not engaged in a vigorous give-and-take, and he might not have fully understood all the consequences. Ike's own NSC meetings were methodical and thorough, with each person at the table presenting his position, followed by debate. He always emphasized the need, as he once put it, to "get them [the people responsible] with their different viewpoints in front of you, and listen to them debate. I don't believe in bringing them in one at a time, and therefore being impressed by the most recent one. . . ."

"Mr. President, were there any changes in the plan that the Joint Chiefs of Staff had approved?" he asked Kennedy.

"Yes, there were. We did want to call off one bombing sally."

"Why was that called off? Why did they change plans after the ships were at sea?"

"Well, we felt it necessary that we keep our hand concealed in this affair," Kennedy explained. "We thought that if it was learned that *we* were really doing this rather than the rebels themselves, the Soviets would be apt to cause trouble in Berlin."

Ike was astonished. "Mr. President, how could you expect the world to believe that we had nothing to do with it?" he asked sharply. "Where did those people get the ships to go from Central America to Cuba? Where did they get the weapons? Where did they get all the communications and all the other things they would need? How could you have possibly kept from the world any knowledge that the United States was involved? I believe there is only one thing to do when you get into this kind of thing—it must be a success."

"I assure you that, hereafter, if we get into anything like this, it is going to be a success."

"Well, I'm glad to hear that," said Eisenhower.

Even as he asked the questions and prodded Kennedy for details, Eisenhower was well aware of the spin coming out of the Kennedy administration, essentially blaming *him* for the invasion and its failure. Kennedy's people were saying, in effect, Ike told him to do it and he trusted Ike. This was a laughable idea on several counts, not the least of which was Kennedy's stated reluctance to adopt plans and organization from Eisenhower's administration. But it was also preposterous on its face. The plan to train Cuban exiles for an invasion was little more than exploratory by the time Ike left office, and there was certainly no strategy in place for an amphibious assault, much less at the difficult site of Bay of Pigs. "See, until you could recognize someone as a government in exile, a Cuban, what could you do from our viewpoint?" he reflected years later. "You might as well go and attack them yourself." Ike had plainly told Kennedy back in January that any effort was contingent on finding the organization and leadership able to actually carry out an overthrow. But he recognized that partisans will attempt to write their own version of history, and, indeed, in some circles he would always be blamed for the Bay of Pigs.

Maybe, in one corner of his conscience, Ike felt some guilt. He recalled how when he had first approved the training of a paramilitary force of Cuban exiles, Goodpaster had told him quite frankly he thought it was a bad idea—the whole affair might gather a momentum of its own with disastrous consequences.

"Not as long as I'm here," Ike replied tartly.

"Yes, sir, that's just the problem," Goodpaster said.

And now that seemed to be a fateful premonition.

Finally, after eating a fried chicken lunch, they walked out of Aspen Lodge and spoke to the waiting press. "I asked President Eisenhower here to bring him up to date on recent events and get the benefit of his thoughts and experience," Kennedy told them.

Of course, they were very interested in hearing Ike's verdict, which he would not give them. "I am all in favor of the United States supporting the man who has to carry the responsibility for our foreign affairs," he said blandly, and left it at that.

As Ike prepared to board the helicopter back to Gettysburg, Kennedy suggested they get together for a golf game in the near future—which they never did.

In the coming days Ike's mind was full of thoughts about what had occurred. His worst fears that Kennedy would dismantle the National Security Council system had been realized. He had tried, during their two meetings, to impart how important it was to have a strong and well-organized system for the NSC—how the process itself could protect a president from acting precipitously and making mistakes. But Kennedy's people— and Kennedy himself—had been so eager to unspool the red tape they thought clogged Ike's administration, they ultimately dismantled a vital bulwark against disastrous error.

Kennedy helicoptered back to the White House, growing angrier the more he went over events in his head. He felt betrayed by his military leadership and the CIA; he complained loudly, "How could I have been so stupid?"

He put in a call to James Killian, who was in New York for

a meeting. "What are we going to do?" he asked. "What are we going to do about the CIA? Can't we change its name?" Killian recalled he was "just floundering as to what to do." He was also looking for scapegoats, and he found them in Allen Dulles, the CIA head, and Richard Bissell, who planned the operation. He called them into his office and said, "You must go."

"I knew how deeply embarrassed and angry President Kennedy was at the outcome," said Killian. "I also think he learned a lot about the need to make extra careful precautions. And I think also he developed a skepticism of the assurances from his own military which stayed with him from that point on as president." Be that as it may, learning on the job is a consequential matter when it comes to the presidency of the United States.

Kennedy also called Clark Clifford, who agreed the president had received bad advice, and things had to change. "I have to have the best possible intelligence," he told Clifford. "This has come early; I would hope that I could live it down, but it's going to be difficult to do."

McGeorge Bundy would later suggest Kennedy's personality played a role in the calamity, saying, "The President was incurably willing to decide"—that is, if a decision had to be made, it was hard for him to wait, especially on weekends when the full contingent of advisors wasn't around. While being decisive is certainly a good quality for a president to have, Bundy was suggesting sometimes it is wiser to wait and receive more guidance before acting.

From that time on, Kennedy was more open about seeking Ike's advice, but he ignored one warning, probably to his regret. Back in December 1960, when the two men had their first post-election meeting, Kennedy had asked if Ike thought he should set up a meeting with Khrushchev. Ike had counseled that he wait until his presidency was more established, cautioning Kennedy about Khrushchev's many faces and manipulations. Kennedy chose to ignore his advice, arranging for a June 1961 summit with the Soviet leader in Vienna. It was a brutal comeuppance, as Kennedy confessed to Scotty Reston, calling it the "worst thing in my life . . . he savaged me." In particular, one exchange was alarming. "It is up to the U.S. to decide whether there will be war or peace," Khrushchev said. Pushed to his limits, Kennedy snapped, "Then, Mr. Chairman, there will be war. It will be a cold winter." Two months later the Berlin Wall went up.

Sir Isaiah Berlin, a professor of social and political theory at Oxford University, recalled, "My impression was that he thought he was a duelist, with Khrushchev at the other end. There was a tremendous world duel being carried on by these two gigantic figures. An enormous rapier had been thrust against him, and he was always on a *qui vive* of some sort. . . . He was the man who was going to rescue civilization and Khrushchev was the man who was going, in some way, to shoot it down, unless he could teach him a lesson. . . ."

Looking on, Ike was furious about the Berlin Wall, and deeply worried about Kennedy's deliberately contentious relationship with Khrushchev. This was not a time for melodrama, he thought, and whenever he got the chance he tried to be the "cooler head," but in some respects it was already too late.

Milton observed later, "The great armament race did not begin until Kennedy became president . . . because as a result of the Bay of Pigs fiasco, President Kennedy worried that the leaders of the Soviet Union, and especially Chairman Khrushchev, would underrate him, and therefore he took a number of actions, including vast expenditures in the military field. . . . President Eisenhower most certainly tried his best to reduce the inflammatory nature of the cold war, to hold down military expenditures and to reason together."

Milton's analysis speaks to the nature of presidential gravi-tas. How does one credibly show strength when conflicts arise with such a volatile and well-armed foe, and against irrational demands? As it turned out, Kennedy would pay for the Bay of Pigs fiasco with the Cuban Missile Crisis, one of the worst con-flicts of his presidency, and the only time before or since Ameri-cans truly feared we were on the brink of a nuclear attack.

Unknown to Kennedy, when he met with Khrushchev in June, the Soviet leader had already made arrangements with Castro to place Soviet nuclear-armed missiles in Cuba, ostensibly to protect it from further U.S. aggression. On October 14, a U-2 spy plane flying over Cuba took photos of intermediate-range missile sites being built—so situated that missiles would have the capacity of reaching any part of the United States. Kennedy was informed of the sites on October 16, and told Congress it was the first he knew of it.

Kennedy's critics in Congress immediately called it a disas-trous failure of intelligence, arguing that missile sites did not just spring up overnight; somehow American intelligence had missed months of activity. The question now was what to do about it. Although the Soviet minister of foreign affairs, An-drei Gromyko, assured Kennedy in a White House meeting the missile sites were for defensive purposes only, the Americans could not let them stand a mere ninety-one miles from Ameri-can shores. Meanwhile, many of Kennedy's advisors were rec-ommending a direct attack on the missile sites, if not a full invasion of Cuba. Kennedy held back.

In a strong letter to Khrushchev on October 22, Kennedy wrote, "In our discussions and exchanges on Berlin and other international questions, the one thing that has most concerned me has been the possibility that your Government would not correctly understand the will and determination of the United

States in any given situation, since I have not assumed that you or any other sane man would, in this nuclear age, deliberately plunge the world into war which it is crystal clear no country could win and which could only result in catastrophic consequences to the whole world, including the aggressor." He assured Khrushchev the Americans would do anything in their power to prevent the breach of security posed by missiles in Cuba.

Khrushchev's response was to emphasize that the missiles were for defense, not aggression, and to warn against any power play the Americans might be considering. He concluded, "I hope that the United States Government will display wisdom and renounce the actions pursued by you, which may lead to catastrophic consequences for world peace."

In a call to Eisenhower on October 22, hours before addressing the American people about the crisis, Kennedy worried out loud about the stakes. "What about if the Soviet Union—Khrushchev—announces tomorrow, which I think he will, that if we attack Cuba that it's going to be nuclear war?" he asked Eisenhower. "And what's your judgment as to the chances they'll fire these things off if we invade Cuba?"

Sounding calm and certain, Ike responded. "Oh, I don't believe that they will. Something may make these people [the Soviets] shoot them off. I just don't believe this will. . . . I will say this. I'd want to keep my own people very alert."

"Well, we'll hang on tight," Kennedy replied with a sour laugh.

In his speech to the Americans at seven that evening—which he knew would be seen around the world—Kennedy described the evidence of Soviet missiles in Cuba and called for their removal. He also announced the establishment of a naval quarantine around the island until the Soviet Union agreed to dismantle the missile sites and consent that no further missiles would be shipped to Cuba. He followed up with a second letter to Khrushchev, informing him that Soviet ships bound for Cuba would be subject to the quarantine and not be allowed to proceed. Any Soviet ship continuing toward Cuba would risk being fired on by a U.S. Navy vessel.

Khrushchev's response was full of outrage. "You, Mr. President, are not declaring a quarantine, but rather are setting forth an ultimatum and threatening that if we do not give in to your demands you will use force. Consider what you are saying! And you want to persuade me to agree to this! What would it mean to agree to these demands? It would mean guiding oneself in one's relations with other countries not by reason, but by submitting to arbitrariness. You are no longer appealing to reason, but wish to intimidate us."

This was the most dangerous moment of the crisis. With Castro now demanding that the Soviets use nuclear weapons to attack the United States if they invaded Cuba to remove the missile sites, and Khrushchev angered by the quarantine as his ships were stalled in the water, the situation was explosive. Recalling the atmosphere in the White House during those days, Ted Sorensen reflected, "I have been asked many times, was I scared? I didn't have time to be scared. Every minute, we were thinking, trying to come up with some solution . . . Nothing seemed to deter Khrushchev from this reckless gamble." He added that in those days the Cabinet Room, where they were meeting, was not a reinforced concrete shelter (which it later became). "So, we knew sitting around that table if we made the wrong decision, if we simply provoked Khrushchev further, that it might well be our last weekend."

Yet Eisenhower's view ended up being correct. Khrushchev did not want a nuclear confrontation; he sought a face-saving compromise that would also protect Cuba from U.S. aggression. And Kennedy was willing to give him that. In the coming three days, while the public rhetoric remained bullish, negotiations went on behind the scenes. Khrushchev's final demand, which Kennedy felt he could live with, was an agreement to remove missile sites in exchange for a promise we would not attack Cuba, and also an agreement to remove "analogous" (Khrushchev's word) missiles in Turkey. Upon approval of Castro, U.S. officials could conduct inspections to ensure the sites had been removed.

Ike was at the farm, sitting on the porch with his old friend George Allen, when the president phoned on October 28 to say that a tentative deal had been reached: the missile sites would be removed in exchange for the United States agreeing that it would never invade Cuba.

After Ike listened, he said, "Now the only thing I would suggest, Mr. President, is this. What you say you will do, whether it is an inspection by us, or whatever concessions we are prepared to make, do this very specifically: Make sure it is written down. And then by all means do everything you say you are going to do. Because if you don't do it, pretty soon you will find that you can't possibly do it. . . . Mr. President, don't sign a blank check."

"We will agree we will not invade Cuba provided there are none of these offensive weapons allowed to stay there," Kennedy said.

But Ike pressed him. "Other conditions might come up," he argued, "when you would have to enter Cuba sometime, and I think you ought to define the circumstances in which you might go in."

"Well," said Kennedy, "the Soviets are agreeing that we can go on land and make land inspections."

"All right, then. There is one thing you must do. Because if we don't do it, they will say it is because you are weak."

But the land inspections never happened. Castro immediately protested that Khrushchev might have agreed but it was, after all, his country. And Kennedy relented—really, he had no choice without stirring up the aggressions all over again. Overall, Eisenhower thought Kennedy had handled the crisis well.

Still, Kennedy's presidency seemed to be a constant effort to pry the bear's jaws from the neck of the free world. He never quite found his bearings. "He was an odd blend of liberalism and conservatism, of impulsiveness and wisdom, of pragmatism and idealism," Milton observed, and it never gelled. By the fall of 1963, with the political parties turning their attention to the 1964 presidential election, Kennedy's approval ratings had slipped to their lowest level ever, and the trend was continuing downward. Republicans thought he was politically vulnerable.

NOVEMBER 19, 1963, MARKED the one hundredth anniversary of the Gettysburg Address, and President Kennedy was asked to speak at the ceremony. He declined, citing a prescheduled political trip to Texas. And so Eisenhower rose to the occasion, giving what for him was an unusually poetic speech. "Lincoln had faith that the ancient drums of Gettysburg, throbbing mutual defiance from the battle lines of the blue and the gray, would one day beat in unison, to summon a people, happily united in peace, to fulfill, generation by generation, a noble destiny. His faith has been justified—but the unfinished work of which he spoke in 1863 is still unfinished; because of human frailty, it always will be."

Three days after Eisenhower's speech, the human frailty he mentioned would be deeply felt when President Kennedy was assassinated in Dallas. The assassination, apparently carried out by a lone gunman, Lee Harvey Oswald, occurred while the president and first lady rode in an open car motorcade and was captured on film. It traumatized the nation. The youth and vigor of the president, and the sight of small children romping in the White House, had become a feature of American life that transcended politics. Kennedy might have been politically vulnerable, but personally he was beloved around the world. To watch him die in such a brutal way drove the nation into an extended period of mourning. Schools closed, churches filled, and Americans spent days fixated on their television screens, trying to make sense of what had happened. Newsreels showed scenes of people openly sobbing on the streets.

The day after the assassination, Ike came to Washington to pay his respects and view the casket, which was lying in state. Afterward, he had lunch with President Johnson. "I need you more than ever now," Johnson said, and Ike gave him the best advice he could—to be his own man—something that would require enormous patience and skill. Grateful, Johnson asked Ike if he could write a memo with advice for him going forward. Ike found a desk and wrote it out in longhand before finding a secretary to type it up.

Among his other suggestions, one would prove to be the wisest move of Johnson's transition. Here Ike's instincts were perfect, and his devotion to the national good transcended partisanship. He suggested Johnson call a joint session of Congress: "Point out first that you have come to this office unexpectedly and you accept the decision of the Almighty," he advised. Then, he wrote, tell them it would be your mission to carry out "the noble objectives so often and so eloquently stated by your great predecessor." Johnson's address to Congress, five days after Kennedy's death, followed Ike's script and was both humble and steadfast, winning him an enormous amount of goodwill from the American people.

Kennedy's funeral and burial took place on November 25. President Hoover was too frail to attend, but Truman and Eisenhower were seated together in the same pew in St. Matthew's Cathedral, located fewer than ten blocks north of the White House. They were old men—Truman seventy-nine and Eisenhower seventy-three—and any disagreements they might have had with the young president dissipated like wisps of incense swung from the priest's thurible. Ike might have thought of other times, in war command, when he had experienced the heartbreaking task of burying young men. But this event was shattering in its own way, with enormous consequences to the nation. Johnson, who had once so eagerly sought the presidency, looked haggard and ill that day, Lady Bird gripping his arm protectively.

The solemnity of the moment finally led to a rapprochement between Truman and Eisenhower. Before the funeral, Ike asked Truman, who was attending with his daughter Margaret, if they would like to ride with him and Mamie in their car, and they agreed. Afterward, as the Eisenhowers prepared to drop off the Trumans at Blair House, where they were staying, Margaret asked their plans. They were headed back to Gettysburg, Ike said. "It's a long drive," said Margaret. "Wouldn't you like to come back to Blair House with us and have a drink and a sandwich?" And the Eisenhowers accepted.

Over sandwiches the two ex-presidents spoke intimately about the experiences they shared, and became so engaged in conversation the hours melted away. There was no great moment of reconciliation, but rather a mutual understanding of who they were, historically, if not personally, and how very much they had in common. "On that day," mused Clifton

Daniel, a journalist and Margaret Truman's husband, "they shared something very much in common; they shared with Jack Kennedy the fact that all of them had been President, and this engenders a greatness of spirit in people sometimes they don't otherwise have."

Ike continued to be a counselor to President Johnson, who took far greater advantage of his expertise than Kennedy had. Ike was alarmed at the prospect of Barry Goldwater being LBJ's Republican opponent in the 1964 election—"I have the feeling that that man is dangerous," he told Merriman Smith. He was particularly worried about Goldwater's hard-line stand on foreign affairs. Behind the scenes Ike enlisted his brother Milton and a group of moderate Republican stalwarts from his administration to advocate for a more mainstream candidate. At the convention Milton placed Pennsylvania governor William Scranton's name in nomination. But Goldwater won the nomination on the first ballot. Unhappy with the result, Ike nonetheless played the good soldier, even filming a campaign video with Goldwater, in which he called claims of Goldwater being a warmonger "tommyrot." He never said it openly, but Ike probably wasn't unhappy when Johnson won the election in 1964. At least LBJ was the devil he knew.

As the situation in Vietnam grew worse, Johnson called Ike to the White House time and time again, seeking advice more from the general than the ex-president. Ike gave it as best he could, discussing strategic matters—always emphasizing the need to overwhelm the enemy with a show of force—something Johnson was never able to accomplish.

There was some misunderstanding about Ike's attitudes toward Vietnam. Johnson liked to say he was merely continuing the policies of Eisenhower and Kennedy. Milton, who was friendly with Johnson, challenged him on this point, describing

Ike's actual policy, which was not interventionist. Johnson was astonished. If that were true, he asked, why was the former president supporting him now? Milton explained that as a former president, Ike felt it was his duty to support the president— not to be a troublemaker in a sensitive global matter.

And yet, as Ike's former special assistant Arthur Larson pointed out, Johnson saw a political advantage in tying his actions in Vietnam with Ike's policies. "It is routine for every administration to blame the troubles of its initial years on the mess that it inherited," Larson wrote. "And President Johnson has tried to picture a 500,000-man war as the inevitable lineal descendent of a 600-man economic and technical aid program under Eisenhower in Vietnam." Johnson wanted to be seen with Ike, sought the reflected glow of his military reputation, but it was not enough to save his presidency.

No doubt Ike commiserated with Johnson about the war protest movement. He felt, in the manner of many of his contemporaries, that the youth were lacking in respect and unwilling to help protect their precious freedoms. He didn't understand them. "No one could hate war more than I," he wrote to his grandson David, "but I get very upset when I find people who are quite willing to enjoy the privileges and rights afforded by this country but publicly announce their readiness to flout their responsibilities."

Ike always had time for Johnson, but it's not as if he sat in a rocking chair waiting for the phone to ring. In addition to a heavy writing schedule—a two-part presidential memoir, his diary, and a book of personal stories, *At Ease: Stories I Tell to Friends*—he had an ambitious speaking schedule. The weight of office having been lifted, those around him observed he grew warmer and mellower with age. Still, Ike kept his edge. When *People* magazine interviewed him and Mamie on the occasion of their fiftieth wedding anniversary, the interviewer asked Ike whether he would marry the same girl if given a chance to do it all over again. Ike roared. "That's the worst question I ever heard! There's only one possible answer."

On one occasion Charlie Halleck, who had remained close to Ike, talked him into giving a speech in Indiana at a barbecue to lay the cornerstone for the Halleck Center. Ike obliged, out of friendship, but he didn't anticipate the enormous crowd. Seventeen thousand people lined up at twelve serving stations to pile barbecue chicken and the fixings on their plates. As Ike walked toward the stage, plate in hand, he was swarmed by enthusiastic fans.

He turned to Halleck with a shocked look on his face. "Why, Charlie, that lady was pawing at me there!" Halleck laughed. "Mr. President, I remember one time you complained to Mamie about people grabbing at you and pawing at you, but she reminded you that if they didn't you wouldn't like it." Ike just smiled.

Everywhere Ike spoke, he received a similar reception. "He was President, he was General, he was everything," Halleck said. "And the people just idolized him. They realized, even the wild-eyed right-wingers, that he'd been a terrific president. I wish to hell we had him back."

Even as his political influence faded, Ike's *presence* in the American heartland remained visceral. *New York Times* reporter Tom Wicker, recalling a time he accompanied Ike on a speaking tour, felt it: "He was a presence—special, not ordinary. The crowds felt it when he emerged from the plane to speak. . . . Even at close quarters, it was possible to turn your eyes away from Eisenhower—but you *knew* he was there anyway."

In his memoirs and other writings, Ike attempted to identify and answer the chief questions facing the nation. In *Wag-*

ing Peace: "Will a great self-governing people such as ours—a people that in three and a half centuries converted a vast wilderness into the richest and most powerful political grouping on earth—continue to practice, in affluence, the pioneering virtues and be guided by the moral values that in leaner times brought us, by the middle of the twentieth century, to an unparalleled pinnacle of power?" He continued to urge the nation and its citizens to be clear-eyed, thoughtful, loyal to the highest principles—strong in resolve, cautious in action, in it for the long haul.

It was in Ike's nature to be reflective, and he often looked back on his years in office, summarizing in his own mind what had been achieved there. As he wrote in an October 18, 1966, letter to Hagerty, "A few days ago, when asked for a list of accomplishments of the Republican administration, I dashed this off from the top of my head, along with a few comments. I thought you might be interested. All the best, as ever. DE." A lengthy list was followed by the reminder, "All this was done with a Congress controlled by an opposition party for six years, the other two having only a nominal Republican majority."

BY 1968, IKE'S HEALTH was failing, and he suffered another heart attack in April. Recuperating, he watched with interest the Republican primary. Nixon was engaged in a heated battle for the nomination with Nelson Rockefeller and to a lesser degree Ronald Reagan. Everyone was wondering why Ike hadn't endorsed his former vice president, and some speculated maybe he wouldn't. Here again the old awkwardness that had defined their relationship emerged. Nixon refused to ask for an endorsement, not wanting to be pushy—seeking approval without having to beg for it. Ike held back until July 18, short weeks before the convention, and finally gave his endorsement, to Nixon's great relief. On the first night of the convention, Ike made a pretaped statement to delegates at the convention from his comfortable suite at Walter Reed Army Hospital in Washington. He had another heart attack the next day. When he accepted the nomination, Nixon called on the delegates to "win this one for Ike."

Ike seemed content and even happy at Walter Reed, ensconced in the relatively plush and spacious presidential suite—Ward 8. He lived to see Nixon elected president, and in a photo with Nixon taken in the hospital after his inauguration, Ike, while thin, was grinning widely in the old way, delight suffusing his face. During the coming month, he began to fail, and two days before he died, he weakly summoned Milton to his side. Motioning him to lean close, he whispered, "I want you to know how much you have always meant to me, how much I have valued your counsel." Milton left the room, dissolving in tears.

Both John and David have recalled the same incredible deathbed scene. As he neared the end, Ike ordered the blinds closed to shut out the sun. Then he asked to be lifted up, and as they struggled to pull him up he murmured disgustedly, "Two strong men," as if to chide them for having trouble managing his frail body. At last raised, he said, "I want to go; God take me." Soon after, he lapsed into a final unconsciousness. He died at 12:25 P.M. on March 28, 1969.

THE AMERICAN PEOPLE TUNED in to their televisions to say goodbye. On March 29, TV cameras were trained on the National Cathedral in Washington as the solemn pallbearers—including Omar Bradley, John Moaney, Milton and Edgar, and others—carried Ike's coffin inside for the first stage of five days of official ceremonies, planned with military precision in 1966. Ike's body, dressed in his Army uniform and resting in the eighty-dollar Army-issue casket he had requested, lay in the Bethlehem Chapel for twenty-four hours, as the public filed by. Then on the afternoon of March 30, a dramatic processional formed to take the casket to the Capitol, where it would lie in state. Thousands of people lined the streets as the casket was transferred to a horse-drawn caisson, which had originally been used to carry canons. (The previous day this same caisson had transported two Vietnam War casualties to Arlington National Cemetery.)

Years out of office and recently away from the limelight, in death Ike was resurrected as the beloved figure and tireless patriot who had so captured the American imagination after his victory in World War II. His passing triggered an emotional outpouring of nostalgia in those who remembered him from that time. Life then was imbued with a moral clarity and sense of national purpose that seemed absent in the chaotic 1960s. The grip of an unwinnable war and the bedlam of civil unrest marked a new era that had many longing for the past. And so Ike's star rose in his leave-taking. As his body lay in state in a flag-draped coffin in the Capitol Rotunda, more than forty thousand ordinary Americans lined up in unseasonably cold weather to pay their respects. The people filed quietly by, averaging as many as two thousand an hour long into the night and continuing until the afternoon of the second day. Although the Eisenhower family had requested that people donate to charity in lieu of flowers, the flowers poured in; there were so many that an Army detail of an officer and four enlisted men were charged with handling the floral arrangements.

On March 31, a majestic funeral procession formed to take

Ike to the National Cathedral for the funeral. After Ike died, Mamie had reached out to Chuck Yeager, the famous brigadier general and test pilot, asking if he could organize a flyby down Pennsylvania Avenue on the day of the funeral. As he recounted many years later, Yeager responded, "Yes, ma'am." He called the Pentagon and Andrews Air Force Base to set it up and was told by a two-star general, "You aren't allowed to fly down Pennsylvania Avenue so you will not be doing so." Not so easily dissuaded, Yeager led two flights of four F-4s to Andrews in preparation.

The skies above Washington were overcast and foggy on March 31, so it looked like a no-go for Yeager. To his surprise he received a call from General John Paul McConnell, the chief of staff of the Air Force, who was overseeing the funeral activities, asking him to do the flyby.

"Sir," asked Yeager, "can you see the Capitol Dome?"

"Just barely," said McConnell.

"I can fly," said Yeager.

And so Yeager led the formation down Pennsylvania Avenue, skirting the treetops as the crowds look heavenward in awe.

After the ceremony, the casket was taken by procession to Union Station for the trip home to Abilene, Ike's final resting place. Fearing accidents, officials didn't notify the public of the train route, but people found out anyway. Crowds lined the railway stops along the route, high school bands playing and children waving flags. By the time the train finally pulled into the rail yard in Abilene, the small town of eight thousand had been transformed to an elaborate stage for their favorite son. On April 2, a final religious service and parade brought Ike to his resting place in a small chapel on the grounds of his presidential library, a few yards from his childhood home.

"The hero has come home," a somber Walter Cronkite told

American television viewers. "It has been noted more than once these past five days that the nation mourns but does not weep. Today's ceremonies in this midwestern town mark the end of a life, an era, and an age. You may feel regret that the age is past, but there can be no complaints about the quality of the life."

A banner hangs over Ike's grave, with the prayer he recited at his 1953 inaugural address. Three quotations are engraved on the marble walls. To the right of his tomb is the warning from the first year of his presidency, which he chose to make immortal:

> Every gun made, every warship launched, every rocket fired signifies, in the final sense, a theft from those who hunger and are not fed, those who are cold and are not clothed. This is not a way of life at all. . . . Under the cloud of threatening war, it is humanity hanging from a cross of iron.

SOME YEARS AFTER EISENHOWER'S death his brother Milton wrote that after all the challenges and conflicts Ike had faced during his presidency, it was too bad he hadn't lived long enough to hear his time in office referred to as "the good old days." It's human nature to look longingly at the past. But today, fifty-six years after Ike delivered his farewell address, the nation, at a critical point in history, is giving the man and his words another look. The YouTube video of Ike's speech, with wavy black-and-white video and scratchy sound, has garnered more than half a million views, and many other videos including commentary are also available for a new generation to see and hear. Left to languish at various periods of our Cold War history, and reemerging as we engaged in new wars in Afghanistan and Iraq, Ike's final message still speaks to us today. But what does it all mean?

Ike's farewell address, delivered three days before the end of his presidency, has often been called prophetic, and it became one of the most-quoted presidential speeches in history. However, it's hard to talk about our takeaway lessons from Ike's military-industrial complex speech without sounding glib. It has become like a Rorschach test on American policy. Depending on where you stand on military spending, troop strength, the role of industry, and, yes, politics, you see something different. For those who oppose war, Ike's words seem to be a "guns versus butter" argument concluding we should reduce the military in favor of domestic growth. For those zeroing in on fraud and waste in government, it evokes backroom deals and quid pro quo between powerful industries and congressional committees. Since the speech has been so often and so eagerly co-opted by various antiwar movements, it has left many people puzzling about how the man who commandeered the largest military force in our history could give such a speech at all.

To get clarity, you have to understand the man. Here's what Ike did *not* mean:

He did not mean America should retreat or be isolationist.

He did not mean we should spend less on the military in favor of domestic spending.

He did not mean industry had no vital role to play in military readiness.

Eisenhower's speech was a call for balance, fiscal restraint, and vigilance. And through the many debates in Washington about defense authorization and appropriation, those guidelines are a fitting template.

Robert Gates, the Kansan who served as secretary of defense between December 2006 and July 2011, for both the

George W. Bush and Obama presidencies, kept a picture of Eisenhower in his office. In a speech at the Eisenhower Library in 2010 to celebrate the 65th anniversary of the allied victory in Europe, he seemed to be channeling Ike's farewell: "Does the number of warships we have, and are building, really put America at risk when the U.S. battle fleet is larger than the next thirteen navies combined—eleven of which are our partners and allies? Is it a dire threat that by 2020, the United States will have only twenty-times more advanced stealth fighters than China?" Gates said if Ike were alive, he'd be asking that same question—just as he had in 1961.

Eisenhower had been talking about these same themes for his entire presidency. He saw budget priorities holistically—not as one pot for military and a separate pot for domestic spending. Rather, he believed that the national interest, including national security, was not reliant solely or even primarily on how many weapons systems we had, but more fundamentally on how stable our nation was. A healthy economy, he thought, was a national security issue. So were civil rights, education, and infrastructure. Our greatness as a nation, not just our military might, was our bulwark against the dangers of the world.

"Crises there will continue to be," he said in the farewell. "In meeting them, whether foreign or domestic, great or small, there is a recurring temptation to feel that some spectacular and costly action could become the miraculous solution to all current difficulties. . . ." That message seems relevant now. Although the United States has a bigger military budget than the next seven countries combined, those who suggest placing limits on spending are accused of wanting to hollow out our defense capabilities. Congress is notoriously gun-shy about refusing support for any new weapons system on the docket, fearing that folks back home will question its commitment to national security. (In the 2016 Republican primary debates, Senator Ted Cruz's reluctance to rubber-stamp the National Defense Authorization Act earned him rounds of criticism for being weak on defense. This is a typical reaction in politics.)

Eisenhower would advise that smarter isn't necessarily bigger—and that might be truer than ever now, an era when defense needs are more diverse, when size alone does not necessarily give us an edge in fighting radical terrorism, and when our enemies are just as likely to be in cyberspace as on the ground. As Ike said in the speech, "Together we must learn how to compose differences, not with arms, but with intellect and decent purpose." The old commander would argue that success on D-Day was not just a matter of overwhelming force, although we had that. It was also a matter of brilliant strategy. In the war room leading up to the invasion, Ike hunkered down over charts and maps and weather reports, knowing that strength was effective only if he got the details right. He prized his advisors and welcomed even the most heated debates, believing that in the scrum of dissent, valuable new insights were revealed.

Eisenhower placed great trust in the wisdom of the people—in their "decent purpose" and practice of democracy. He had a deep regard for the Founding Fathers. He especially relied on the words of George Washington, who seemed remarkably foresighted when he warned in *his* farewell address against excessive partisanship and factionalism: "[D]omination of one faction over another, sharpened by the spirit of revenge, natural to party dissension, which in different ages and countries has perpetrated the most horrid enormities, is itself a frightful despotism." Washington, too, worried about excess, whether in military influence or partisanship. The question then as now is whether we can hold true to our common ideals even in the midst of discord.

David Eisenhower, Ike's grandson, in a 2011 piece for the *Los Angeles Times* titled "A Tale of Two Speeches," reflected on the two men—Eisenhower and Kennedy—who gave historic speeches within three days of one another in 1961. Eisenhower observed that these were political opponents, and their contrasts in philosophy and style were obvious. But he emphasized that the "addresses converged on key points, namely on questions of citizenship in the modern age and on the belief that the American system of self-government can rise to any challenge." It's a message his grandfather would have approved of.

THE LAST WORD

2017

November 10, 2016
The White House
11:00 a.m.

Under unseasonably warm and sunny skies, president-elect Donald J. Trump stepped out of his black SUV at the South Lawn entrance of the White House, away from the press cameras, less than two days after the American people chose him to be their forty-fifth president. He was there for a historic appointment with the President of the United States. His wife Melania, who accompanied him, was scheduled to spend the time touring the White House with First Lady Michele Obama. Trump's son-in-law, Jared Kushner, married to his daughter Ivanka, was in tow as well to meet with White House Chief of Staff Denis McDonough.

The President-elect and First Lady-to-be walked in through the South Lawn entrance and were greeted by President and Mrs. Obama in the Diplomatic Reception Room, the setting most often used to welcome visiting foreign dignitaries. An oval room, the walls are papered with an antique scenic wallpaper featuring scenes of Boston Harbor, West Point, Niagara Falls, and New York Harbor. It's the decor First Lady Jacqueline Kennedy chose in her redecorating effort of 1962.

The Obamas cordially welcomed the Trumps to the White House, what will become their new home. After a campaign marred by inflammatory rhetoric, public dissent, and divisions both within and between the two parties, this first meeting face to face was pleasant. With the history of animosity between the two men and rhetorical jabs back and forth that had just ended two days before, the two couples chatted comfortably like they were at a cocktail party. After a few minutes, the President and President-elect headed to the West Wing and the Oval Office, while the First Lady and Melania Trump went to tour the residence and to talk about raising children in the most famous home in the country.

President-elect Trump and President Obama met privately in the Oval Office in a ritual of peaceful transition that is the hallmark of our democracy. They had been vigorous opponents on the campaign trail—Obama as Hillary Clinton's most combative surrogate, who believed his legacy was at stake; and Trump, as the champion of many who wanted to see Obama's achievements undone—but the two men had never met personally before they shook hands on this day. Their meeting, which was expected to last no more than twenty minutes, stretched on for an hour and a half as Obama described the enormity of the job—its organizational structure, its foreign-policy complexities, and its domestic challenges. Trump, who has never been shy, listened more than he talked, soaking in the reality of the job, asking questions about specifics. When the press was allowed in, they saw two men, sitting side by side in high-back chairs, sober and at ease. In brief statements each expressed deep respect and seriousness about the task that was before them. "My number one priority," said Obama, "is to try to facilitate a transition that assures our president-elect is successful." Trump, uncharacteristically deferential, replied, "It was a great honor being with you, and I look forward to being with you many, many more times." Beneath the clatter of the press cameras, he said softly, almost inaudibly, referring to Obama, "He is a good man."

And so the careful orchestration of presidential transition, which Ike had so valued, began once again—the Oval Office veteran and the newcomer joined in common cause.

AT THE BEGINNING, NO one thought it could happen—no one gave Trump a chance in a field of seventeen Republican hopefuls, and less of a chance up against the Clinton machine in the general election. But on January 20, 2017, the improbable will happen. Donald J. Trump will be sworn in as the forty-fifth president of the United States after an historic campaign—clearly one of the most nontraditional and most negative campaigns the country has ever seen on both sides. The anti-establishment, populist if not nationalist, blunt-spoken, hard-charging billionaire businessman from New York captured the imagination of voters who, exit polls show, were seriously fed up with Washington on both sides of the aisle.

Hillary Clinton, while well-funded and backed by even some wary Republicans, proved to be a poor campaigner, the embodiment of the establishment, and weighed down by investigations and questions about her honesty. President Barack Obama tried to help. While he leaves office with much higher approval ratings than his predecessor George W. Bush had when he left office, the world is a much more dangerous and uncertain place. Global hotspots appear to only be getting hotter. The threat of terrorism is on the rise. Our country has a record-high national debt. There are serious questions about the future and viability of his signature health care law, Obamacare. The U.S. economy has sputtered along but never fully hit all cylinders in recovery. And thousands of U.S. troops are still fighting in two wars that the Obama administration took credit for ending. (Though technically the administration said the troops are not engaged in "combat operations.")

Now Donald Trump has the mandate and President Obama is blocked from the third Democratic term he was hoping for to try to keep his policies and executive orders intact. And Democrats are left to lick their wounds and to try to pick up the pieces in time for the midterms and then the next presidential battle.

This election did follow a normal script in one way. American voters frequently act like a pendulum from election to election. Swinging one way to correct or change what was lacking in the previous president, and then swinging back the other way after four or eight years—always looking for change . . . sometimes hope and change. Donald Trump's success seemed to be a direct swing from the professorial President Obama, "No Drama Obama," as he was called, the president accused by Republicans of not being a forceful leader on the world stage. Trump, with his bold, kick-the-table-over, not politically correct, nonpolitician, New York businessman style, attracted attention and votes from people sick of both parties.

The Clinton camp eventually ended up with the same messaging they tried to make stick in her first presidential run in 2008. "Do you want Donald Trump answering the red phone in the White House at three in the morning?" Voters said "yes" when the name in the ad was the new senator Barack Obama in 2008—and despite increased fears about the state of the world, they also said "yes" to the opinionated billionaire Trump in 2016.

Trump becomes only the fifth president to never have been elected to public office before his inauguration. The previous four: Zachary Taylor, Ulysses S. Grant, Herbert Hoover, and Dwight D. Eisenhower.

On social media and cable TV news this election cycle, many people of all political persuasions say they are largely disappointed by the failures of our system and have been more dismissive of experience and gravitas than ever before. While campaigning for her, President Obama said, "There has never been any man or woman more qualified for this office than Hillary Clinton." The former First Lady, former senator, and former secretary of state faced those headwinds and fell victim to the atmosphere in the country.

Eisenhower fans may argue with President Obama's declarative statement, but the key question is how President-elect Trump plans to make decisions inside the Oval Office. Ike's final mission in office in 1961 was to make sure incoming President-elect Kennedy knew the challenges of the job, knew the weight of the decisions and the mere fact that the job—and that weight—never leave you as president. Eisenhower's biggest worry about Kennedy was that he had a "seat-of-the-pants attitude"—as Ike put it, JFK viewed the presidency as "an institution that one man could handle with an assistant here and another there." Once in office, Kennedy felt the election pendulum swinging for change and disregarded Ike's warnings, choosing to dismantle his carefully built national security apparatus designed for key aides to debate tough decisions laying out pros and cons in front of the President.

Within three months of taking office, Kennedy fell into the Bay of Pigs fiasco because either he didn't have the advisors in place to tell him it was folly—or wasn't listening to them. In desperation, he called Ike to Camp David for help. And Ike gave him the Abilene version of "I told you so" with a big grin, before offering sage advice to the young president.

Donald Trump has made big business decisions and has

taken advice from a small circle of advisors and family members, but has never had the weight of the world on his shoulders in crisis. We live in a fast-moving, Internet, social media, twenty-four-hour news world where decisions are talked about, debated, discarded, and then resurrected—even before they are actually made by world leaders. But the job of president of the United States is performed mostly *outside* the view of the media—much to the news media's chagrin. And as Eisenhower noted throughout his time in office, sitting behind that desk in the Oval Office is grave and serious business.

On the campaign trail, Trump touted Eisenhower several times at rallies, always adding, "I like Ike." He pointed to Eisenhower deporting more than one million illegal immigrants from Mexico in a 1954 operation as proof that Trump's controversial immigration policies could work. (There are now more than 12 million illegal immigrants in the U.S., and the 1954 operation, which was roundly criticized, was in conjunction with the Mexican government.) On foreign policy, Trump has talked tough but also expressed a healthy skepticism about getting involved militarily around the world. Finding the balance to promote peace *was* vintage Eisenhower.

In this transition time since his election, President-elect Trump has been urged to take a step back from the noisy clamor of day-to-day modern politics to try to draw inspiration from history. In particular, Eisenhower may provide a template for how to govern during a time when the international landscape is hostile and dangerous as it is now. One of the biggest gifts Ike had was ignoring the loudest voices in the room in favor of deliberate and wise counsel. Campaigning and governing are two very different things. The decisions President Trump makes will shape the world.

From that first visit to the Eisenhower Cabin at Augusta

National in 2013 . . . to the Eisenhower Library in Abilene, Kansas, numerous times . . . through a tumultuous presidential election with twists and turns . . . to now ten days before the forty-fifth president is sworn into office, it has been a real joy rediscovering the thirty-fourth president and the messages he had back then that clearly translate to today. Every president is peppered with questions, problems, decisions to be made, and every president comes from his or her own perspective—but the one question aides said Ike always asked was, "Is it good for America?" Let's hope that question drives most discussions inside the White House and that the new president remembers the paperweight on Eisenhower's Oval Office desk: gently in manner, strong in deed.

ACKNOWLEDGMENTS

PRESIDENT EISENHOWER KNEW HOW to tap into the power of others, to encourage them to be their best, to work toward an objective, and to make sure they got credit. This book could NOT have happened without the amazing work and writing of my coauthor, Catherine Whitney. Her tireless hours of work and research, and her ability to capture my voice and writing style as we bounced copy back and forth, refining every last word, has been remarkable. From the first time we sat down to walk through the premise and scope of the book, Catherine had a gleam in her eye that rediscovering Eisenhower was as important to her as it was to me. She lived, breathed, and slept Eisenhower for many months, and this book is the result of that dedication. Catherine is a real pro.

A special thank-you to Sydney Soderberg, our researcher at the library in Abilene, who was invaluable as well. Sydney helped us find "nuggets" of information inside the vast expanse of documents and oral histories that really made the book come to life. In a true Kansas way, Sydney welcomed us like we were family every visit we made to Abilene. A former mayor of nearby Salina, Sydney could be doing anything she wanted—but we were ecstatic she signed on to dig out research treasures about Ike for us.

I am particularly grateful for the tremendous support of the staff at the Eisenhower Library and Museum in Abilene. Thank you to former director Karl M. Weissenbach, and Tim Rives, the deputy (now acting) director, who both helped me originally formulate the idea for the book. Thanks to William Snyder, curator of the museum, Samantha Kerner, communications director, and Kathy Struss, audiovisual archivist. The John F. Kennedy Library and the Truman Library were also instrumental in our research. In particular, I want to thank Maryrose Grossman, audio/visual archivist at the John F. Kennedy Library.

The Columbia University Oral History Project's dedication to preserving the voices of previous administrations is a noble effort—and it made Ike's presidency feel as if it were happening in real time. Very special thanks to David A Olson, archivist for the Columbia Center for Oral History, Rare Books and Manuscript Library, Columbia University.

Writers of history stand on the shoulders of many others, and I am deeply grateful for the rich library of books and media about Ike's life, produced by authors, editors, documentarians, photographers, and others, who endeavored, as I have, to shine a bright light on Ike's important legacy. These contributions, including those of Ike's grandchildren, have meant a great deal to me.

What started almost four years ago, after that fateful trip to Augusta National, is now a reality. It happened because of some great teamwork. Not only Catherine and Sydney and the team above from Abilene, but also my manager, Larry Kramer, and book agent, Claudia Cross, helped get this book to the finish line.

Special thanks to Peter Hubbard, my editor at William Morrow. From the start, he grasped my vision for the book, and his dedication, patience, and insight have been invaluable. My deepest appreciation to Peter and to the entire team at William Morrow.

And thank you to my wife, Amy, and sons Paul and Daniel, for putting up with my schedule during a crazy election cycle while also working on this book.

Hopefully, this book will bring the thirty-fourth President of the United States into new focus for a new generation. We can ALWAYS learn from our past.

APPENDIX

EISENHOWER'S FAREWELL ADDRESS TO THE NATION

January 17, 1961

Good evening, my fellow Americans.

First, I should like to express my gratitude to the radio and television networks for the opportunities they have given me over the years to bring reports and messages to our nation. My special thanks go to them for the opportunity of addressing you this evening.

Three days from now, after half a century in the service of our country, I shall lay down the responsibilities of office as, in traditional and solemn ceremony, the authority of the Presidency is vested in my successor. This evening, I come to you with a message of leave-taking and farewell, and to share a few final thoughts with you, my countrymen.

Like every other—Like every other citizen, I wish the new President, and all who will labor with him, Godspeed. I pray that the coming years will be blessed with peace and prosperity for all.

Our people expect their President and the Congress to find essential agreement on issues of great moment, the wise resolution of which will better shape the future of the nation. My own relations with the Congress, which began on a remote and tenuous basis when, long ago, a member of the Senate appointed me to West Point, have since ranged to the intimate during the war and immediate post-war period, and finally to the mutually interdependent during these past eight years. In this final relationship, the Congress and the Administration have, on most vital issues, cooperated well, to serve the nation good, rather than mere partisanship, and so have assured that the business of the nation should go forward. So, my official relationship with the Congress ends in a feeling—on my part—of gratitude that we have been able to do so much together.

We now stand ten years past the midpoint of a century that has witnessed four major wars among great nations. Three of these involved our own country. Despite these holocausts, America is today the strongest, the most influential, and most productive nation in the world. Understandably proud of this pre-eminence, we yet realize that America's leadership and prestige depend, not merely upon our unmatched material progress, riches, and military strength, but on how we use our power in the interests of world peace and human betterment.

Throughout America's adventure in free government, our basic purposes have been to keep the peace, to foster progress in human achievement, and to enhance liberty, dignity, and integrity among peoples and among nations. To strive for less would be unworthy of a free and religious people. Any failure traceable to arrogance, or our lack of comprehension, or readiness to sacrifice would inflict upon us grievous hurt, both at home and abroad.

Progress toward these noble goals is persistently threatened by the conflict now engulfing the world. It commands our whole attention, absorbs our very beings. We face a hostile ideology global in scope, atheistic in character, ruthless in purpose, and insiduous [insidious] in method. Unhappily, the danger it poses promises to be of indefinite duration. To meet it successfully, there is called for, not so much the emotional and transitory sacrifices of crisis, but rather those which enable us to carry forward steadily, surely, and without complaint the burdens of a prolonged and complex struggle with liberty the stake. Only thus shall we remain, despite every provocation, on our charted course toward permanent peace and human betterment.

Crises there will continue to be. In meeting them, whether foreign or domestic, great or small, there is a recurring temptation to feel that some spectacular and costly action could become the miraculous solution to all current difficulties. A huge increase in newer elements of our defenses; development of unrealistic programs to cure every ill in agriculture; a dramatic expansion in basic and applied research—these and many other possibilities, each possibly promising in itself, may be suggested as the only way to the road we wish to travel.

But each proposal must be weighed in the light of a broader consideration: the need to maintain balance in and among national programs, balance between the private and the public economy, balance between the cost and hoped-for advantages, balance between the clearly necessary and the comfortably desirable, balance between our essential requirements as a nation and the duties imposed by the nation upon the individual, balance between actions of the moment and the national welfare of the future. Good judgment seeks balance and progress. Lack of it eventually finds imbalance and frustration. The record of many decades stands as proof that our people and their Government have, in the main, understood these truths and have responded to them well, in the face of threat and stress.

But threats, new in kind or degree, constantly arise. Of these, I mention two only.

A vital element in keeping the peace is our military establishment. Our arms must be mighty, ready for instant action, so that no potential aggressor may be tempted to risk his own destruction. Our military organization today bears little relation to that known of any of my predecessors in peacetime, or, indeed, by the fighting men of World War II or Korea.

Until the latest of our world conflicts, the United States had no armaments industry. American makers of plowshares could, with time and as required, make swords as well. But we can no longer risk emergency improvisation of national defense. We have been compelled to create a permanent armaments industry of vast proportions. Added to this, three and a half million men and women are directly engaged in the defense establishment. We annually spend on military security alone more than the net income of all United States corporations.

Now this conjunction of an immense military establishment and a large arms industry is new in the American experience. The total influence—economic, political, even spiritual—is felt in every city, every Statehouse, every office of the Federal government. We recognize the imperative need for this development. Yet, we must not fail to comprehend its grave implications. Our toil, resources, and livelihood are all involved. So is the very structure of our society.

In the councils of government, we must guard against the acquisition of unwarranted influence, whether sought or unsought, by the military-industrial complex. The potential for the disastrous rise of misplaced power exists and will persist. We must never let the weight of this combination endanger our liberties or democratic processes. We should take nothing for granted. Only an alert and knowledgeable citizenry can compel the proper meshing of the huge industrial and military machinery of defense with our peaceful methods and goals, so that security and liberty may prosper together.

Akin to, and largely responsible for the sweeping changes in our industrial-military posture, has been the technological revolution during recent decades. In this revolution, research has become central; it also becomes more formalized, complex, and costly. A steadily increasing share is conducted for, by, or at the direction of, the Federal government.

Today, the solitary inventor, tinkering in his shop, has been overshadowed by task forces of scientists in laboratories and testing fields. In the same fashion, the free university, historically the fountainhead of free ideas and scientific discovery, has experienced a revolution in the conduct of research. Partly because of the huge costs involved, a government contract becomes virtually a substitute for intellectual curiosity. For every old blackboard there are now hundreds of new electronic computers. The prospect of domination of the nation's scholars by Federal employment, project allocations, and the power of money is ever present—and is gravely to be regarded.

Yet, in holding scientific research and discovery in respect, as we should, we must also be alert to the equal and opposite danger that public policy could itself become the captive of a scientific-technological elite.

It is the task of statesmanship to mold, to balance, and to integrate these and other forces, new and old, within the principles of our democratic system—ever aiming toward the supreme goals of our free society.

Another factor in maintaining balance involves the element of time. As we peer into society's future, we—you and I, and our government—must avoid the impulse to live only for today, plundering for our own ease and convenience the precious resources of tomorrow. We cannot mortgage the material assets of our grandchildren without risking the loss also of their political and spiritual heritage. We want democracy to survive for all generations to come, not to become the insolvent phantom of tomorrow.

During the long lane of the history yet to be written, America knows that this world of ours, ever growing smaller, must avoid becoming a community of dreadful fear and hate, and be, instead, a proud confederation of mutual trust and respect. Such a confederation must be one of equals. The weakest must come to the conference table with the same confidence as do we, protected as we are by our moral, economic, and military strength. That table, though scarred by many fast frustrations— past frustrations, cannot be abandoned for the certain agony of disarmament—of the battlefield.

Disarmament, with mutual honor and confidence, is a continuing imperative. Together we must learn how to compose differences, not with arms, but with intellect and decent purpose. Because this need is so sharp and apparent, I confess that I lay down my official responsibilities in this field with a definite sense of disappointment. As one who has witnessed the horror and the lingering sadness of war, as one who knows that another war could utterly destroy this civilization which has been so slowly and painfully built over thousands of years, I wish I could say tonight that a lasting peace is in sight.

Happily, I can say that war has been avoided. Steady progress toward our ultimate goal has been made. But so much remains to be done. As a private citizen, I shall never cease to do what little I can to help the world advance along that road.

So, in this, my last good night to you as your President, I thank you for the many opportunities you have given me for public service in war and in peace. I trust in that—in that—in that service you find some things worthy. As for the rest of it, I know you will find ways to improve performance in the future.

You and I, my fellow citizens, need to be strong in our faith that all nations, under God, will reach the goal of peace with justice. May we be ever unswerving in devotion to principle, confident but humble with power, diligent in pursuit of the Nation's great goals.

To all the peoples of the world, I once more give expression to America's prayerful and continuing aspiration: We pray that peoples of all faiths, all races, all nations, may have their great human needs satisfied; that those now denied opportunity shall come to enjoy it to the full; that all who yearn for freedom may experience its few spiritual blessings. Those who have freedom will understand, also, its heavy responsibility; that all who are insensitive to the needs of others will learn charity; and that the sources—scourges of poverty, disease, and ignorance will be made [to] disappear from the earth; and that in the goodness of time, all peoples will come to live together in a peace guaranteed by the binding force of mutual respect and love.

Now, on Friday noon, I am to become a private citizen. I am proud to do so. I look forward to it.

Thank you, and good night.

NOTES

INTRODUCTION: FINDING IKE

xiii *The library and museum are built*: After their beloved mother's death in 1946, the Eisenhower brothers decided to memorialize the property and keep it intact. They made it a gift to the Eisenhower Foundation, which had been created to honor Ike—then General Eisenhower. The library, museum, and chapel came later, but to this day the humble house is the centerpiece; millions of visitors have walked in the front door and experienced Ike's early life.

xiv *The historian Jon Meacham*: From *The Roosevelts: An Intimate History*, a film by Ken Burns, PBS, 2014.

xvii *glasses slipping down*: Oral history with Dr. Gabriel Hauge by Ed Edwin, March 10, 1967, p. 49, Columbia University Oral History Project, Dwight D. Eisenhower Library.

xviii *In 2014, the scholars*: 2014 Survey of the American Political Sciences Association's President and Executive Politics Section.

PROLOGUE: THE VISIT

1 *Kennedy came alone*: Press accounts, such as William J. Eaton, "Kennedy to Get a Big Ike 'Hello,'" UPI; Edward T. Folliard, "Kennedy, Eisenhower Talk 3½ Hours in Policy Briefing at White House," *Washington Post*.

1 *"The general doesn't know any more about politics"*: Reported in the *Kansas City Times*, October 24, 1952.

2 *Eisenhower grumbled*: Emmet John Hughes, *The Ordeal of Power: A Political Memoir of the Eisenhower Years* (London: Macmillan, 1975).

2 *things deteriorated*: In *Eisenhower: The Inside Story* (New York: Harper & Brothers, 1956), Robert J. Donovan points out that top hats had been the style for one hundred years, and Truman thought it was his place to set the style, since he was the president. Ike insisted on a homburg and quipped that tradition wasn't the issue. "If we were going back to tradition, we would wear tricornered hats and knee britches."

2 *"I'm glad I wasn't"*: J. B. West, *Upstairs at the White House: My Life with the First Ladies* (New York: Coward, McCann & Geoghegan, 1973).

2 *Now Ike was determined*: Carl M. Brauer, *Presidential Transitions: Eisenhower Through Reagan* (New York: Oxford University Press, 1986).

2 *Kennedy hadn't particularly distinguished*: John T. Shaw, *JFK in the Senate: Pathway to the Presidency* (New York: St. Martin's Griffin, 2015). Shaw

writes, "A national celebrity because of his famous family, celebrated war record, and impressive literary prowess, Kennedy struggled to find a role in the upper chamber that was commensurate with his ambition and promise." Shaw adds that Kennedy showed "a reluctance to immerse himself in the drudgery of legislative affairs."

3 *Ike had been depressed*: Dwight D. Eisenhower, *Waging Peace: The White House Years 1956–1961* (Garden City, NY: Doubleday, 1965).

4 *Was Ike trying to dump*: Kenneth Crawford first reported the suggestion in *Newsweek*. The following week at Ike's press conference, Crawford meant to ask him about it, and he was sweating because he thought there was a good chance Ike would deny the story. Instead, Ike "said yes, he had told Nixon that maybe the best thing for him, Nixon, would not be to remain in the Vice Presidency, and that he had asked him to consider paddling his own canoe." Oral history with Kenneth Crawford by John Luter, June 13, 1967, pp. 19–20, Columbia University Oral History Project, Dwight D. Eisenhower Library. Also, according to Milton Eisenhower, Ike's suggestion was sincere. Milton noted that Ike had come to admire Nixon, and he "genuinely thought that the vice presidency was not a good political stepping stone to the Presidency." Ike was considering Nixon for secretary of defense. Oral history with Milton Eisenhower by John Luter, September 6, 1967, pp. 46–47, Columbia University Oral History Project, Dwight D. Eisenhower Library.

4 *she felt sorry*: Oral history interview of Pierre Salinger by Theodore White, July 19, 1965, John F. Kennedy Presidential Library.

4 WE LIKE IKE: Nancy Gibbs and Michael Duffy, *The Presidents Club: Inside the World's Most Exclusive Fraternity* (New York: Simon & Schuster, 2012).

4 *"clique of young, so-called"*: Tom Wicker, "Eisenhower Mocks Kennedy Record," *New York Times*, October 9, 1960.

4 *"With every word he utters"*: Gibbs and Duffy, *The Presidents Club*.

5 *Upon Kennedy's victory*: Oral history with Pierre Salinger by Theodore White, July 19, 1965, John F. Kennedy Library. Both telegrams are on file at the Dwight D. Eisenhower Library.

5 *"We are facing"*: Speech by John F. Kennedy on national defense in the U.S. Senate, February 1960, as he was launching his presidential campaign, John F. Kennedy Library and Museum.

7 *Honestly, Eisenhower hadn't*: James Hagerty's notes from the meeting, recounted by Eisenhower, Dwight D. Eisenhower Library; also oral history with Clark Clifford by Larry J. Hackman, December 16, 1974, John F. Kennedy Library. Clifford recalled being told by his and Ike's mutual friend George Allen that Ike was impressed with Kennedy. "And apparently, because of the great difference in their ages—I think President Kennedy being the youngest president ever elected and President Eisenhower being the oldest president ever elected—Allen said prior to his talk Eisenhower had considered Kennedy a 'young whippersnapper.' So the talk they had was good."

7 *"Sure it's a big job"*: Thomas E. Cronin, *On the Presidency: Teacher, Soldier, Shaman, Pol* (Boulder, CO: Paradigm, 2009).

8 *He hoped Kennedy*: Stephen E. Ambrose, *Eisenhower: Soldier and President* (New York: Simon & Schuster, 1990).

8 *The two men discussed*: James Hagerty notes from the meeting, recounted by Eisenhower, Dwight D. Eisenhower Library.

8 *Kennedy was in favor*: Ibid. This conversation will be revisited at Eisenhower and Kennedy's second meeting on January 19, and has tremendous historical relevancy in the blame game over the Bay of Pigs.

9 *In his 1959 U.S. visit*: Oral history with Barbara Eisenhower by Carol Hegeman and Lawrence Eckert, August 20 and September 11, 1983, pp. 6–7, Eisenhower National Historic Site, National Park Service.

9 *Watching Kennedy closely*: James Hagerty notes from the meeting, recounted by Eisenhower, Dwight D. Eisenhower Library; also Joint Statement by the

President and President-Elect Kennedy, December 6, 1960, in *Public Papers of the President: Dwight D. Eisenhower: 1960*, doc. 369.

10 *Ike could not emphasize enough*: Oral history with Milton Eisenhower by Herbert Parmet, June 19, 1969, Columbia University Oral History Project, Dwight D. Eisenhower Library.

11 *Ike was a "leavener"*: Oral history interview with Sherman Adams by Herbert Parmet, July 31 and August 3, 1969, p. 48, Columbia University Oral History Project, Dwight D. Eisenhower Library.

11 *the only way to win*: Campaign rally speech, Civic Auditorium, Seattle, Washington, October 17, 1956.

11 *Under Ike's watch*: Stephen I. Schwartz, ed., *Atomic Audit: The Costs and Consequences of U.S. Nuclear Weapons Since 1940* (Washington, D.C.: Brookings Institution Press, 1998).

12 *As he walked*: James Hagerty notes from December 6, 1960, Dwight D. Eisenhower Library.

CHAPTER 1: THE MEASURE OF IKE

15 *"If I'm lucky"*: Oral history interview with Mamie Eisenhower by Maclyn Burg and Dr. John Wickman, July 15–16, 1972, p. 70, Dwight D. Eisenhower Library.

16 *A White House aide*: William B. Ewald Jr., "Eisenhower," *American Experience*, PBS WGBH Educational Foundation 1993, http://www.pbs.org/wgbh/americanexperience/features/transcript/eisenhower-transcript/.

16 *Ida was bright*: Tim Horan, "Eisenhower Stories Abound," *Salina Journal*, May 29, 2016.

18 *The Eisenhowers' religion*: Jerry Bergman, "Steeped in Religion: President Eisenhower and the Influence of the Jehovah's Witnesses," *Kansas History* 21, no. 3 (Autumn 1998): 148–67; also John R. Hertzler, "The 1879 Brethren in Christ Migration from Southwestern Pennsylvania to Dickinson County, Kansas," *Pennsylvania Mennonite Heritage* 8, no. 1 (January 1980): 11–18; also, Eisenhower's own account in his *At Ease: Stories I Tell to Friends* (Garden City, NY: Doubleday, 1967).

18 *During Eisenhower's administration*: "Eisenhower's Faith: An Interview with Billy Graham," *Link*, September 1969, pp. 5–7; also Frederick Fox, "The National Day of Prayer," *Theology Today* 30 (July 1973): pp. 258–60.

18 *he spent the first Day of Prayer*: Robert S. Alley, *So Help Me God: Religion and the Presidency, Wilson to Nixon* (Richmond, VA: John Knox Press, 1972).

18 *It was supposed to be*: Oral history with Merriman Smith by John Luter, January 3, 1968, p. 74, Columbia University Oral History Project, Dwight D. Eisenhower Library.

19 *Living right across*: Eisenhower, *At Ease*.

19 *it isn't surprising*: On May 10, 2004, Congressman Todd Russell Platts read into the Congressional Record a remembrance by the historian John Burke Jovich, written on the thirty-fifth anniversary of Ike's death, including an ode to his "Everyman" style: "He was also very much a common man who preferred watching 'Gunsmoke' on the back porch of his Gettysburg farmhouse while eating a TV dinner atop a tray, as opposed to hosting a formal dinner at the White House."

19 *"I was raised"*: Eisenhower's remarks upon receiving the Democratic Legacy Award at B'nai B'rith dinner in honor of the fortieth anniversary of the Anti-Defamation League, November 25, 1953.

20 *Ike relished the rural life*: Eisenhower, *At Ease*.

20 *In later years*: Oral history with Barbara Eisenhower by Carol Hegeman and Lawrence Eckert, August 20 and September 11, 1983, Eisenhower National Historic Site, National Park Service.

20 *Ike's first encounter*: Eisenhower, *At Ease*.

21 *"Father was the breadwinner"*: Ibid.

21 *A favorite story*: Ibid.
22 *And the best chore*: Eisenhower's remarks at the Convention of the National Association of Retail Grocers, June 16, 1954.
23 *"In retrospect"*: Television broadcast, "The People Ask the President," from the Sheraton-Park Hotel in Washington, D.C., October 12, 1956.
23 *watching baby Milton*: Interview with Milton Eisenhower at childhood home by Dr. Maclyn Burg, October 15, 1971, Dwight D. Eisenhower Library.
23 *Ike was easily distracted*: Eisenhower, *At Ease.*
24 *love in the Eisenhower*: Ibid.
24 *As he wrote*: Ibid.
24 *Ike described himself*: Ibid.
24 *But an accident*: Ibid.
26 *Ike sent a letter*: Letters to Senator Bristow, August 20, 1910, and October 25, 1910, on file in the Dwight D. Eisenhower Library.
26 *Milton, who was twelve*: Interview with Milton Eisenhower at childhood home by Dr. Maclyn Burg, October 15, 1971, Dwight D. Eisenhower Library.
27 *In his early*: Eisenhower, *At Ease.*
27 *"It would be difficult to overemphasize"*: Ibid.
28 *"Homer and his legendary"*: Ibid.
28 *"the class the stars"*: Michael E. Haskew, *West Point 1915: Eisenhower, Bradley, and the Class the Stars Fell On* (Minneapolis: Zenith Press, 2014).
28 *His disciplinary infractions*: From records of Cadet Dwight D. Eisenhower, USMA, 1915, Dwight D. Eisenhower Library.
30 *Eighteen-year-old Mamie*: Eisenhower, *At Ease.*
31 *As a side*: Merle Miller, *Ike the Soldier: As They Knew Him* (New York: G. P. Putnam's Sons, 1987).
32 *"I understand that Mr. Ike Jr."* : Letters to Mamie. Although Ike Jr. was nicknamed "Icky," in his correspondence Ike sometimes spelled it "Ikky."
32 *Temperamentally, they were*: Eisenhower, *At Ease.*
32 *"He plays a good hand"*: Susan Eisenhower, *Mrs. Ike: Portrait of a Marriage* (New York: Farrar, Straus & Giroux, 2011).
33 *Ann Whitman recalled*: Miller, *Ike the Soldier.*
33 *Conner, who had served*: Eisenhower, *At Ease.*
34 *"I am certain I was born standing"*: John S. D. Eisenhower, *Strictly Personal* (Garden City, NY: Doubleday, 1974).
35 *"This is the best officer"*: Efficiency Report Dwight D. Eisenhower—0-3822—Major Infantry, records at the Dwight D. Eisenhower Library.
36 *"MacArthur could never see"*: Miller, *Ike the Soldier.*
37 *He spoke long and seriously*: Eisenhower, *At Ease*; also oral history with John S. D. Eisenhower by Carol Hegeman, January 26, 1984, Eisenhower National Historic Site, National Park Service.
37 *Ike was napping*: Oral history interview with Mamie Eisenhower by Maclyn Burg and Dr. John Wickman, July 15–16, 1972, pp. 84–86, Dwight D. Eisenhower Library.
38 *"Tempers are short"*: Ferrell, ed., *The Eisenhower Diaries.*
39 *"Dad would make a tee"*: Oral history with John S. D. Eisenhower by Carol Hegeman, January 26, 1984, Eisenhower National Historic Site, National Park Service.
40 *On March 10, 1942*: Ferrell, ed., *The Eisenhower Diaries.*
40 *"The sight of my mother"*: Eisenhower, *At Ease.*
40 *Ike presented*: Ibid.
41 *"What's your job"*: Oral history with John S. D. Eisenhower by Carol Hegeman, January 26, 1984, p. 24, Eisenhower National Historic Site, National Park Service.

CHAPTER 2: IKE IN COMMAND

42 *"Darling," he wrote Mamie*: Mamie kept Ike's letters in a box (and never looked at them again, she said). But she saved them all.

42 *The social side*: Eisenhower recounted this story in a speech at the Pilgrims Dinner, New York City, May 22, 1963. Complete copy in 1962–63 Signature File, box 23, Dwight D. Eisenhower Library.

43 *He battled loneliness*: Letters to Mamie, September 15, 1942.

43 *The chief stumbling*: Dwight D. Eisenhower, *Crusade in Europe* (Garden City, NY: Doubleday, 1948).

44 *"I will clamp down"*: Ibid.

44 *The operation would*: Ibid.

46 *"I worried like all the rest"*: Oral history interview with Mamie Eisenhower by Maclyn Burg and Dr. John Wickman, July 15–16, 1972, p. 97, Dwight D. Eisenhower Library.

46 *"Ike depended a great deal"*: Oral history interview with Mamie Eisenhower by Maclyn Burg and Dr. John Wickman, July 15–16, 1972, pp. 110–11, Dwight D. Eisenhower Library.

46 *When FDR arrived*: Eisenhower, *Crusade in Europe*.

47 *"FDR also liked Ike"*: Jean Edward Smith, *Eisenhower in War and Peace* (New York: Random House, 2012).

48 *"He's not the greatest soldier"*: Joseph E. Persico: *Roosevelt's Centurions: FDR and the Commanders He Led to Victory in World War II* (New York: Random House, 2013).

49 *The devil, of course*: Eisenhower, *Crusade in Europe*.

50 *For Assaulting Army*: Ibid.

50 *Unfortunately, once Patton*: Ibid.

51 *"When I think of the beaches"*: Eisenhower, *At Ease*.

52 *So it was very bad news*: Ibid.

53 *Ike slumped in his chair*: John S. D. Eisenhower, *Strictly Personal* (Garden City, NY: Doubleday, 1974).

53 *"Okay, we'll go"*: There are a number of versions about what Ike actually said in that moment. In his analysis of the record, "Like Footprints in the Sand: Searching for Eisenhower's Climactic D-Day Words," Tim Rives, the deputy director of the Dwight D. Eisenhower Presidential Library, cites a few of the versions: Lieutenant General Bedell Smith, Ike's chief of staff, recalled, "Well, we'll go"; Major General Frances "Freddie" De Guingand, Montgomery's chief of staff, recalled, "We will sail tomorrow"; the intelligence officer, Major General Kenneth Strong, recalled, "Okay, boys, we will go"; Ike himself recalled, "Okay, we'll go," in a later interview with Walter Cronkite.

54 *That day, in a moment*: Eisenhower's written apology in the event of Overlord's failure is at the Dwight D. Eisenhower Library and on display at the museum.

54 *"We saw hundreds of"*: Captain Harry C. Butcher, *My Three Years with Ike: The Personal Diary of Captain Harry C. Butcher, USNR, Naval Aide to General Eisenhower, 1942 to 1945* (New York: Simon & Schuster, 1946).

54 *Ike's feeling for his*: John Thompson, *Chicago Tribune* war series, 1944.

55 *"I found the men"*: Eisenhower, *Crusade in Europe*.

55 *"Honey," Mamie always asked*: Oral history interview with Mamie Eisenhower by Maclyn Burg and Dr. John Wickman, July 15–16, 1972, p. 112, Dwight D. Eisenhower Library.

56 *The Germans never*: Eisenhower, *Crusade in Europe*.

56 *"The present situation"*: Ibid.

57 *To inspire confidence*: Ibid.

57 *"General, there is nothing"*: Jean Edward Smith, *Eisenhower in War and Peace* (New York: Random House, 2012); also oral history with John S. D. Eisenhower by Carol Hegeman, January 26, 1984, Eisenhower National Historic Site, National Park Service.

58 *"During his recitation"*: Dwight D. Eisenhower, *Mandate for Change: The White House Years 1953–1956* (Garden City, NY: Doubleday, 1965).

58 *According to Churchill*: Winston Churchill, *Triumph and Tragedy: The Second World War*, vol. 6 (Boston: Houghton Mifflin, 1953).

59 *"If we have a nuclear exchange"*: John Eisenhower, "Eisenhower," *American Experience*, PBS WGBH Educational Foundation, 1993.

59 *In August Ike accepted*: Oral history with John S. D. Eisenhower by Carol Hegeman, January 26, 1984, pp. 34–35, Eisenhower National Historic Site, National Park Service. (John accompanied his father on the trip.)

59 *MacArthur boasted*: Oral history interview with Joseph Alsop by John Luter, June 14, 1972, Columbia University Oral History Project, Dwight D. Eisenhower Library.

CHAPTER 3: A NONPOLITICIAN IN THE POLITICAL ARENA

61 *"I felt that the Republican Party"*: Oral history with Thomas E. Dewey by Pauline Madow, December 1, 1970, p. 2, Columbia University Oral History Project, Dwight D. Eisenhower Library.

62 *When the Columbia board of trustees*: Dwight D. Eisenhower, *At Ease: Stories I Tell to Friends* (Garden City, NY: Doubleday, 1967).

64 *"He was a soldier"*: Oral history interview with Mamie Eisenhower by Maclyn Burg and Dr. John Wickman, July 15–16, 1972, p. 134, Dwight D. Eisenhower Library.

64 *"I fired him because"*: Merle Miller, *Plain Speaking: An Oral Biography of Harry S. Truman* (New York: Black Dog and Leventhal, 1974).

65 *"I am amused to note"*: Robert H. Ferrell, ed., *The Eisenhower Diaries* (New York: Norton, 1981).

65 *Dewey told him*: Oral history with Milton Eisenhower by Herbert Parmet, June 19, 1969, p. 5, Columbia University Oral History Project, Dwight D. Eisenhower Library.

66 *Perhaps the turning point*: Ibid., p. 3; also Eisenhower, *At Ease*.

66 *"He was absolutely devoted"*: Oral history with Milton Eisenhower by Robert F. Ivanov, November 6, 1975, p. 34, Columbia University Oral History Project, Dwight D. Eisenhower Library.

67 *"You know, Governor"*: Oral history interview with Sherman Adams by Michael Birkner, March 3, 1985, Columbia University Oral History Project, Dwight D. Eisenhower Library.

67 *Breaking with the pro-Taft*: Lucius Clay, who was intimately involved at this point, had to explain to the New Hampshire folks that "'if we really want to lose him as a candidate, just serve him with an ultimatum that to win the nomination he's got to come back and campaign in New Hampshire.' But we carried New Hampshire hands down." Oral history with Lucius D. Clay by Jean Smith, April 17, 1971, pp. 905–6, Columbia University Oral History Project, Dwight D. Eisenhower Library; also Jean Edward Smith, *Lucius C. Clay: An American Life* (New York: Henry Holt, 1990).

67 *"Viewing it"*: Ferrell, ed., *The Eisenhower Diaries*.

68 *"Which one?"*: Oral history with J. Earl Schaefer by E. Alan Thompson, February 24, 1969, Columbia University Oral History Project, Dwight D. Eisenhower Library.

69 *"I want to know where a man"*: Oral history with Milton Eisenhower by Herbert Parmet, June 19, 1969, pp. 10–11, Columbia University Oral History Project, Dwight D. Eisenhower Library.

69 *He delivered the announcement*: Oral history interview with Mamie Eisenhower by Maclyn Burg and Dr. John Wickman, July 15–16, 1972, p. 145, Dwight D. Eisenhower Library. Milton also wrote about the day in his memoir, describing fifty thousand people showing up in a driving rain. Milton S. Eisenhower, *The President Is Calling: A Veteran Advisor for the Presidency Suggests Far-Reaching Changes* (Garden City, NY: Doubleday, 1974).

69 *"If he had a weakness"*: Oral history with James Hagerty by Ed Edwin, March 2, 1967, Columbia University Oral History Project, Dwight D. Eisenhower Library.
70 *Ike had the media*: Ibid.
71 *Ike's people aggressively*: Oral history with James Hagerty by Ed Edwin, March 2, 1967, Columbia University Oral History Project, Dwight D. Eisenhower Library.
71 *He was closeted*: Oral history with Lucius D. Clay by Jean Smith, April 17, 1971, p. 907, Columbia University Oral History Project, Dwight D. Eisenhower Library.
71 *Ike's first act*: Ike's spontaneous meeting with Taft was described by Milton: Oral history with Milton Eisenhower by Herbert Parmet, June 19, 1969, pp. 13–14, Columbia University Oral History Project, Dwight D. Eisenhower Library; also by Hagerty: Oral history with James Hagerty by Herbert Parmet, April 9, 1969, p. 47, Columbia University Oral History Project, Dwight D. Eisenhower Library.
72 *In the selection of his vice president*: Oral history with James Hagerty by Ed Edwin, March 2, 1967, Columbia University Oral History Project, Dwight D. Eisenhower Library; also oral history with Lucius D. Clay by Jean Smith, April 17, 1971, pp. 908–9, Columbia University Oral History Project, Dwight D. Eisenhower Library; also oral history with Milton Eisenhower by Herbert Parmet, June 19, 1969, p. 15, Columbia University Oral History Project, Dwight D. Eisenhower Library.
72 *"Politics is a funny thing"*: Oral history with James Hagerty by Ed Edwin, March 2, 1967, Columbia University Oral History Project, Dwight D. Eisenhower Library.
72 *"What do you mean"*: Oral history with James Hagerty by Ed Edwin, March 2, 1967, Columbia University Oral History Project, Dwight D. Eisenhower Library; also oral history interview with Sherman Adams by Ed Edwin, April 10, 1967, pp. 85–86, Columbia University Oral History Project, Dwight D. Eisenhower Library.
74 *When he emerged*: Oral history with Dr. Gabriel Hauge by Herbert Parmet, November 22, 1968, p. 9, Columbia University Oral History Project, Dwight D. Eisenhower Library.
74 *"I had never thought the man"*: Remarks by Harry Truman in Batavia, New York, October 10, 1952, Harry S. Truman Library and Museum.
74 *"a real hair shirt"*: Oral history with Thomas E. Dewey by Pauline Madow, December 1, 1970, p. 16, Columbia University Oral History Project, Dwight D. Eisenhower Library.
74 *"Truman is a man"*: Oral history with John S. D. Eisenhower by Carol Hegeman, January 26, 1984, p. 39, Columbia University Oral History Project, Eisenhower National Historic Site, National Park Service.
75 *When Stevenson declared*: Milton S. Eisenhower, *The President Is Calling*.
75 *"There was a great deal of hue and cry"*: Oral history interview with Sherman Adams by Ed Edwin, April 10, 1967, pp. 95–96, Columbia University Oral History Project, Dwight D. Eisenhower Library; also oral history with Milton Eisenhower by Herbert Parmet, June 19, 1969, pp. 15–19, Columbia University Oral History Project, Dwight D. Eisenhower Library.
75 *He also enjoyed*: Oral history with Dr. Gabriel Hauge by Ed Edwin, March 10, 1967, pp. 26–27, Columbia University Oral History Project, Dwight D. Eisenhower Library.
76 *Trying to run*: Ibid., pp. 15–16.
76 *Wanting to bring new voters*: Oral history with James Hagerty by Ed Edwin, March 2, 1967, Columbia University Oral History Project, Dwight D. Eisenhower Library; also oral history with Dr. Gabriel Hauge by Ed Edwin, March 10, 1967, pp. 34–35, Columbia University Oral History Project, Dwight D. Eisenhower Library.

77 *"He could have been"*: Oral history with James Hagerty by Herbert Parmet, April 9, 1969, p. 48, Columbia University Oral History Project, Dwight D. Eisenhower Library.

77 *noticed a group of nuns*: Oral history with Dr. Gabriel Hauge by Ed Edwin, March 10, 1967, p. 45, Columbia University Oral History Project, Dwight D. Eisenhower Library.

78 *"If we don't get some settlement"*: Oral history with James Hagerty by Ed Edwin, March 2, 1967, pp. 56–57, Columbia University Oral History Project, Dwight D. Eisenhower Library.

78 *"Now don't worry"*: Oral history with John S. D. Eisenhower by Carol Hegeman, January 26, 1984, p. 68, Eisenhower National Historic Site, National Park Service.

78 *On election eve*: http://www.c-span.org/video/?309007–1/eisenhower-campaign-election-eve-program.

79 *During the evening*: Dwight D. Eisenhower: *Mandate for Change: The White House Years 1953–1956* (Garden City, NY: Doubleday, 1965).

79 *it was revealed*: Steve Henn, "The Night a Computer Predicted the Next President," NPR, *All Tech Considered*, October 31, 2012.

80 *He was joined on the course*: David Sowell, *Eisenhower and Golf: A President at Play* (Jefferson, NC: McFarland, 2007).

81 *Afterward, Truman would*: Report of brusque Truman-Eisenhower meeting. *New York Times*, November 19, 1952; also Harry S. Truman, *Memoirs of Harry S. Truman*, vol. 2, *Years of Trial and Hope* (New York: Signet Books, 1956); also Steve Neal, *Harry and Ike: The Partnership That Remade the Postwar World* (New York: Touchstone, 2001).

81 *The women were warmer*: Oral history interview with Mamie Eisenhower by Maclyn Burg and Dr. John Wickman, July 15–16, 1972, p. 152, Dwight D. Eisenhower Library.

81 *Used to traveling*: Oral history with Wilton Persons by Stephen J. Wayne, May 29, 1974, Columbia University Oral History Project, Dwight D. Eisenhower Library.

82 *"I appreciate your"*: Eisenhower, *Mandate for Change*.

82 *"This is the first time"*: The exchange provoked a flurry of newspaper articles, such as this overly optimistic front page of the New York *Monthly Bulletin*, December 11, 1952: "Exchange of Messages Solves Far East Problems."

83 *"They knew he wasn't kidding"*: Oral history with James Hagerty by Ed Edwin, March 2, 1967, p. 87, Columbia University Oral History Project, Dwight D. Eisenhower Library.

83 *After the Korean War*: There is a slight dispute about this number. In an interview on *Meet the Press* on May 8, 2011, historian Doris Kearns Goodwin said, "Eisenhower, having won World War II, could then take enormous pride in the fact that not a single soldier had died in combat during his time." PolitiFact challenged the assertion. Even taking into consideration that her account referred to the period after the Korean War, PolitiFact noted that at the Vietnam Veterans Memorial, there is the name of Air Force Technical Sergeant Richard B. Fitzgibbon Jr., with a casualty date of June 8, 1956. Technically, though, Sergeant Fitzgibbon was not a "combat" death. Louis Jacobson, "Doris Kearns Goodwin Says No U.S. Combat Deaths under Eisenhower," PolitiFact, May 10, 2011.

CHAPTER 4: IKE'S HIDDEN CARD

84 *The mood inside*: Carl M. Brauer, *Presidential Transitions: Eisenhower Through Reagan* (New York: Oxford University Press, 1986); also Harry S. Truman, *Off the Record: The Private Papers of Harry S. Truman* (Columbia: University of Missouri Press, 1997).

85 *Richard Nixon, who took*: Edward T. Folliard, "Ike Takes Helm in a 'Time of Tempest': Says 'We Are Linked to All Free Peoples,'" *Washington Post*, January 21, 1953.

86 *Hoover called his successor*: Nancy Gibbs and Michael Duffy, *The Presidents Club: Inside the World's Most Exclusive Fraternity* (New York: Simon & Schuster, 2012).

86 *Roosevelt cared little*: Ibid.

86 *Hughes loved the lofty*: Robert H. Ferrell, ed., *The Eisenhower Diaries* (New York: Norton, 1981).

87 *Ike didn't like words to*: Ibid.

87 *"It sounds like I'm giving"*: Halford Ryan, ed., *The Inaugural Addresses of Twentieth-Century American Presidents* (New York: Praeger, 1993).

87 *he made it very clear*: Emmet John Hughes, *The Ordeal of Power: A Political Memoir of the Eisenhower Years* (London: Macmillan, 1975).

87 *at church that morning*: Eisenhower, *Mandate for Change*.

88 *a runaway train*: Bob Cohen, "The Wreck of the Federal Express." (Washington, D.C. Chapter, National Railways Historical Society, 1999).

89 *"Speaking as one who has marched"*: Robert Donovan, *Eisenhower: The Inside Story* (New York: Harper & Brothers, 1956).

90 *Once all the hoopla*: Oral history with John S. D. Eisenhower by Carol Hegeman, January 26, 1984, p. 105, Eisenhower National Historic Site, National Park Service.

91 *"He had this vein"*: Oral history with Ann Whitman, February 15, 1991, p. 6, Columbia University Oral History Project, Dwight D. Eisenhower Library.

91 *Ike hated them*: Ibid, p. 14.

91 *"Do you like jumping?"*: Dwight D. Eisenhower, *At Ease: Stories I Tell to Friends* (Garden City, NY: Doubleday, 1967).

91 *Richard Stout made a joke*: *New Republic*, December 15, 1952, under the pseudonym "TRB."

92 *The misquoted version*: Many people, hearing the misquoted version, thought that Wilson was just another imperious corporate titan who would sublimate America to industry's will. In fact, his words expressed a sense of humility and public spirit.

93 *"bellicose counterpart"*: Martin J. Medhurst, ed., *Eisenhower's War of Words: Rhetoric and Leadership* (East Lansing: Michigan State University Press, 1994).

93 *He even reviewed*: Ibid.; also, Ike's own account: "Foster made no important move without consulting the President," Ike wrote in a *Reader's Digest* piece, "Some Thoughts on the Presidency," in November 1968.

94 *Kay Bailey Hutchison*: "Women's History Month: Oveta Culp Hobby," *Texas Humanities,* March 2012.

94 *"Come on"*: Oral history with James Hagerty by Ed Edwin, March 2, 1967, p. 56, Columbia University Oral History Project, Dwight D. Eisenhower Library.

94 *"Every president has to have"*: Oral history with James Hagerty by Herbert Parmet, April 9, 1969, p. 59, Columbia University Oral History Project, Dwight D. Eisenhower Library.

95 *"Governor Adams was a combination"*: Oral history with Bryce Harlow by James F. C. Hyde Jr., May 30, 1974, p. 7, Columbia University Oral History Project, Dwight D. Eisenhower Library.

95 *"It was an education"*: Oral history with Maxwell Raab by David Horrochs, May 13, 1973, Columbia University Oral History Project, Dwight D. Eisenhower Library.

95 *"Are you telling me"*: Oral history interview with Sherman Adams by Herbert Parmet, July 31 and August 3, 1969, Columbia University Oral History Project, Dwight D. Eisenhower Library.

96 *Adams, knowing*: Oral history interview with Sherman Adams by Ed Edwin, April 10, 1967, Columbia University Oral History Project, Dwight D. Eisenhower Library.

96 *The aspect of Ike's character*: Fred I. Greenstein, *The Hidden-Hand Presidency: Eisenhower as a Leader* (1982; reprint, Baltimore: Johns Hopkins University Press, 1994).

97 *"It's his Army"*: James C. Hagerty, *The Diary of James C. Hagerty: Eisenhower in Mid-Course, 1954–1955* (Bloomington: Indiana University Press, 1983).

98 *Zwicker endured being called*: Richard H. Rovere, *Senator Joe McCarthy* (New York: Harcourt, Brace, 1959).

98 *"McCarthy was such an evil"*: Oral history with Milton Eisenhower by John Luter, June 21, 1967, p. 65, Columbia University Oral History Project, Dwight D. Eisenhower Library.

98 *But Ike believed*: In a letter to his friend Ed Hazlett that has great resonance for today's political environment, Ike wrote that politicians (like McCarthy) have "learned a simple truth of American life. This is that the most vicious kind of attack from one element always creates a very great popularity, amounting to almost hero worship, in an opposite fringe of society." Letter to Hazlett, July 21, 1953.

98 *"Do you take a junior senator"*: Hagerty, *The Diary of James C. Hagerty*.

98 *he called McCarthy*: Ibid.

101 *"Tell the full medical"*: Ibid., p. 28.

102 *Treatment for heart attacks*: R.E. Gilbert, "Eisenhower's 1955 heart attack: medical treatments, political effects, and the 'behind the scenes' leadership style." (PubMed.gov, March 27, 2008).

102 *"There's never been a president"*: Oral history interview with Sherman Adams by Ed Edwin, April 10, 1967, Columbia University Oral History Project, Dwight D. Eisenhower Library.

103 *In January 1956 he hosted*: Dwight D. Eisenhower, *Mandate for Change: The White House Years 1953–1956* (Garden City, NY: Doubleday, 1965); also oral history with James Hagerty by Ed Edwin, February 6, 1968, pp. 309–10, Columbia University Oral History Project, Dwight D. Eisenhower Library; oral history with Milton Eisenhower by Herbert Parmet, June 19, 1969, pp. 32–34, Columbia University Oral History Project, Dwight D. Eisenhower Library.

103 *John Eisenhower leaned against . . . but Mamie*: Oral history with Lucius D. Clay by Jean Smith, April 17, 1971, p. 929, Columbia University Oral History Project, Dwight D. Eisenhower Library.

104 *The television age*: Gary Richard Edgerton and Peter C. Rollins, ed., *Television Histories: Shaping Collective Memory in the Media Age* (Lexington: University Press of Kentucky, 2001).

104 *Ironically, almost as soon as*: About second terms it is interesting to note that Milton favored making the presidency a one-term position. The power of the president, he wrote, is not in his winning a second term in the future, but in the *now*. He believed that a one-term office would free the presidency from political calculations: Milton S. Eisenhower, *The President Is Calling: A Veteran Advisor for the Presidency Suggests Far-Reaching Changes* (Garden City, NY: Doubleday, 1974).

105 *there's often a certain freedom*: Oral history with James Hagerty by Herbert Parmet, April 9, 1969, p. 42, Columbia University Oral History Project, Dwight D. Eisenhower Library.

106 *On vacation*: Oral history with James Hagerty by Herbert Parmet, April 9, 1969, pp. 11–12, Columbia University Oral History Project, Dwight D. Eisenhower Library.

107 *In a press briefing*: Ibid, p. 12.

108 *suffered a mild stroke*: "President Suffers 'Mild Stroke', Will Need Several Weeks' Rest; Nixon Denies He'll Take Charge." Associated Press, November 27, 1957.

109 *The call from the president*: Oral history with Wilton Persons by John Luter,

June 23, 1970, pp. 55–57, Columbia University Oral History Project, Dwight D. Eisenhower Library.

109 *"Jerry, you'll have to take"*: Ibid.

110 *This inner steel*: Oral history with James Hagerty by Ed Edwin, February 6, 1968, pp. 416–17, Columbia University Oral History Project, Dwight D. Eisenhower Library.

111 *bucolic family life*: Oral history with Barbara Eisenhower by Carol Hegeman and Lawrence Eckert, August 20 and September 11, 1983, Eisenhower National Historic Site, National Park Service. In her oral history, Barbara describes scenes of family life: sitting together on the porch (p. 25), Mamie's needlepoint and Ike's painting (p. 30), singing Christmas carols (p. 45), etc.

112 *"We have a big thirteen-ring"*: Oral history with Howard K. Smith by John Luter, January 19, 1967, p. 21, Columbia University Oral History Project, Dwight D. Eisenhower Library.

112 *"He put on a mask"*: Oral history with Andrew J. Goodpaster Jr. by Malcolm S. McDonald, April 10, 1982, Columbia University Oral History Project, Dwight D. Eisenhower Library.

112 *"President Eisenhower's standing"*: Arthur Larson, *Eisenhower: The President Nobody Knew* (New York: Charles Scribner's Sons, 1968).

CHAPTER 5: FAREWELL IN BLACK AND WHITE

118 *Hagerty had arranged a "dummy"*: Oral history with James Hagerty by Ed Edwin, March 2, 1967, pp. 176–77, Columbia University Oral History Project, Dwight D. Eisenhower Library.

118 *That first time*: However, an odd item appeared in the *Eugene Register-Guard* on September 5, 1956, titled "Ike Not Likely to Use TV Makeup." In it Hagerty adamantly denies that Ike had used makeup for years, claiming he didn't need it. This is almost certainly not the case.

119 *"Whenever you get in the sunset"*: Oral history with Malcolm Moos by T. H. Baker, November 2, 1972, p. 6, Columbia University Oral History Project, Dwight D. Eisenhower Library.

119 *Among Moos's first*: Ibid., p. 11.

120 *As he wrote to Milton*: Correspondence file, Dwight D. Eisenhower Library.

120 *"The business of"*: Oral history with Bryce Harlow by James F. C. Hyde Jr., May 30, 1974, p. 132, Columbia University Oral History Project, Dwight D. Eisenhower Library.

120 *Milton had once joked*: Oral history with Milton Eisenhower by Herbert Parmet, June 19, 1969, p. 41, Columbia University Oral History Project, Dwight D. Eisenhower Library.

120 *"when he had finished"*: Milton S. Eisenhower, *The President Is Calling: A Veteran Advisor for the Presidency Suggests Far-Reaching Changes* (Garden City, NY: Doubleday, 1974.)

121 *"I want to thank you"*: A story related by Eisenhower in a speech at the Lotos Club, New York City, December 6, 1962. In one transcript of the speech, Ike says, "My fellow Americans," but in another version he says, "Ladies and gentlemen," which seems more accurate for that setting.

121 *"You know that General MacArthur"*: As an example, Moos cited MacArthur's famous Guild Hall speech in London. Oral history with Malcolm Moos by T. H. Baker, November 2, 1972, Columbia University Oral History Project, Dwight D. Eisenhower Library.

121 *The reporter James "Scotty" Reston*: Oral history with James Hagerty by Herbert Parmet, April 9, 1969, p. 31, Columbia University Oral History Project, Dwight D. Eisenhower Library.

121 *But Robert S. Kieve*: Oral history with Robert S. Kieve by Dr. Thomas Soapes, April 10, 1978, p. 14, Columbia University Oral History Project, Dwight D. Eisenhower Library.

121 *Howard K. Smith defended*: Oral history with Howard K. Smith by John Luter, January 19, 1967, p. 24, Columbia University Oral History Project, Dwight D. Eisenhower Library.

122 *"Absolute pedant"*: Oral history with Robert S. Kieve by Dr. Thomas Soapes, April 10, 1978, p. 14, Columbia University Oral History Project, Dwight D. Eisenhower Library.

122 *"When those explosions came"*: Oral history with Malcolm Moos by T. H. Baker, November 2, 1972, p. 18, Columbia University Oral History Project, Dwight D. Eisenhower Library.

122 *Milton had a confidential*: "It's often been said . . . that I was his confidante and his primary advisor," Milton would say. "The first of these is true, the second is not. It just happens that my brother and I have very much the same philosophy. We began working together intimately in the 1930s, a working relationship which both of us enjoy in mutual respect. . . . But by no means was I his advisor." Oral history with Milton Eisenhower by John Luter, June 21, 1967, Columbia University Oral History Project, Dwight D. Eisenhower Library.

122 *Ike's personal secretary*: Oral history with Ann Whitman, February 15, 1991, Columbia University Oral History Project, Dwight D. Eisenhower Library.

126 *one draft*: The various drafts of Eisenhower's farewell address are available at the Eisenhower Library and online at www.eisenhower.archives.gov.

126 *He could hear the bustle*: the Eisenhower Library and Museum was already built and ready to receive papers and other items in Abilene, Kansas. During Eisenhower's era, gifts from foreign governments were allowed, and the museum showcases a remarkable display of elaborate gifts.

127 *Relief surely mingled*: This mood would be nicely captured in a piece by Saul Pett of the Associated Press on January 19, 1961. Pett also listed the nitty-gritty details, such as the sparse furniture the Eisenhowers would be taking.

127 *At the party*: Edward T. Folliard, "Some Memories of Soldier President Ike," Dwight D. Eisenhower Library.

128 *He could be dragging*: Oral history with James Hagerty by Ed Edwin, April 17, 1968, p. 556, Columbia University Oral History Project, Dwight D. Eisenhower Library.

128 *"I suppose one of"*: Oral history with James Hagerty by Herbert Parmet, April 9, 1969, p. 45, Columbia University Oral History Project, Dwight D. Eisenhower Library.

128 *"You've done so much"*: Oral history with Wilton Persons by Stephen J. Wayne, May 29, 1974, Columbia University Oral History Project, Dwight D. Eisenhower Library.

CHAPTER 6: INTIMACY AND INTERDEPENDENCE

133 *An early draft*: Farewell address drafts, speech file, Dwight D. Eisenhower Library.

134 *"Good man, but wrong business"*: Recounted in Harry S. Truman, *Memoirs*, vol. 2, *1946–1952: Years of Trial and Hope* (New York: Da Capo Press, 1955).

136 *In his diary*: Robert H. Ferrell, ed., *The Eisenhower Diaries* (New York: Norton, 1981).

138 *Every Tuesday at 8:30*: Oral history with Bryce Harlow by John T. Mason Jr., February 27, 1967, p. 61, Columbia University Oral History Project, Dwight D. Eisenhower Library.

138 *"the care and feeding of members"*: Ibid., pp. 124–25.

139 *"I used to say to department fellows"*: Oral history with Bryce Harlow by James F. C. Hyde Jr., May 30, 1974, Dwight D. Eisenhower Library.

140 *As the historian*: Doris Kearns Goodwin, *Lyndon Johnson and the American Dream* (New York: HarperCollins, 1976).

140 *Eisenhower set out to woo*: Oral history with Bryce Harlow by James F. C.

Hyde Jr., May 30, 1974, Dwight D. Eisenhower Library; also, in *Sam Rayburn: A Biography* (New York: Hawthorn Books, 1975), Alfred Steinberg described how Eisenhower would invite Rayburn and Johnson to the residence, and how Nixon felt neglected for never being invited during the eight years he was vice president.

140 *"Us three Texans"*: Oral history with James Hagerty by Joe Frantz, November 16, 1971, LBJ Library.

141 *Privately, he said of Johnson*: Stephen Hess, "What Congress Looked Like Inside the Eisenhower White House," Brookings Institution, January 6, 2012.

141 *"Any jackass can kick down"*: Said during a 1953 conversation with reporters.

141 *"when I agree with you"*: Johnson quoted himself saying this to Eisenhower in his White House tapes. Michael Beschloss, *Reaching for Glory: Lyndon Johnson's Secret White House Tapes 1964–1965* (New York: Simon & Schuster, 2001).

142 *"He saw himself"*: Michael R. Beschloss, "Dwight D. Eisenhower and John F. Kennedy: A Study in Contrasts," in Robert A. Wilson, ed., *Power and the Presidency* (New York: PublicAffairs, 1999).

144 *Ike expressed his frustration*: Ferrell, ed., *The Eisenhower Diaries*.

145 *In the Senate*: Robert A. Caro, *Master of the Senate: The Years of Lyndon Johnson* (New York: Knopf, 2002).

145 *"the high-water mark"*: Ibid.

146 *Eisenhower even tried*: Samuel W. Rushay Jr., "The Ike & Harry Thaw: A Presidential Aide Sought to Restore Cordiality between Two Presidents," *Prologue*, Fall/Winter 2013; also, an account of Truman declining Ike's invitation to a dinner honoring Churchill: "Truman Declines an Invitation to Ike's Dinner for Churchill," *Washington Post and Times-Herald*, May 5, 1959; additionally, in a memo to Hagerty, dated October 21, 1959, Homer H. Gruenther, an Eisenhower aide, strongly disputes a *New York Times* account of the apparent snub in Kansas City, which Gruenther assures Hagerty never happened.

147 *"Bryce, let me explain"*: Oral history with Bryce Harlow by John T. Mason Jr., February 27, 1967, pp. 138–39, Columbia University Oral History Project, Dwight D. Eisenhower Library.

148 *Mamie did her part*: Susan Eisenhower, *Mrs. Ike: Portrait of a Marriage* (New York: Farrar Straus & Giroux, 2011); also oral history interview with Mamie Eisenhower by Maclyn Burg and Dr. John Wickman, July 15–16, 1972, Dwight D. Eisenhower Library.

148 *"I've always thought"*: Oral history with Robert B. Anderson by Herbert Parmet, March 11, 1970, pp. 16–18, Columbia University Oral History Project, Dwight D. Eisenhower Library.

149 *One of these*: David Sowell, *Eisenhower and Golf: A President at Play* (Jefferson, NC: McFarland, 2007).

150 *Smith wrote in her memoir*: Margaret Chase Smith, *Declaration of Conscience* (Garden City, NY: Doubleday, 1972).

151 *"I directed the secretary"*: Oral history with Milton Eisenhower by Robert F. Ivanov, November 6, 1975, pp. 6–7, Columbia University Oral History Project, Dwight D. Eisenhower Library.

152 *Cooperation was his natural*: Oral history with Milton Eisenhower by Herbert Parmet, June 19, 1969, Columbia University Oral History Project, Dwight D. Eisenhower Library.

152 *"He judged the legislation"*: Oral history with Wilton Persons by Stephen J. Wayne, May 29, 1974, Columbia University Oral History Project, Dwight D. Eisenhower Library.

153 *"The problems a president faces"*: "Republicans: The Loneliness of Office," *Time*, November 14, 1960; also Gibbs and Duffy, *The Presidents Club*.

CHAPTER 7: THE HOSTILE LANDSCAPE

155 *"That fellow in the White House"*: Oral history with James Hagerty by Ed Edwin, March 2, 1967, Columbia University Oral History Project, Dwight D. Eisenhower Library.

156 *In a famous speech*: From the Pamphlet Collection, J. Stalin, *Speeches Delivered at Meetings of Voters of the Stalin Electoral District, Moscow* (Moscow: Foreign Languages Publishing House, 1950).

156 *"This develops the war spirit"*: Dwight D. Eisenhower, *Mandate for Change: The White House Years 1953–1956* (Garden City, NY: Doubleday, 1965).

156 *his strongest rhetoric*: Speech to the American Legion at Madison Square Garden, New York, August 25, 1952.

157 *Shortly before the election*: Oral history with Milton Eisenhower by Robert F. Ivanov, November 6, 1975, pp. 10–11, Columbia University Oral History Project, Dwight D. Eisenhower Library.

158 *Zhukov was easily offended*: Dwight D. Eisenhower, *At Ease: Stories I Tell to Friends* (Garden City, NY: Doubleday, 1967).

159 *Dulles warned Ike*: Oral history with James Hagerty by Ed Edwin, February 6, 1968, p. 328, Columbia University Oral History Project, Dwight D. Eisenhower Library,

159 *"Well, he did [die]"*: Evan Thomas, *Ike's Bluff: President Eisenhower's Secret Battle to Save the World* (New York: Little, Brown, 2012).

160 *Ike confessed to speechwriter*: Robert Schlesinger, *White House Ghosts: Presidents and Their Speechwriters* (New York: Simon & Schuster, 2008).

162 *"I'm tired of babying"*: Truman's letter to Secretary of State James Byrnes, January 5, 1946.

162 *Named Project Solarium*: Oral history with Andrew J. Goodpaster Jr. by Malcolm S. McDonald, April 10, 1982, p. 15, Columbia University Oral History Project, Dwight D. Eisenhower Library.

165 *On Saturday, Ike worked*: After a meeting at Quantico related to the Korean armistice, Hagerty described the events leading up to the day and Ike's speech, which were taken down and preserved in a confidential memo, now at the Dwight D. Eisenhower Library.

166 *"You have a row of dominos set up"*: Oral history with Charles Halleck by Thomas Soapes, April 26, 1977, Columbia University Oral History Project, Dwight D. Eisenhower Library; also oral history with James Hagerty by Ed Edwin, March 2, 1967, Columbia University Oral History Project, Dwight D. Eisenhower Library; also on the domino theory, oral history with Dean Elie Abel by Don North, December 10, 1970, p. 16, Columbia University Oral History Project, Dwight D. Eisenhower Library.

166 *According to the recollections*: Oral history with Dean Elie Abel by Don North, December 10, 1970, p. 16, Columbia University Oral History Project, Dwight D. Eisenhower Library.

166 *it was almost impossible*: Eisenhower, *Mandate for Change*.

166 *"Vietnam represents"*: Speech to the Conference on Vietnam luncheon, at the Hotel Willard in Washington, D.C., June 1, 1956.

167 *In his rhetoric*: Oral history with Andrew J. Goodpaster Jr. by Malcolm S. McDonald, April 10, 1982, pp. 7–8, Dwight D. Eisenhower Library.

168 *When the president flew to Geneva*: "The Presidency: The Return of Confidence," *Time*, cover story, July 4, 1955.

168 *More than one person noted*: Thomas, *Ike's Bluff*.

169 *"How can this fat"*: Francis Beckett, *Macmillan* (London: Haus, 2006).

169 *One evening there was a stag*: Eisenhower, *Mandate for Change*; also John S. D. Eisenhower, *Strictly Personal* (Garden City, NY: Doubleday, 1974).

170 *Joseph Alsop once noted*: Oral history interview with Joseph Alsop by John Luter, June 14, 1972, Columbia University Oral History Project, Dwight D. Eisenhower Library.

170 *"Don't worry about"*: Eisenhower, *At Ease.*
170 *It was during the Geneva*: John S. D. Eisenhower, *Strictly Personal* (Garden City, NY: Doubleday, 1974).
171 *The success of the*: Vladislav M. Zubok, "Soviet Policy Aims at the Geneva Conference, 1955," in Gunter Bischof and Saki Dockrill, eds., *Cold War Respite: The Geneva Summit of 1955* (Baton Rouge: Louisiana State University Press, 2000).
172 *Ike remained tremendously popular*: Oral history with Howard K. Smith by John Luter, January 19, 1967, p. 5, Columbia University Oral History Project, Dwight D. Eisenhower Library.
173 *On display were the wonders*: http://www.c-span.org/video/?110721–1/nixon khrushchev-kitchen-debate.
175 *"Talk is cheap"*: Kennedy speech to the American Legion Convention in Miami Beach, Florida, October 18, 1960.
175 *"What in the world is Camp David?"*: Sergei Khrushchev, English language ed., *Memoirs of Nikita Khrushchev*, vol. 3 (University Park: Pennsylvania State University, 2007).
175 *Seated side by side*: Oral history with Admiral Evan P. Aurand by John T. Mason Jr., May 1, 1967, pp. 111–12, Columbia University Oral History Project, Dwight D. Eisenhower Library.
176 *Before Khrushchev left*: Oral history with James Hagerty by Ed Edwin, March 2, 1967, Columbia University Oral History Project, Dwight D. Eisenhower Library.
176 *their time together*: There are a number of accounts of the Camp David visit, including Ike's own in *Mandate for Change*; also Sergei Khrushchev, ed., *Memoirs of Nikita Khrushchev*, vol. 3; also oral history with James Hagerty by Ed Edwin, March 2, 1967, p. 205, Columbia University Oral History Project, Dwight D. Eisenhower Library.
177 *"When Stalin was still alive"*: W. Dale Nelson, *The President Is at Camp David* (Syracuse, NY: Syracuse University Press, 1995).
177 *Barbara Eisenhower was struck*: Oral history with Barbara Eisenhower by Carol Hegeman and Lawrence Eckert, August 20 and September 11, 1983, pp. 6–7, Eisenhower National Historic Site, National Park Service.
177 *David, who was*: David Eisenhower with Julie Nixon Eisenhower, *Going Home to Glory: A Memoir of Life with Dwight D. Eisenhower 1961–1969* (New York: Simon & Schuster, 2010).
178 *In a press conference*: "Khrushchev Speaks of His Gettysburg Visit," National Press Club, September 27, 1959, Dwight D. Eisenhower Library.
178 *Ike had a gift*: Hagerty recalled a trip they made to Taiwan, where they were to be hosted at a state dinner by Generalissimo and Madame Chiang Kai-shek. Ike loved Chinese food, and he was like an excited kid anticipating the meal. "Oh, boy, oh, boy," he enthused. "I'll bet this is going to be the finest Chinese dinner anybody has ever had!" Well, wouldn't you know, in honor of the president they had flown in steak from Kansas City. Ike was so disappointed that Hagerty managed to send out for Chinese later. Oral history with James Hagerty by Ed Edwin, March 2, 1967, p. 67, Columbia University Oral History Project, Dwight D. Eisenhower Library.
178 *what was the appeal*: Oral history with Andrew J. Goodpaster Jr. by Malcolm S. McDonald, April 10, 1982, pp. 8–10, Columbia University Oral History Project, Dwight D. Eisenhower Library.
179 *"he never tried to whip up"*: Ibid., p. 16.
180 *"Khrushchev had his"*: Oral history with Admiral Evan P. Aurand by John T. Mason Jr., May 1, 1967, p. 14, Columbia University Oral History Project, Dwight D. Eisenhower Library.
180 *Reading the draft*: Oral history with Malcolm Moos by T. H. Baker, November 2, 1972, pp. 31–32, Columbia University Oral History Project, Dwight D. Eisenhower Library.

181 *Privately, Ike was angry*: Oral history with Merriman Smith by John Luter, January 3, 1968, p. 41, Columbia University Oral History Project, Dwight D. Eisenhower Library.

182 *"My boy"*: Oral history with James Hagerty by Ed Edwin, March 2, 1967, Columbia University Oral History Project, Dwight D. Eisenhower Library.

CHAPTER 8: DUST TO DUST

183 *JFK had pounded away*: Oral history with Milton Eisenhower by John Luter, September 6, 1967, pp. 41–43, Columbia University Oral History Project, Dwight D. Eisenhower Library.

184 *Kennedy's administration would acknowledge*: Richard Reeves, "Missile Gaps and Other Broken Promises," *New York Times*, February 10, 2009.

184 *Asking for a key*: Dwight D. Eisenhower, *Mandate for Change: The White House Years 1953–1956* (Garden City, NY: Doubleday, 1965).

185 *He encouraged the report's author*: J. Robert Oppenheimer, "Atomic Weapons and American Policy," *Foreign Affairs* 31, no. 4 (July 1953).

185 *Khrushchev knew it, too*: Oral history with James Hagerty by Ed Edwin, March 2, 1967, Columbia University Oral History Project, Dwight D. Eisenhower Library.

186 *Knowing the stakes was*: Oral history with James Hagerty by Herbert Parmet, April 9, 1969, Columbia University Oral History Project, Dwight D. Eisenhower Library.

186 *"If the Russians press us"*: Oral history with Howard K. Smith by John Luter, January 19, 1967, p. 14, Columbia University Oral History Project, Dwight D. Eisenhower Library.

188 *"[E]ven in the event"*: Robert H. Ferrell, ed., *The Eisenhower Diaries* (New York: Norton, 1981).

189 *A new economy*: Dee Garrison: *Bracing for Armageddon: Why Civil Defense Never Worked* (New York: Oxford University Press, 2006).

189 Life *magazine*: "How You Can Survive Fallout," *Life*, September 15, 1961.

189 *"fallout shelter for everyone"*: Kennedy speech October 1961; also oral history with Admiral Evan P. Aurand by John T. Mason Jr., May 1, 1967, Columbia University Oral History Project, Dwight D. Eisenhower Library; also Kenneth D. Rose, *One Nation Underground: The Fallout Shelter in American Culture* (New York: New York University Press, 2001).

190 *In a letter to Winston Churchill*: On file at the Eisenhower Library.

191 *Americans panicked*: Yanek Mieczkowski, *Eisenhower's Sputnik Moment: The Race for Space and World Prestige* (Ithaca, NY: Cornell University Press, 2013).

191 *Ike knew we were*: Oral history with James Killian by Stephen White, November 9, 1969, pp. 41–42, Columbia University Oral History Project, Dwight D. Eisenhower Library.

192 *Politics aside*: Association for Educational Communications and Technology. www.aect.site-ym.com.

193 *called the Gaither Report*: David L. Snead, "The Gaither Committee, Eisenhower, and the Cold War." (*Foreign Affairs*, May/June 1999).

CHAPTER 9: THE MILITARY-INDUSTRIAL COMPLEX

195 *JFK's false*: James Ledbetter, *Unwarranted Influence: Dwight D. Eisenhower and the Military-Industrial Complex* (New Haven, CT: Yale University Press, 2011); also Danielle Sarver Coombs and Bob Batchelor, eds., *We Are What We Sell: How Advertising Shapes American Life and Always Has* (New York: Praeger, 2014).

196 *Science advisor James Killian*: James R. Killian, *Sputnik, Scientists, and Eisenhower: A Memoir of the First Special Assistant to the President for Science and Technology* (Cambridge, MA: MIT Press, 1977).

197 *"We don't want"*: Presidential press conference May 14, 1953, Dwight D. Eisenhower Library.

197 *Ike's granddaughter*: Susan Eisenhower: "50 Years Later—A Reflection on the Farewell Address," *Washington Post*, January 16, 2011.

199 *In a June 1959 meeting*: Notes on Legislative Leadership Meeting, June 2, 1959, Dwight D. Eisenhower Library Diary Series, Box 42.

199 *The National Security Council report*: "A Report to the National Security Council–NSC 68," April 12, 1950, President's Secretary's File, Truman Papers.

200 *"Thank God Korea"*: Thomas G. Patterson, *On Every Front: The Making and Unmaking of the Cold War* (New York: Norton, 1992).

200 *Undue influence*: Congressional inquiries were halfhearted. Indeed, no "undue influence" was found, at least not directly. But an article in the *Washington Post* soon after Ike left office listed in detail exactly how much influence there was, quoting an Eisenhower associate calling the military-industrial complex a "floating power" largely free of restraint. " 'Influencers' Still Busy as Eisenhower Warned," *Washington Post and Times Herald*, March 29, 1961. Also, Milton shared Ike's views, and experienced the problems of undue influence himself when Ike was out of office. Ike was concerned about the influence of industry on government. When Milton became chairman of the Republican Critical Issues Conference, a group that was Ike's brainchild, he cited an example of wanting a man of a leading corporation to become chairman of one of the study groups, but his board of directors would not allow it because the corporation wouldn't allow him to do anything critical of the administration because they had so many contracts. Oral history with Milton Eisenhower by John Luter, June 21, 1967, pp. 54–61, Columbia University Oral History Project, Dwight D. Eisenhower Library.

201 *Every community that housed*: Alex Roland, *The Military-Industrial Complex* (Washington, D.C.: American Historical Association, 2002). The congressional resistance to any cutbacks was strong because of local interests. For example, the interests of Senator Henry "Scoop" Jackson's home state, Washington, made him particularly critical of what he saw as Ike's weak defense budget. Nicknamed "the senator from Boeing," Jackson also had the naval shipyards in Bremerton and the Hanford plutonium weapons plant in his state.

202 *When Ike appointed*: Oral history with James Killian by Stephen White, November 9, 1969, pp. 1–3, Columbia University Oral History Project, Dwight D. Eisenhower Library.

202 *"My scientists"*: Ibid., p. 68.

202 *"badly impaired by the Oppenheimer case"*: Oppenheimer, who had overseen the laboratory at Los Alamos during World War II and been instrumental in the development of the atom bomb, had a change of heart after the war and became a strong opponent of the development of the hydrogen bomb. He was called before Congress, with suggestions of communist sympathies lingering in the air, and ultimately stripped of his security clearance. Ferrell, ed., *The Eisenhower Diaries*.

203 *"We had many, many hours"*: Oral history with James Hagerty by Ed Edwin, February 9, 1968, Columbia University Oral History Project, Dwight D. Eisenhower Library.

203 *Crafting the original*: Oral history with Malcolm Moos by T. H. Baker, November 2, 1972, Columbia University Oral History Project, Dwight D. Eisenhower Library.

203 *Ike's naval aide*: Oral history with Malcolm Moos by T. H. Baker, November 2, 1972, Columbia University Oral History Project, Dwight D. Eisenhower Library.

204 *As a side note*: Christian Davenport, "Pentagon Not Properly Tracking 'Revolving Door' Data, Report Says," *Washington Post*, April 7, 2014.

204 *The third leg*: Oral history with Malcolm Moos by T. H. Baker, November 2, 1972, Columbia University Oral History Project, Dwight D. Eisenhower Library.

204 *Ralph E. Williams*: Memorandum from file, Ralph E. Williams, October 31, 1960, Eisenhower Library.

208 *"Ike, I think"*: Oral history with Dean Elie Abel by Don North, December 10, 1970, p. 8, Columbia University Oral History Project, Dwight D. Eisenhower Library.
208 *"I don't know whether"*: Oral history with James Killian by Stephen White, November 9, 1969, p. 67, Columbia University Oral History Project, Dwight D. Eisenhower Library.
208 *Bryce Harlow once*: Oral history with Bryce Harlow by John T. Mason Jr., February 27, 1967, p. 136, Columbia University Oral History Project, Dwight D. Eisenhower Library.
209 *"Surely, it is impressive"*: Walter Lippmann, "Today and Tomorrow: Eisenhower's Farewell Warning," *Washington Post*, January 19, 1961.
209 *Ike "was striving"*: Oral history with Malcolm Moos by T. H. Baker, November 2, 1972, Columbia University Oral History Project, Dwight D. Eisenhower Library. After Ike left office, Bryce Harlow sent him an optimistic letter describing the military-industrial complex section of the speech as turning out to be "curiously yeasty"—citing interest from two young members of Congress. However, it took some time for Ike's warning to take root. In the *Reader's Guide to Periodical Literature*, there is no listing for the term *military-industrial complex* from 1961 until 1969, when it regained prominence during the Vietnam War and was widely misinterpreted.

CHAPTER 10: AN UNKNOWABLE SUCCESSOR
213 *However, there is reason*: Thurston Clarke, *Ask Not: The Inauguration of John F. Kennedy and the Speech That Changed America* (New York: Henry Holt, 2004).
213 *"both a stinging reply"*: Ibid.
214 *Truman also despised*: Matthew Algeo, *Harry Truman's Excellent Adventure: The True Story of a Great American Road Trip* (Chicago: Chicago Review Press, 2009).
215 *As a World War II hero*: Kennedy's book *Profiles in Courage* (New York: Harper & Brothers, 1956) was a national bestseller and was awarded the Pulitzer Prize in 1957.
215 *Rose Kennedy*: June 15, 1959, letter to Jackie, Correspondence of Rose Kennedy, John F. Kennedy Library and Museum.
215 *In 1956, Ike*: "Kennedy's Outlay Held 'Immoral,'" UPI. The account sources Kennedy's Republican opponent, Vincent J. Celeste, who said Eisenhower told him to make the "immoral" charge.
216 *"go out there"*: Oral history with Malcolm Moos by T. H. Baker, November 2, 1972, pp. 29–30, Columbia University Oral History Project, Dwight D. Eisenhower Library.
216 *Ike's relationship with Johnson*: Gary A. Donaldson, *The Secret Coalition: Ike, LBJ, and the Search for a Middle Way in the 1950s* (New York: Carrel Books, 2014).
216 *Bryce Harlow perhaps*: Oral history with Bryce Harlow by Bill Hartigan of the John F. Kennedy Library, June 3, 1997, p. 1, Dwight D. Eisenhower Library.
218 *"the men around President Kennedy"*: Oral history with Clark Clifford by Larry J. Hackman, December 16, 1974, John F. Kennedy Library.
218 *Ike found the media's slavish*: Craig Allen, *Eisenhower and the Mass Media: Peace, Prosperity, and Prime-Time TV* (Chapel Hill: University of North Carolina Press, 1993).
218 *Kennedy, too, was an avid*: David Sowell, *Eisenhower and Golf: A President at Play* (Jefferson, NC: McFarland, 2007).
219 *Arthur Larson once*: Arthur Larson, *Eisenhower: The President Nobody Knew* (New York: Charles Scribner's Sons, 1968).
219 *He retained Allen Dulles*: Correspondence files, Dwight D. Eisenhower Library; also Hagerty meeting notes.

220 *Kennedy's most surprising*: Oral history with Clark Clifford by Larry J. Hackman, December 16, 1974, John F. Kennedy Library.

221 *He warned Dillon*: In an oral history with Dixon Donnelley on July 30, 1964, for the John F. Kennedy Library, Douglas Dillon blithely remarked about Eisenhower's reaction to his becoming secretary of state: "I can't conceive that President Eisenhower really had any particular feeling other than surprise because when I did resign from the Department of State he wrote me a most friendly and laudatory letter thanking me for my service in the Department, and I certainly didn't get any impression at that time that he thought I was doing anything wrong." However, the letter in question disputes his account, and is on file at the Dwight D. Eisenhower Library.

222 *Kennedy had asked Clifford*: Oral history with Clark Clifford by Larry J. Hackman, December 16, 1974, John F. Kennedy Library; also oral history with Wilton Persons by Stephen J. Wayne, May 29, 1974, Dwight D. Eisenhower Library, pp. 21–22, describing his working relationship with Clifford.

224 *With the economy collapsing*: Exchange of Letters Between President Hoover and President-Elect Roosevelt, December 17, 1932, American Presidency Project.

224 *Of his own transition*: Carl M. Brauer, *Presidential Transitions: Eisenhower Through Reagan* (New York: Oxford University Press, 1986).

225 *"Poor Ike"*: Richard E. Neustadt, *Presidential Power: The Politics of Leadership* (Cambridge: Cambridge University Press, 1960).

225 *"chip on his shoulder"*: Brauer, *Presidential Transitions*.

226 *"I think that we ought"*: This statement about changing the timing of the inauguration was made at Ike's final press conference, January 18, 1961.

226 *"throws away much of"*: Quote by Thomas H. Kuchel, Republican of California in press accounts.

226 *"Very interesting"*: Tom Wicker, "State of the Union; Dirksen . . . Democrats Critical of Message; G.O.P. Applauds Statesmanship," *New York Times*, January 12, 1961.

228 *"Now look, you're going to"*: Oral history with Andrew Goodpaster, Ann Whitman, Raymond Saulnier, Elmer Staats, Arthur Burns, and Gordon Gray by Hugh Heclo and Anna Nelson, Dwight D. Eisenhower Library.

229 *One of these*: J. B. West: *Upstairs at the White House: My Life with the First Ladies* (New York: Coward, McCann & Geoghegan, 1973). The story was recently reprised by Kate Andersen Brower in *First Women: The Grace and Power of America's Modern First Ladies* (New York: Harper, 2016).

230 *"Eisenhower didn't like"*: Attributed to Timothy J. Naftali lecture, "The Peacock and the Bald Eagle: The Remarkable Relationship Between JFK and Eisenhower."

230 *Pressured to finally attend*: Robert H. Ferrell, ed., *The Eisenhower Diaries* (New York: Norton, 1981).

230 *"I don't think"*: Oral history with Wilton Persons by Stephen J. Wayne, May 29, 1974, Columbia University Oral History Project, Dwight D. Eisenhower Library.

231 *"He was not very good"*: Oral history with Kenneth Crawford by John Luter, June 13, 1967, p. 12, Columbia University Oral History Project, Dwight D. Eisenhower Library.

231 *"I came this morning"*: Final news conference, transcript, American Presidency Project, http://www.presidency.ucsb.edu.

232 *He began with*: Whitney Shoemaker, "White House Reporter Jack Romagna Is Fired," *Fort Scott Tribune*, June 1, 1962.

234 *"You know, I've seen"*: Oral history with Admiral Evan P. Aurand by John T. Mason Jr., May 1, 1967, p. 58, Columbia University Oral History Project, Dwight D. Eisenhower Library.

CHAPTER 11: THE DAY BEFORE

235 *The morning of*: David Eisenhower with Julie Nixon Eisenhower, *Going Home to Glory: A Memoir of Life with Dwight D. Eisenhower 1961–1969* (New York: Simon & Schuster, 2010).

235 *"If I've done nothing"*: Christopher Matthews, *Kennedy and Nixon: The Rivalry That Shaped Postwar America* (New York: Simon & Schuster, 1996).

235 *"If you give me a week"*: Ike told Merriman Smith he didn't mean it that way. Basically, he overthought the question. Oral history with Merriman Smith by John Luter, January 3, 1968, pp. 44–45, Columbia University Oral History Project, Dwight D. Eisenhower Library; also, Gabriel Hauge pointed out that Ike "would never undercut anyone in public," so it's unlikely he meant it as a slam against Nixon—"Maybe it was a poor wisecrack." Oral history with Dr. Gabriel Hauge by Ed Edwin, March 10, 1967, p. 117, Columbia University Oral History Project, Dwight D. Eisenhower Library.

236 *"The President is a man"*: Ann Whitman Diary Series, August 30, 1960, Eisenhower Library.

237 *To Kennedy's eye*: Kennedy dictated his account of the meeting to his secretary, Evelyn Lincoln. John F. Kennedy Library.

237 *For their private meeting*: Dwight D. Eisenhower, *Waging Peace: The White House Years 1956–1961* (Garden City, NY: Doubleday, 1965).

239 guerilla glory: Oral history with Milton Eisenhower by John Luter, September 6, 1967, p. 112, Columbia University Oral History Project, Dwight D. Eisenhower Library.

239 *"was very much like a child"*: Michael H. Hunt, *Ideology and U.S. Foreign Policy* (New Haven, CT: Yale University Press, 1987).

240 *"They saw him as a champion"*: Eisenhower, *Waging Peace*.

241 *"If you can't stand up"*: Kennedy campaign speech in Johnstown, Pennsylvania, October 15, 1960, John F. Kennedy Library. As a historical note, Nixon felt tricked by Kennedy at the debate. He knew Kennedy had been briefed on Cuba by the CIA and was aware that the United States was training exiles. By claiming the U.S. was doing nothing, he bated Nixon, aware that the vice president could not respond without breaching national security. Nixon held a grudge about this, as evidenced by his remarks twelve years later (on the Nixon tapes) about how much to brief his Democratic opponent in the 1972 election. https://www.nixonlibrary.gov/forresearchers/find/tapes/watergate/wspf/343-036.pdf.

243 *"Tell your Dad"*: John S. D. Eisenhower, *Strictly Personal* (Garden City, NY: Doubleday, 1974).

244 *One Republican hostess*: Daz and Richard Harkness, "New Faces, New Leases, New Frontiers." Richard Harkness, an NBC News Washington correspondent, wrote a regular column on Washington social doings.

244 *The big event*: Recounted in Todd Purdum, "From That Day Forth," *Vanity Fair*, January 17, 2011 (from the *Vanity Fair* Kennedy archive).

245 *Back at the White House*: John S. D. Eisenhower, *Strictly Personal*.

CHAPTER 12: THE PASSAGE

247 *An informal attitude*: John S. D. Eisenhower, *Strictly Personal* (Garden City, NY: Doubleday, 1974).

248 *"Doesn't Ike look"*: Arthur M. Schlesinger Jr., *A Thousand Days: John F. Kennedy in the White House* (Boston: Houghton Mifflin, 1965).

248 *former president Herbert Hoover*: *Raleigh Dispatch*, January 20, 1961.

249 *Ike leaned over*: Thurston Clarke, *Ask Not: The Inauguration of John F. Kennedy and the Speech That Changed America* (New York: Henry Holt, 2004).

249 *Malcolm Moos once*: Oral history with Malcolm Moos by T. H. Baker, November 2, 1972, p. 27, Columbia University Oral History Project, Dwight D. Eisenhower Library.

250 *Theodore Sorensen's central*: Clarke, *Ask Not*; also, Richard Tofel, *Sounding the Trumpet: The Making of John F. Kennedy's Inaugural Address* (Chicago: Ivan R. Dee, 2005).

250 *Over the years*: Sorensen wrote about "Ask Not" in *Counselor: A Life at the Edge of History* (New York: Harper, 2008). However, according to Thurston Clarke, the "Ask not" line was not in Sorensen's original draft.

250 *Sorensen would also offer*: Ted Sorensen, *Kennedy* (New York: Harper & Row, 1965).

250 *At the time*: Oral history with Malcolm Moos by T. H. Baker, November 2, 1972, pp. 26–27, Columbia University Oral History Project, Dwight D. Eisenhower Library.

251 *It might be added*: Ike's speech at the Lotos Club, New York City, December 6, 1962.

251 *Edward R. Murrow would*: Edward Bliss Jr., ed., *In Search of Light: The Broadcasts of Edward R. Murrow* (London: Palgrave Macmillan, 1968).

252 *"In retrospect"*: Clarke, *Ask Not*.

253 *Moaney, an African American*: Interview with Master Sergeant John A. Moaney by Dr. Maclyn Burg, July 21, 1972, Dwight D. Eisenhower Library.

253 *"Leaving the White House"*: David Eisenhower with Julie Nixon Eisenhower, *Going Home to Glory: A Memoir of Life with Dwight D. Eisenhower 1961–1969* (New York: Simon & Schuster, 2010).

254 *The next day*: Letter from Kennedy, Dwight D. Eisenhower Library.

255 *On his first day*: Oral history with Merriman Smith by John Luter, January 3, 1968, pp. 69–71, Columbia University Oral History Project, Dwight D. Eisenhower Library.

256 *According to Schlesinger*: Schlesinger, *A Thousand Days*.

256 *"new Presidents frequently"*: Carl M. Brauer, *Presidential Transitions: Eisenhower through Reagan* (New York: Oxford University Press, 1986).

257 *"The cabinet as such"*: Oral history with Richard K. Donahue by John F. Stewart. John F. Kennedy Library.

257 *Admiral Arleigh Burke*: Oral history with Admiral Arleigh A. Burke by Joseph E. O'Conner, January 20, 1967, John F. Kennedy Library.

257 *Kennedy's time in the*: Michael R. Beschloss, "Dwight D. Eisenhower and John F. Kennedy: A Study in Contrasts," in Robert A. Wilson, ed., *Power and the Presidency* (New York: PublicAffairs, 1999).

257 *As Ike would write*: Dwight D. Eisenhower, *Mandate for Change: The White House Years 1953–1956* (Garden City, NY: Doubleday, 1965).

CHAPTER 13: A SPRING DAY AT CAMP DAVID

258 *"Shangri-La was just"*: DDE Papers as President, name series Box 18, Swede Hazlett, 1953.

259 *"When I saw them"*: W. Dale Nelson, *The President Is at Camp David* (Syracuse, NY: Syracuse University Press, 1995).

259 *By almost every account*: Richard Neustadt, *Presidential Power and the Modern Presidents* (New York: Free Press, 1990).

260 *Senator William Fulbright*: Ibid.

260 *"[F]or God's sake"*: Oral history with Samuel E. Belk by William M. Moss, June 1, 1974, John F. Kennedy Library.

261 *Kennedy gathered his team*: Oral history with McGeorge Bundy by Richard Neustadt, March 1964 and May 1964, John F. Kennedy Library.

261 *As a side*: Dean Rusk as told to Richard Rusk, *As I Saw It* (New York: Norton, 1990).

261 *In a speech*: John F. Kennedy Library, White House Audio Recordings 1961–1963.

262 *Now face-to-face*: Dwight D. Eisenhower, *Waging Peace: The White House Years 1956–1961* (Garden City, NY: Doubleday, 1965).

263 *His response troubled*: Thomas Preston: *The President and His Inner Circle*:

Leadership Style and the Advisory Process in Foreign Affairs (New York: Columbia University Press, 2001).

264 *"See, until"*: Interview transcript of Eisenhower discussing his meeting with Kennedy, conducted by Captain A. Ross Wollen for the *Pointer,* a publication of the Corps of Cadets, West Point, New York. Dwight D. Eisenhower Post-Presidential Papers, 1965, Dwight D. Eisenhower Library.

265 *"Not as long as I'm"*: Oral history with Andrew J. Goodpaster Jr. by Malcolm S. McDonald, April 10, 1982, Columbia University Oral History Project, Dwight D. Eisenhower Library; also, historian Irwin F. Gellman, author of *The President and the Apprentice: Eisenhower and Nixon 1952–1961* (New Haven, CT: Yale University Press, 2015), has written that any historical record blaming Ike for the invasion is suspect. "In World War II, Eisenhower had directed the largest and most complex amphibious invasion in world history. He knew how to do 'this kind of thing.' To think that he would have approved such a sloppily planned operation as the Bay of Pigs attack is, on its face, absurd." "It's Time to Stop Saying that JFK Inherited the Bay of Pigs Operation from Ike," History News Network, December 5, 2015.

265 *As Ike prepared*: Robert H. Ferrell, ed., *The Eisenhower Diaries* (New York: Norton, 1981).

265 *would dismantle*: Oral history with John McCone by Dr. Thomas Soapes, July 26, 1975, Columbia University Oral History Project, Dwight D. Eisenhower Library.

265 *But Kennedy's people*: Oral history with Admiral Arleigh A. Burke by Joseph E. O'Conner, January 20, 1967, John F. Kennedy Library.

266 *"What are we going to do?"*: Oral history with James Killian by Stephen White, November 9, 1969, pp. 25–26, Columbia University Oral History Project, Dwight D. Eisenhower Library.

266 *Kennedy also called Clark*: Oral history of Clark Clifford by Larry J. Hackman, December 16, 1974, John F. Kennedy Library.

266 *"The President was incurably"*: Oral history of McGeorge Bundy by Richard Neustadt, March 1964 and May 1964, John F. Kennedy Library.

267 *It was a brutal*: Frederick Kempe, *Kennedy, Khrushchev, and the Most Dangerous Place on Earth—Berlin 1961* (New York: Putnam's Sons, 2011); also Richard Reeves, *President Kennedy: Profile of Power* (New York: Simon & Schuster, 1993).

267 *Milton observed*: Oral history with Milton Eisenhower by Robert F. Ivanov, November 6, 1975, pp. 3–4, Columbia University Oral History Project, Dwight D. Eisenhower Library.

268 *Unknown to Kennedy*: Cuban Missile Crisis: John F. Kennedy Library, https://www.jfklibrary.org.

269 *In a call*: Recording of telephone conversation, dictation belt 30.2, John F. Kennedy Library.

271 *After Ike listened*: Recording, microsites, jfklibrary.org.cmc/oct28/doc3.html.

272 *Kennedy's approval ratings*: "Presidential Approval Ratings—Gallup Historical Statistics and Trends," Gallup.com; although Gallup recorded 56 percent for Kennedy it was a low point.

272 *"Lincoln had faith"*: Address at the Centennial of Lincoln's Gettysburg Address, November 19, 1963, Dwight D. Eisenhower Library archives, post-presidential speeches.

273 *"I need you more"*: November 23, 1960, Presidential Papers of Lyndon B. Johnson, LBJ Library.

274 *The solemnity of the moment*: Brian Burnes, *Harry S. Truman: His Life and Times* (Kansas City, MO: Kansas City Star Books, 2003).

274 *"On that day"*: Oral history of E. Clifton Daniel by J. R. Fuchs, May 3 and 4, 1972, Truman Library.

275 *"I have the feeling"*: Oral history with Merriman Smith by John Luter, January 3, 1968, p. 52, Columbia University Oral History Project, Dwight D. Eisenhower Library.

275 *"There was some misunderstanding"*: Oral history with Milton Eisenhower by Robert F. Ivanov, November 6, 1975, Dwight D. Eisenhower Library. Decades later, near the end of his life, McGeorge Bundy admitted he had made many mistakes in orchestrating what he called "a great failure." Gordon M. Goldstein, *Lessons in Disaster: McGeorge Bundy and the Path to War in Vietnam* (New York: Times Books, 2008).

276 *"It is routine"*: Arthur Larson, *Eisenhower: The President Nobody Knew* (New York: Charles Scribner's Sons, 1968).

276 *"No one could hate war"*: David Eisenhower with Julie Nixon Eisenhower, *Going Home to Glory: A Memoir of Life with Dwight D. Eisenhower 1961–1969* (New York: Simon & Schuster, 2010).

276 *When* People *magazine*: Ibid.

277 *On one occasion*: Oral history with Charles Halleck by Thomas Soapes, April 26, 1977, pp. 36–37, Columbia University Oral History Project, Dwight D. Eisenhower Library.

277 *Even as his*: Tom Wicker, *Dwight D. Eisenhower* (New York: Times Books, 2002).

277 *In* Waging Peace: Eisenhower, *Waging Peace*.

278 *It was in Ike's nature*: The list of his accomplishments, as written to Hagerty: "Among them: statehood of Alaska and Hawaii, building the St. Lawrence Seaway, end of the Korean War (and thereafter no American killed in combat), largest reduction of taxes to that time, first civil rights law in 80 years, prevention of Communist efforts to dominate Iran, Guatemala, Lebanon, Formosa, South Vietnam, reorganization of the Defense Department, initiation and great progress in most ambitious road program by any nation in all history, slowing up and practical elimination of inflation, initiation of space program with successful orbit in less than three years, starting from scratch, initiation of strong ballistic missile program, conceiving and building the Polaris program, with ships operating at sea within a single administration, starting federal medical care for the aged, the Kerr-Mills bill, desegregation in Washington DC and armed forces without laws, fighting for responsible fiscal and financial policies throughout eight years, extension of OASI (Old Age Insurance Coverage) to over 10 million people, intelligent application of federal aid to education, the Defense Education Bill, preservation for the first time in American history of adequate military establishment after cessation of war, using federal power to enforce orders of a federal court in Arkansas, with no loss of life, good will journeys to more than a score of nations in Europe, Asia, Africa, South America, South Africa and in the Pacific, establishment of the Department of Health, Education and Welfare, initiation of plans for social progress in Latin America after obtaining necessary authorization from Congress for $500 million, later called Alliance for Progress, and the Atoms for Peace Proposal." Oral history with James Hagerty by Ed Edwin, March 2, 1967, Columbia University Oral History Project, Dwight D. Eisenhower Library.

278 *Here again the old awkwardness*: Jim Newton, *Eisenhower: The White House Years* (New York: Anchor Books, 2011).

279 *Motioning him to lean*: Milton S. Eisenhower, *The President Is Calling: A Veteran Advisor for the Presidency Suggests Far-Reaching Changes* (Garden City, NY: Doubleday, 1974).

279 *Both John and David*: John S. D. Eisenhower, *Strictly Personal* (Garden City, NY: Doubleday, 1974); and David Eisenhower with Julie Nixon Eisenhower, *Going Home to Glory*.

279 *The American people*: "Former President Dwight D. Eisenhower's State Funeral, 28 March–2 April," in B. C. Mossman and M. W. Stark, *The Last Salute: Civil and Military Funerals 1921–1969* (Washington, DC: Department of Army, 1991).

281 *After Ike died*: Yeager's account was published on his wife, Victoria's, website, www.victoriayeager.com/flying-pennsylvania-ave-wash-dc-for-generalmamie

-eisenhower; also Colleen Madonna Flood Williams, *Chuck Yeager* (Philadel-phia: Chelsea House, 2003).

281 *"The hero has come"*: Part 7 of funeral coverage, www.youtube.com/watch?v =mbzVGqOxq4s.

282 *To the right*: "The Chance for Peace" address before the American Society of Newspaper Editors, Washington, D.C., April 16, 1953.

284 *In a speech*: archive.defense.gov/speeches/speech.aspx?speechid =1467.

286 *"addresses converged"*: David Eisenhower, "A Tale of Two Speeches" (The *Los Angeles Times*, January 25, 2011).

INDEX

ABOUT THE AUTHOR

Courtesy of the author

The Baier family—Amy, Daniel, Paul, and Bret—at the National
World War II Memorial in Washington, D.C.

BRET BAIER is the Chief Political Anchor for Fox News Channel and the Anchor and Executive Editor of *Special Report with Bret Baier*. He has previously served Fox News as Chief White House Correspondent, and as National Security Correspondent based at the Pentagon. He has reported from seventy-four countries, and has reported from Iraq twelve times and Afghanistan thirteen times. Baier is the *New York Times* bestselling author of *Special Heart: A Journey of Faith, Hope, Courage and Love*. He lives with his family in Washington, D.C.

CATHERINE WHITNEY is the *New York Times* bestselling coauthor of more than fifty books. She lives in New York.